Avoiding The Ageing Parent Trap

Essential Information & Solutions

Brian Herd

16pt

Copyright Page from the Original Book

Copyright © Brian Herd

First published 2021

Copyright remains the property of the authors and apart from any fair dealing for the purposes of private study, research, criticism or review, as permitted under the Copyright Act, no part may be reproduced by any process without written permission.

All inquiries should be made to the publishers.

Big Sky Publishing Pty Ltd

PO Box 303, Newport, NSW 2106, Australia

Phone: 1300 364 611

Email: info@bigskypublishing.com.au

Web: www.bigskypublishing.com.au

Cover design and typesetting: Think Productions

Printed in China

 A catalogue record for this book is available from the National Library of Australia

For Cataloguing-in-Publication entry see National Library of Australia.

TABLE OF CONTENTS

DISCLAIMER	i
TESTIMONIALS	ii
FOREWORD	v
ABOUT THE AUTHOR	x
ACKNOWLEDGEMENTS	xviii
PREFACE	xxii
CHAPTER 1: WHAT COULD POSSIBLY GO WRONG?	1
CHAPTER 2: FAMILY PLANNING & GOVERNANCE	6
CHAPTER 3: THE HUMAN SIDE – RELATIONSHIPS	41
CHAPTER 4: PARENT PERSONALITIES	93
CHAPTER 5: YOU AND YOUR SIBLINGS	128
CHAPTER 6: TALES FROM THE FAMILY TRENCHES	154
CHAPTER 7: WHERE AND HOW WILL THEY LIVE?	189
CHAPTER 8: MONEY, MONEY, MONEY	338
CHAPTER 9: THE LAW OF FAMILY	396
CHAPTER 10: ELDER ABUSE	430
CHAPTER 11: SEXUAL EXPRESSION	472
CHAPTER 12: THE END	505
CHAPTER 13: THE LAST WORD	532
ABOUT THE AUTHOR	537

DISCLAIMER

I used to think this part of a book was just another way of saying, *Don't believe a single word I say. You can believe my words but don't think that anything I say is an answer to your problem.* My book is just a collage of information mixed with experience. It is not advice or suggestions about what you should do, or not do. It is always best to seek your own advice on your circumstances and not rely on anything contained, as they say, 'herein'. Now that's what I call good advice.

While the stories in this book do not change over time, the legal and financial issues may. For example, aged care fees change twice every calendar year, in March and September. For clarity then it is important to understand that the information in this book is current as at October 2020.

Be aware also that, given that the law can be different between the States and Territories, you should always seek advice on the law as it applies in your State or Territory.

TESTIMONIALS

When I read Brian's wise words, I felt like Alice in Wonderland gazing in amazement at the litany of rabbit holes and traps for young (and old) travellers in the strange and complicated world of ageing and aged care. I now appreciate the plethora of potential pitfalls that my family and friends face and will encourage them to take action now! Many of them will find this book in their Christmas stocking or birthday bounty.

Dr Greg Timbrell, Higher Education Advisory, Queensland University of Technology

This insight inducing book delves into recesses of our future lives many of us should recognise in order to avoid. It is essential, if not compulsory reading for anyone who harbours a desire to avoid the inevitable consideration of planning a future where you are parenting your parents. Pitfalls and perilous progressions are artfully described in an entertaining yet very serious guidebook on life as the adult child parenting parents. Avoid reading this at your peril, or approach this aspect of your future armed with the great wisdom Brian Herd offers to educate you. Your choice, now or later.

Dr Anthony French FRACP, Geriatrician, Brisbane

An engaging and insightful read – Brian unapologetically calls a spade a spade; not afraid to delve into complex issues and emotions that (on occasion) can make you cringe. He presents real-life, and often confronting scenarios while offering the kind of sage advice that comes only from years of experience, practice and self-reflection. Brian expertly navigates a challenging and ever changing landscape with ease and aplomb.

Joanna Lezanski, Relationships Australia

Whether you are an ageing parent, or the child of ageing parents, this is the essential workbook to understand estate planning from Retirement villages and residential aged care, family carers, Centrelink, Wills and Enduring Power of Attorneys, disintegration of family relationships, to the financial pitfalls to avoid. Brian has tackled a subject about which very little has been written, in an entertaining and informative work, crafted from his experience as an elder lawyer, in which he uses true life stories to illustrate the conundrum that faces families of ageing parents. It is both engaging and frighteningly realistic.

Jon Attenborough, former Managing Director, Simon & Schuster Australia

FOREWORD

BY NOEL WHITTAKER AM, FINANCE EXPERT AND BESTSELLING AUTHOR

I am privileged to have known Brian Herd for more than 30 years. Over that time we have shared the stage at conventions, and discussed in depth the challenges that can arise when some family members age, and major decisions are required to be made by family and friends who are inexperienced in this area, and who may have competing interests and hidden agendas.

I also enjoy Brian's monthly newsletters which invariably lead me to reflect on what a difficult space elder law has become, as people age, and blended families and cultural differences become much more common. For years I have been saying to Brian 'this stuff is just so important – you need to write a book about it!'

Brian finally succumbed to my pleadings, and the book you are holding in your hands is the product of many years of experience in the elder law area. But let me make one point clear – this is a book that will challenge you. Brian raises points about dealing with your aged parents that may never have occurred to you, or which you've been pushing to the back of your mind because they're too scary to think about.

But the sad reality is that ignoring important issues in the early stages, is a recipe for facing much more difficult challenges in the future. In this book Brian highlights major issues that most people will face when dealing with their older parents, and provides helpful suggestions of ways to make the situation better. The book is also chock full of real-life case studies to illustrate the points.

So take this book as an invaluable guide to navigate your way through the difficult elder parent scenario. Believe me, the effort you spend in reading it, and then using the principles discussed in it will repay the time spent 100 times over.

BY HON DR KAY PATTERSON AO, AGE DISCRIMINATION COMMISSIONER

'The time has come, Brian Herd said, to talk of many things: of wills – and cash – and EPOs – of RADS – and mother's rings'. (With apologies to Lewis Carroll.[1])

This book is a no-holds-barred, frank call to action for both parents and children to confront the well-trodden but often unpredictable course of our life's journey – particularly towards the end, or as Brian would say, 'our celestial transfer'.

With a professional lifetime of working in the area of elder law, Brian Herd brings to life, using plenty of real-life examples, the common traps for young (and older) players in navigating this complex area. With his quintessential and oftentimes irreverent humour, Brian alerts us to the consequences of failing to heed his call to 'challenge your parents to become partners in this almost mandatory need to anticipate events, educate ourselves, converse, communicate and action, or implement, a strategic plan'.

He deals with a multitude of possibilities, problems and pitfalls related to planning and caring for ageing relatives. He covers, among other topics, the complications arising from various combinations and permutations of families, the failing mental capacity of your parent(s), the never-ending variation of caring, craven, controlling, carefree or concerned offspring, the financial and legal issues involved in residential aged care and retirement village living, lack of knowledge about the implications of gifting money, undocumented loans and some, perhaps, taboo topics such as intimacy and sex in life. The list goes on.

This book should be required reading for all law students, lawyers, accountants, financial planners and advisers. Equally important, it should be read by older people preparing their enduring documents (wills, powers of attorney and advanced care directives) and their families. Brian stresses the importance of doing this as cooperatively as possible – 'better to have discussed than never to have discussed at all' would be his mantra.

This is a much needed and timely clarion call from a lawyer who has seen it all and tells it like it is – warts and all. Just when the going gets tough while reading this tome, a wicked aside or clever anecdote inspires you to read on.

Brian, thank you for making such a complicated topic so educational and enjoyable. Hopefully the families wise enough to read this book will be able to navigate successfully through the crests and troughs of the ageing voyage.

***

[1] Carroll L, 'The Walrus and the Carpenter' in *Through the Looking Glass: and what Alice found there* (1872) 73, p 75.

ABOUT THE AUTHOR

My qualifications to be your tea leaves soothsayer, or crystal ball doomsayer for you and your ageing parents, are a combination of the *personal* and the *professional*.

THE PERSONAL

I am in my 68th year on earth. Most significantly, I am a baby boomer, a term I abhor but which many of us identify with. I am also a parent of adult children.

Along with my four siblings, I am also the product of two, very matured aged parents (90 & 91). They recently took up residency in an aged care facility and, until my father's recent death, they remained confident they would each receive a message from the Queen on their respective 100th birthday. Regrettably now, from my mum's point of view, given the Queen's current age, it may well be the King.

All their parenting lives, they had been sacrificial exemplars for their children – hard working, dedicated, loving, caring, supportive and, all the while, mostly due to the growing-up needs of their children, poor. They had their usual bouts of annoyance and irritation with each other, often over trivia – was it a Tuesday or a Wednesday? To this we have coined an acronym – 'DIM' – Does it Matter! which we all dutifully sound out to them when a bout was brewing.

While they got frustrated with each other, made worse by their limitations, it was obvious that they loved each other. While my mum is in relatively good health, albeit living with a synergy of increasing frailty and fragility, side by side with her constant constellation of companions—the medicos and the medication. Their social lives revolved around frequent contact with their children, extended family and excursions to their friendly stable of health professionals. Until recently, their 25-year-old car sat forlornly in their garage, like a sphinx, a symbol of the past.

Along with my siblings, my family world now includes being to my parents what they have been to me, in a time of their increased dependency and reliance. Life has again come full circle.

As a result, with grown up children, I no longer wait for that dreaded call from the childcare centre – 'Your child is sick, please come quickly and take her home'. Now the looming spectre is a call from the 'adult care centre', a hospital – 'Your mother has had a fall, she can't go home, and we've done all we can for her, but she can't stay here. There are others more deserving and she's a "bed blocker",' etc.

Parenting is always a constant process of event management, or, sometimes, crisis management, whether it is for your children or your parents. Occasionally, events can transcend both spheres of life and all at the same time. "The question is ... *are you ready*?

THE PROFESSIONAL

I am a lawyer and have been for over 35 years. For many years, I have been a happy lawyer. I practice in Elder Law or law relating to older people and I've waited a long time to write this book so that I could distil all those years of experience. Contrary to my perception of public perception, I think that makes me useful. It has given me the opportunity to give credence to that mantra, 'Doing well, by doing good'.

My coming to Elder Law is a story in itself and the result of some epiphanies.

THE BOWEL BOOK

Some years ago, about 2001, initially more by way of chance, I chose to abandon the traditional lucrative areas of law in the cut and thrust, if not, trench warfare of commercial law and litigation. A combination of factors drew me to a new and emerging area of legal practice known as Elder Law (which is not necessarily immune from warfare).

The first was happenstance. Why she chose me I don't remember, but a DON (Director of Nursing) from a small aged care facility called me one day. Her voice had a tired, desperate tone. She needed help to resolve a simmering dispute between the facility and the six adult daughters of a resident. The daughters, or at least some of them, were alleging that the facility was starving their mother to death.

There I was sitting in the DON's office, discussing what was clearly a distressing experience for her. At one point, she pushed an open book across the table to me and, almost pleadingly said, 'See, this is proof she's not starving'. I naturally responded, 'What's that?' As quick as you like, she responded, 'It's our bowel book!' When I regained my composure, I repeated myself, 'What's that?' It was, she carefully explained, a comprehensive record of each resident's bowel movements for every day of their lives in the facility. She pointed to the page she had opened and took me to the record of the resident which, it seemed, clearly showed regular and, regular amounts of, movement.

There was more. She then handed me a small, laminated card. It was, she almost proudly explained, their 'stool tool'-pictures (in vivid colour) of the surprisingly broad types of stools we humans are capable of producing. Each variety, apparently, painted a picture of the health (or otherwise) of a resident. Every member of staff was required to pin the tool to their uniform each day on their rounds for a ready reckoning of the quality of a resident's movement. In the resident's case, they were distinctly conventional, with no hint of abnormalities.

This was my first foray into the bowels of aged care and, as it turned out, it was a revelation and the start of my voyage into the deep recesses of ageing.

A WAY FINDER

Since then, I have devoted myself to the calling of Elder Law or law relating to older people and their families. I follow the mantra – 'Doing Well by Doing Good'. For many lawyers, the aspiration of doing good has become slightly perverted – it has become more about winning, not good over evil, or right over wrong – just winning. With families, the last environment you want to create is that of winners and losers. With that attitude, everyone is a loser.

I see myself as a law bringer, a fact giver and, ultimately, a way finder. I first came across 'way finding' as a profession when I happened to sit next to a woman on an aircraft. After we came to an understanding about the use of our mutual arm rest, she made the usual entrée enquiry – 'and what do you do?' I told the truth – 'I'm a lawyer'. Her head turned quietly away in silence, slightly deflated. Ah, such is my lot in life.

I then reciprocated the query. She came back to life, enthusiastically replying, 'I am a way finder'. That Pauline Hanson look of 'Please explain' was written all over my face. I had esoteric visions of a spruiker, life coach or some personal stylist. But it was far more utilitarian. She had been a psychologist and an industrial designer, (a curious combination in itself), but now, she combined them both to undertake way finding. Put simply, it involved being engaged by large institutions to advise them on how people could find their way more easily around their sprawling edifice. As an example, she was on her way to New

Zealand to ply her trade for a large public hospital.

So it is that, in addressing the convoluted needs and demands of families with the smorgasbord of personalities, sense of entitlement, and agendas, not to mention the various amounts of goodness and badness exposed in the stress of addressing parent problems, I would like this book to represent a personal and a professional plea – no winners and losers please, just some way finding.

ACKNOWLEDGEMENTS

NOEL WHITTAKER

As his foreword recounts, we have known each other for a long time. We have matured together. His expertise, enthusiasm and entreaties to do this book, kept me going in those many hours of just me and my laptop. He is a fine motivator for the power of knowledge as a basis for good decision making in our lives. He loves to help, as he has done for many others, for many years. I have been privileged to be helped so generously.

JON ATTENBOROUGH

Jon was quietly enjoying his retirement when, at the suggestion of Noel, I contacted him at a time when I was at the pointy end of publishing. Having been in a senior role with Simon & Schuster for many years, Jon was 'the man'. As with Noel, Jon freely took the time to apply his broad editorial skills to the manuscript and was instrumental in restraining my enthusiasm for words. His many comments and insights were crucial and constructive and I cannot thank him enough for his generosity and expertise.

GREG TIMBRELL

Greg is a friend who, fortunately, is not a lawyer. He is a fine musician, IT guru, academic and, as I discovered, gifted editor. His willingness to review the manuscript and share his often, which I am sure he won't mind me saying, pedantic, but invariably correct, comments and suggestions were, mostly, gratefully received. My safari with him through the intricacies of parsing, transitive verbs, conjunctive adverbs and the many other delights of English grammar and punctuation, was eye opening (if not watering, at times). He knows his stuff as they say and he deserves all the accolades and acknowledgements he brings to his craft.

SUE FIELD

Sue is a lawyer who, some years ago, joined the exclusive club of academia in the prized area of Elder Law for which she is recognised Australia wide. She was also, once, an employee of mine. Her expertise and encouragement in reviewing the manuscript was very helpful from a fellow travellers point of view. Again I thank her for her efforts and enthusiasm for my project and I suspect I will be called upon in a future time to reciprocate.

MY FIRM – CRH LAW

Throughout the many hours producing this book, I have also been running a legal practice with my fellow partners, Joanne O'Brien and Margaret Arthur. I thank them and all the other staff who continually encouraged me and forgave me for my occasional absences in pursuit of this passion.

MY CLIENTS

Much of what you read about in this book derives from the many varied and interesting clients and families I have worked with (and against) over my many years. Without them sharing their stories with me and seeking my help, this book would have remained just an idea. I thank them for what they have given me, intentionally and unintentionally, and the opportunity to tell you their stories.

PREFACE

LOVE THEM OR LOATH THEM?

Many commentators on ageing parents speak of them as our 'loved ones'. Could they sometimes be also our 'loathed ones'?

'I literally just want to kill him!' she exclaimed.

They were an angry set of words and potentially, quite alarming. Remarkably, the words fell out of the mouth of a 64-year-old, retired school principal who had led an exemplary, untarnished life and had been much respected and admired as an educator and pillar of her community.

It was the climax of a brooding monologue started a mere ten minutes before in response to my seemingly innocuous question, 'How's your father?' As she went on, her diatribe gathered momentum, quickly turning into a fulminating tirade. It was excruciating to listen to. The corners of her lips lathered, her pupils were dilated, she had sharp body movements, her facial muscles were taught, her complexion that of a toffee apple and with a glare looking for a victim to zap.

What could have possibly transformed this eminent educator, honourable citizen and dutiful daughter into a raging, salivating wreck? Simple, really – her 88-year-old father who she described as manipulative, conniving and nasty.

She also harboured a personal loss of opportunity. Her retirement dreams were being sacrificed on the altar of care – for her parent. To add to her sense of deprivation, her much cherished time with the grandkids was also being stolen from her.

They can evoke and provoke the full suite of human, painful emotions. Pain can cause tears but, the most tears are usually shed at the pathos of our parents' mutation – their passing from the parents we once knew. The ravages of that long-life disease, Alzheimer's, can make them strangers to us and even strangers to themselves. They can live in a yet to be discovered parallel universe, moving further and further away as the years pass by.

SHARING MY EXPERIENCE

Both hers, and many other's circumstances will be dissected, analysed and revealed in this book. She is but a stark example of what I regard as one of the greatest social challenges of our generation – the interplay between us, our ageing parents and our siblings. Our parents used to manage us and our siblings, but the circle of life is just that, a circle.

We may yearn for our families to be akin to a Neapolitan cake, where layers of different coloured sponge, sugar coated, live harmoniously and functionally in one happy whole.

Realistically, our families can be more like the layers of a traditional wedding cake, where marzipan (denial) suffocates the inner brooding boiled fruit cake (dysfunction) and the layers, which vertically diminish in size upwards, are then supported by fragile Roman columns. As a final touch, at the top, and on the smallest layer, we replace effigies of the smiling couple with those of our frowning parents.

The book is unashamedly focussed on, and directed to, people just like you and me, the adult children of ageing parents. It throws up for us the inevitable, not the possible, later-life scenarios that will arrive on your doorstep. It also throws out to you a carrot – to cooperate, if not, collaborate, with your siblings because, to put it as kindly as possible, without that, your parents' lives will be miserable and yours will be worse.

It aims to open your eyes to the fate of many families who have come to my office and what may lay ahead for you. I would hope that it will provoke you to do something to prepare or plan for those days ahead. It is also a book of stories with an underlying moral – unveiling real and complex family lives that often derive their complexity from the simplest family cohort, sparked by the smallest flint of disagreement about just one thing – ageing parents.

Here is just a taste of what is to come.

While having lots of children may seem like a good 'later life' insurance for parents to meet their needs down the track, it has a potential downside. I recently had to dowse the flames of an inferno that had erupted in a family involving a mother in her 90's and her seven adult daughters. The mother lived in her own home of some 58 years, with limited financial means and on the cusp of requiring high care. She had vehemently asserted, to all who would listen, that she never wanted to grace the halls of an aged care facility but simply wanted to see out her days in her home. When making her Enduring Power of Attorney, it took a herculean effort for the solicitor to convince her not to appoint all seven daughters. So, as is often the case, she opted for the seemingly simple, quick fix – she appointed just one – her eldest daughter.

And, as is often the case as well, that daughter turned out to be the renegade, the black sheep, emboldened in addition with the legal power of being the Enduring Power of Attorney. Six of the daughters were adamant that their mother's wishes should be respected. In fact, one of them offered to move in with the mother to look after her 24 hours a day with occasional respite from the others. The eldest daughter would have none of it insisting that the mother must enter residential aged care.

Lawyers prefer to have one or, at best, two clients to represent in any dispute but there they were one day, arrayed before me, the six daughters. While it was not exactly like herding cats, it took some deft footwork to keep them on message and on song and to adopt an agreed strategy. Needless to say, it cost them a lot of money to get to a resolution with their sister which was achieved, ultimately, in a mediation. However, it came at great emotional cost as well.

As you will gather from reading on, in sharing my experiences with you, I am not guaranteeing a stress-free retirement, or a happy and fulfilling time pursuing those later life dreams. What I offer you is a series of predictions and plans. Interspersed with that is information, the most powerful ingredient for knowledge and your know-how and understanding are your best sword and shield for coping.

I have much to share with you.

CHAPTER 1

WHAT COULD POSSIBLY GO WRONG?

THE FIRST SIGN OF TROUBLE

Your phone lights up early one evening at the end of an exhausting, unremunerated day with the grandkids. It's your sister breathlessly announcing to you, *'Mum's had a fall! She's in hospital! They're saying she can't go back home!'* It's one of those perfunctory conversations perforated with exclamations. Those subconscious thoughts you have been suppressing have just surfaced.

If that wasn't enough, two days later, the hospital is now pressing another line—'Your mum can't stay here anymore. We've done all we can for her, and she needs to leave now but she can't go home'. She has become what the hospital fraternity so elegantly describe as a 'bed blocker'. Just to add a final piece to this overwhelming puzzle, the nurse adds, 'By the way, we don't think your mum can make decisions for herself anymore and someone will have to make them for her—who will that be?' Pure shock and awe – denial turns to dread which quickly mutates to panic, a mood that infects the entire extended family.

Later that night, you're lying in bed still in a flailing state of mind, a vast array of questions swirl in no particular order, or urgency, within your feverish brain:
- Is this really happening?
- Who can make decisions for her – I've got three brothers and two sisters?
- Surely, Mum can go home, can't she?
- Where else can she go?
- How will she get there, and will she go willingly?
- How much will it cost?
- What do my siblings think and what can we all do?

- How long will everything take?
- What is 'everything'?
- Who do I need to contact and about what?
- Who should I get advice from and about what?
- Can we access her money and how?
- What are her passwords?
- What if we can't find somewhere for her to go?
- What if she's not happy going anywhere?

This is all so painful. You yearn for sleep, not for its rest, but its escape. Suddenly, your phone lights up. A text arrives from one of your daughters, 'Sorry Mum, I forgot to ask if you can look after the kids again tomorrow?' You drop the phone and stare at the ceiling.

You have arrived. Your family's failures have brought you to this destination. You are in a 'C' change – 'Crisis' – and it will be unlike any other crisis you have ever faced, even before your recent retirement.

People beware! Ask yourself a question – what impact will my parents have on my life?

In one way or another, and to a larger extent than we care to admit, the biggest factor impacting on your happiness in later life will not be your health, your marriage, the travails of your own children or your ceaseless pursuit of answers to the question – 'do I have enough to live on in retirement?' I confidently predict it will be something else – it will be your parents.

We usually only have one set of them (excluding for the moment, the parents-in-law) and their ageing is, for most of us, something for which we have no past experience to call upon. We are babes in the wood. We may have been exposed indirectly to the lives of our grandparents in their later lives but more as bystanders than active players. So it is, ironically, your parents who come with 'form', as they say – they may well have had to look after or support their parents, your grandparents. I know my parents did.

Regrettably, your parents' own experience is seldom applied to their own circumstances. Of all the people who will steadfastly, if not aggressively, avoid confronting their own decline, it is your parents. How often have you heard their snorty retort to your pestering and sometimes, hectoring concerns – 'I'll let you know when I need any help.' They won't.

As such, it is over, and down, to you. There is no time for reflection or, even worse, indecision or avoidance. I entreat you to educate and inform yourself in anticipation of those increasingly complex events your parents and thereby, you, will inevitably have to face.

It comes down to deciding how you want your parents to live, and how you want to live at the same time.

CHAPTER 2
FAMILY PLANNING & GOVERNANCE

THE FAMILY

Families come in all shapes and sizes. They are made up of different ages, personalities, achievements, failures, aspirations, cultures, alliances and, collectively, experience some significant events. They are micro communities full of implied expectations of mutual support.

The events that can befall ageing parents are some of the most difficult and complex for families. Our parents will suffer from what I call, 'frailty creep'. Their dependency will increase imperceptibly at first but then become more pronounced as they age, and the ravages of time starts to assert itself.

It forces us into the mode of parent management, or events management. For business types, I have devised a spin off phrase from the familiar mantra, 'corporate governance' which I call, 'family governance'. To use a business analogy, families are like a corporation where the parents, in the early days at least, were the Board of Directors and the children, the shareholders. As time passes and the parents are forced to give up their controlling roles, the demarcation lines become blurred as the children's roles and influence evolve and they become a de-facto or alternative Board of Directors.

Family governance sounds a worthwhile, if not, deceptively simple concept, but it hides a welter of nuances and intricacies – physical, emotional, practical and financial. Above all, it encapsulates the essence of good management – collaboration with 'the team', the family. Family cooperation and engagement is the oil that greases the creaking engine of our older parents' lives. Done well, it may also help to preserve relationships which are often irreparably fractured by the pressure of parent's circumstances.

FAMILY PERFORMANCE

The diverse parts of a family are called upon to come together as a whole in response to the care needs of their ageing parents.

But, my many years at the coal face of residential aged care, for example, have taught me one salient thing – the quality of care we provide to the elderly is not just a reflection of the quality of the hired carers but the quality of the families and how they relate to those carers. Oddly, the actions and the ability of families to impact on that care appears to be a no-go zone for critics of aged care even in the expansive remit of the Royal Commission. Is poor care always related to poor facilities and staff?

Generally speaking, families hold, and wield, considerable power over the fate of their parents who are placed in the hands of professional care organisations. Yet not all family members conduct themselves for the benefit and in the best interests of their parents. In some cases, they adversely impact on that care.

To understand this provocative proposition, let me place families in certain categories which, again, all arise from my experience:
- Functional families
- Dysfunctional families
- Missing in action families
- Passive families
- Non-existent families
- Helicopter families.

Functional Families

Believe it or not, such families do exist. They are both internally cohesive and externally, act as reasonable and diligent advocates for their parents. They are receptive to, and respect information and advice that they obtain from skilled professionals, including doctors, nurses and care staff. They then make decisions based on that advice, taking into account the best interests and wishes of their parents. But, they are also champions of their parents' cause. When questions need to be asked, they will not engage in rampaging verbal assaults on innocent victims but carefully consider and pursue their concerns with a view to resolution not revolution.

From my experience they tend to have fewer complaints because they are also respected by the caring organisations. If they do complain, it is usually resolved quickly and without ongoing acrimony.

Dysfunctional Families

The needs of elderly parents unmask these families and expose the internal bickering and conflict that has usually characterised them for most of their lives. They disagree on many things particularly their parents' needs. They are prepared to snipe at, and denounce, each other and none of them are prepared to be a point of contact or fulcrum when they are called upon to make decisions or convey information to other members of the family. When information is shared it is often censored or embellished or coated with distorted bias, feeding a never-ending guerrilla war. Meanwhile mum or dad sit helplessly on the sidelines.

Missing in Action Families

These families do exist, but they are, generally, just absent. They are often either hiding from responsibility, feigning '*busyness*', blaming the tyranny of distance or time poverty. They are unavailable, unresponsive or shirk the task of confronting the need for involvement. Vital decisions, let alone important legal approvals e.g., for parents' health care, are difficult to obtain. Just putting together a care plan can be lengthy and protracted akin to negotiations on denuclearisation of the Korean peninsula.

Passive Families

They are closely aligned to the missing family. They are leaderless, can be hard to get hold of, and even when they are, they tend to pass the buck to other members or simply avoid any commitment for fear of being accountable.

They rarely visit their parents and usually only when on holidays (briefly and if it is convenient). They infuriate aged care staff because their recalcitrance and lack of focus can lead to leaving the facility in a 'no man's land' mentality. There is a certain 'out of sight, out of mind' mentality that pervades this family believing, as they do, that their mum or dad are now somebody else's problem.

Non-Existent Families

There are older people in care who have no family whatsoever. They may have had, but by the time they arrive in care, there is no one left to take an interest. They usually have benevolent bureaucrats e.g., Public Trustees, making decisions for them and who visit even less than the passive family. Bureaucrats are also the butt of much criticism by care staff because of their unresponsiveness and lack of attention to efficient, empathetic and effective decisions.

Helicopter Families

Picture an Apache attack helicopter flying into a war zone in full battle set up. It can fly fast over terrain below and then hover almost stealthily before it descends and wreaks havoc amongst those on the ground. You have the classic metaphor for this family.

These families, or some members at least, have a combative attitude to the care of their parents. Any minor indiscretion, actual or perceived, will be met with a withering array of 'military ordinance'. They can be irrationally irate and even threatening. They will resort to outside complaints processes or legal action without considering any alternative informal resolution. A legal analogy might be that of the vexatious litigant.

They seem to take a perverted pleasure in being disruptors or even guardian angels in their rightful and persistent challenge to the system. They also see themselves as honourable, the only ones prepared to stand up for their parents as opposed to their other 'useless' siblings. Indeed, the latter are often too cowed or intimidated to push back from the outrage.

They often cause severe staff distress and anxiety leading to adverse care outcomes and resignations. Staff churning is not a recipe for good care.

FAMILIAR FAMILY FAILINGS

The least successful families in this context fall into a familiar pattern, or a form of gestation:
- Initially, during their parent's early retirement years, the adult children maintain a state of peace, albeit, sometimes artificially. Stability is the theme. Gatherings still occur under the benign and pacifying gaze of the parents.
- As their parents age, and their needs increase, a simmering state of tension starts to ferment between the adult children as they mumble to themselves, or their spouse, about the lack of contribution or involvement of their brothers or sisters.
- A stage of undeclared war can then erupt when a dramatic event befalls a parent and the pressure reaches an intense stage. The admission of one parent to hospital leaving the other at home is a common spark.

- Temporary truces will be negotiated throughout the conflict stage but soon fail under the growing pressure applied by the parent's increasing complexities.
- Ultimately, 'Berlin' walls are erected between the children, communication is minimal, if at all, and, at best, limited to the necessities. There is almost an irrevocable breakdown in relationships.

This pattern is familiar and so destructive. I devote a whole chapter later to the issue of sibling conflict and ways to minimise it.

However, the initial antidote to this malaise lies in the motivation and willingness of the family to understand what is happening and to join together, not for the sake of sibling relationships necessarily, but for the parents' welfare.

MOVING FAMILY MOUNTAINS

For all the inexorable and inevitable scenarios that this book will examine, the seed for dysfunction arising from parental needs and demands is the failure to do anything to confront their parents' future, ahead of that future.

While I don't recall where I first came across it, there is a saying that still moves me personally, every day – 'If you don't invest a little bit of time and money in yourself, you're a bad judge of a good investment'. To this I would add my own personal spin – 'If you don't invest a little bit of time and money in yourself **and your parents**, you're a worse judge of a good investment'.

One of the great stressors for adult children is that our retirement expectations can clash with other's retirement realities – our parents. As with the moon, both groups are in various phases – the boomers are waxing, and the parents are waning. Having devoted countless hours at work and expended buckets of dollars on their children, many boomers carry into their retirement, their gospel of 1001 things to do based on their theme – 'It's our turn now'. The plans for stage 3 of our lives then meet the reality check of those in stage 4 of their lives.

They don't have time to plan for their parent's future.

What to do then?

Motivating You and Your Parents

Despite the apparent reduction in their responsibilities and activities in their later lives, your parents' lives can become full of more 'things' than they ever had in their earlier, active lives.

The biggest 'thing' of all, the top of the tree of things, the king of things in their lives is—'no thing'—also more commonly known as 'nothing'. Your parents' unerring propensity as human beings to do nothing about confronting the future. There is a saying about Australians – 'we will always do the right thing, once we have exhausted all other possibilities'. Death is not the only trigger for the adverse consequences of doing nothing in life. Doing nothing during our lives can have adverse consequences during our lives. Doing nothing is the illegitimate child of avoidance.

And, for adult children, the biggest 'do nothing' is not confronting their parents' later lives.

In my many presentations to boomer networks and organisations, I have attempted to counter this cultural cringe. I have tried various approaches:

Negative psychology

This approach can be effective to motivate, but only temporarily. Even after being motivated, most people find it difficult to follow up and to activate themselves once they resume their lives amongst the pervading noise of the pleasure principle that most of us prefer to pursue.

The doomsday tactic is that 'pestilence and damnation shall follow you to the ends of your days' if you don't follow my teaching and preaching. For lawyers, this is a natural, if not, instinctive fit. We are harbingers of doom and gloom and the advocates for the enlightening power of the 'what ifs' of life. We tend to wear dark glasses, while our clients prefer rainbow coloured ones.

After the 9-11 disaster at the New York Trade Centre, airline travel plummeted. Within six months, however, normal traffic had resumed. In my own experience as well, it is remarkable how many people who may have heard my message, will show up in my office with the words 'We saw you about three years ago and have now decided we should do something.' Why so tardy? – because something happened! – an event.

While negative messages can have a fleeting persuasiveness, which, as a speaker I often see in an audience's 'noddies', they lack longevity because the power in negativity is fear. Fear, however, hardly ever forces us to action, or, at least, any sustained action. More often than not, it leads us to inaction in order to bury the fear sooner. After all, confronting the fear just prolongs it.

Positive psychology

Ageing positively is a fine mantra and one that I thoroughly endorse. Positivity is a good starting inoculation against the scourges of apathy and avoidance. But, just like fear, positivity is a moving thought, not a pre-emptive action. That mindset must be accompanied by doing good things – activity.

There is the apocryphal story of five frogs on a log. One of them decided to jump off. How many remain on the log? Our logic says four. But the reality is five. Why? Because that one frog only decided to jump – it didn't actually jump.

Action requires an attack on the great cultural failing of we humans, summed up in the aphorism – 'We focus too much on the price of doing something as opposed to the cost of doing nothing.' Thought is cheap but action, or at least, useful action, comes with a price upfront – it's called planning.

To many of us it is an over hyped or even dirty word. Its reputation has taken a battering of late if you put 'financial' in front of it. But, can I repeat myself – I've been passionate about this for a very long time and with good reason. All you have to do is sit in a room in my office and read through a selection of my files (families' lives) and know I speak the truth about the failings of doing nothing.

If your parents can't find their way through the good sense of all this, this leaves you to be the disruptor in their lives – you have to move their mountains and bring them along – to get your parents to take control not delegate, avoid, put it off, cross their fingers, close their eyes or pray to their god.

Dusty Springfield had a No 1 worldwide hit song in 1966 entitled *Wishin and Hopin.* I hate that song. While there is nothing wrong with those aspirations in themselves, they don't stimulate or inspire action – there's no Doin!

DO SOMETHING

It has been said that, broadly speaking, there are three types of generic personalities in this world – those who *watch* something happen, those who *wait* for something to happen and those who *make* something happen.

To that typical cross section of humanity, I would add a fourth – those who *don't know (or want to know) that something will happen.* Those who particularly feature in this emerging cohort are the family 'escapees' – adult sons and daughters who live and work in far-away places. The analogy is the grandparent who chooses a lifestyle just a bit too far away for regular grandchild minding.

Nowhere are these human traits more pronounced and ominous than in our association with the lives of our ageing parents.

In our younger lives, some of us might see the perils of waiting or watching as simply a missed opportunity, something akin to the tantalising allure of the share market. But, the events and stories in this book are not an analysis of the vagaries, uncertainties or the unfathomable 'sentiment' of the marketplace. I am not a financial investment advisor, but I am a family investment adviser, to help find, and prepare for, the future life of your family.

For some of us, the challenge of our ageing parents represents the current reality. For many others, it is a forewarning, if not a foreboding, of what is yet to come. For the recalcitrant, it will be disturbing news, not of the fake variety, but the real variety.

As a value-added benefit, think of this. Experts in many fields of human endeavour, such as economists, can do no more than anticipate the future or, at best, identify and explain trends based on empirical evidence. As an elder lawyer however, I am different – I can predict the future for many families.

You need to 'make it happen' – to adopt the revered Scout motto – 'Be Prepared' to avoid the 'C' Change – the crisis event that you suspected would happen but quietly hoped and prayed, would not. The failure to be prepared will result in crisis management – a family condition to avoid at all costs. Without it, trust me as a lawyer, it will cost you emotionally and financially, both individually and collectively.

STORIES

The Law of Late

Being late is almost fashionable for some of us and I love clients who are late – or even better, clients who are too late – it can be good for business.

In life, you can be late for all sorts of reasons and for all sorts of things – such as an appointment. But, being too late for your appointment with the future is particularly problematic. It leads to so much more crisis management, family disarray and the stuff of legendary, lengthy and costly disputes. Curiously, I tend to find that, the wealthier you are, the later you are for this important appointment.

Wealth seems to create a psychological, if not a practical barrier to being on time. It is hard to confront the future and even harder to make decisions about it in advance. Wealth gives a subconscious sense of comfort – money will get me out of trouble. But, it actually just adds layers of complexity which feeds the aversion syndrome.

Here's a story:
- Bob and Jean were wealthy and elderly.
- They had built up a profitable business and property portfolio over their long lives.
- They had the other usual accoutrements of wealth – a company, a family trust and a self-managed superannuation fund.
- So wealthy were they that they provided handsomely throughout their lives for their adult children with generous financial assistance, in varying amounts for such exigencies as buying a child's first home, getting them out of sticky situations, including for one child, a marriage etc.
- Two of the children were employed in the business.
- None of the children had emulated their parents' success, either in business, or in their lives—two of them had children from more than one marriage.

For each of them, contemplating what to do about their Wills was daunting, so much so, they hadn't managed to do one when, unexpectedly, Bob had a heart attack at the wheel of his Mercedes and died shortly after in hospital. Tragically as well, Jean died four days later after a massive stroke and heart failure in the same hospital.

Mind you, they (and one of their children) had been to a presentation I gave on the subject some three years before at their local Probus Club and, according to the feedback I received from them at the conclusion of the presentation, they were enlivened, emboldened and inspired to do something—hmmm.

We became involved when one of their children was going through their parents' personal things and found one of my handouts from the presentation.

This was not the life legacy that Bob and Jean wanted to leave, compounded, as it was, by having:
- No Will
- No succession plan for the business
- No superannuation death benefit nominations
- No idea on who would control the family trust

- No idea of what do about those 'loans/gifts' to their children.

They left a veritable smorgasbord for a lawyer's picnic (more than one) and family disarray. The only certain beneficiaries of their estates were the unintended and undeserving, people like me.

If only the children, just one, had sought to prompt them to do something which was the clear message from the presentation where, remarkably, one of the children was actually present!

My Parents Won't Make a Will – What to do?

We all, mostly, have an aversion to confronting our celestial transfer, also known as death. We live in hope it will never happen or, if it does, it will be a case of 'don't you worry about that'!

For adult children, confident and concerned enough to ensure their parents have, as they say, their affairs in order, getting mum or dad over the line can be a herculean task. But I have some therapy for parental aversion. Like all good therapy it involves a story, and a true one at that from my own files.

Some of you may remember the 1950's when, traditionally, the men worked, and the women were assigned to homemaking and child rearing. In those days, when the newly minted married couple fronted the local branch manager of the Commonwealth Bank to borrow their first 200 pounds to buy their first 300 pounds home, what was the bank's usual response? Sure, they said, we'll lend you that money but, we'll only lend it to the man. Why? – Because he was, and was expected to be, the sole breadwinner. The spouse could not show any capacity to repay the loan. As a result, only the man became the registered proprietor of the new family home.

Well, so what, you may ask? The man had the usual cultural disdain for making a Will. Fifty years later he dies, without a Will leaving his spouse and four adult children on earth. Here's where the trouble starts.

Not having a Will meant the law, not him, determined what happened to his estate when he died. It's called the law of intestacy. It says (in Queensland at least), that, on his death, the first $150,000 and the household chattels will go to his wife and the rest is split between his spouse and his children. Here's where the trouble got worse.

He didn't die with $150,000 but he did die with sole ownership of that lovely family home bought way back in the 1950's. The children were immediately entitled to a share of the house. You guessed it – the consequence was that the house had to be sold and mum was out on the street.

This is not only a true story, but, as with most sad but true stories, a salutary one. Dad's recalcitrance was bad enough, but what really hurt was the flow on effect on mum. But his true legacy was even more serious and long lasting. The relationship between mum and the children was now poisonous and irredeemable. The true legacy of his lethargy and lassitude was the destruction of a previously happy family.

Should we be Working on our Parents and not just our Business?

First created by Michael Gerber of the 'E Myth' fame, many business owners would be familiar with that ubiquitous mantra – work on your business not in your business.

It was devised in the 1980's when the concept of planning, particularly business and strategic planning, emerged as the motivational ethos and cause celebre for success in business. Along the way, some more subtle notions have evolved to temper the seductiveness of this catch cry – the best known of these would be the search for that elusive business 'Yeti' – work/life balance.

But our lives and our businesses are deluged more than ever with the big 'P' word – Planning. Just some examples include business planning, strategic planning, life planning, estate planning, financial planning, career planning, urban planning, party planning and even that old hoary chestnut, family planning, still occasionally raises its head.

But here's a new one to add to the 'P' word descriptor – Parent Planning – not as you might first imagine it – becoming a mum or dad. Rather, it is all about life coming a full circle – when we become mums and dads to our mums and dads and how, without proper planning, this reversal of roles can have a devastating impact on our business let alone our personal lives.

As is so often the case, experience is the best explanation and here are two stories to make the point.

The Myth and the Matriarch

Maureen was a 78-year-old who, after the death of her husband some years ago, became the sole director and shareholder of her large and very successful multi-million dollar family company. She had four adult children, two of whom worked in the business.

She believed subconsciously in an urban myth – if you lost your capacity to make decisions, your next of kin, in this case, her children, could make financial decisions for her. Consequently, she never put in place an Enduring Power of Attorney formally appointing someone to make financial decisions for her if she ever lost capacity to do so.

Regrettably, she suffered an unexpected stroke one day while working in her office, lost her capacity to make decisions and was left in a semi-vegetative state in hospital. When one of the children consulted me about the situation shortly after, they came to a shuddering realisation that, without the mum having made an Enduring Power of Attorney, no one could make financial decisions for her and the business effectively descended rapidly into a large black hole and was on the verge of liquidation.

The only solution was for someone to apply to a Tribunal to be appointed her Administrator to make financial decisions for her. That's when the real trouble started.

None of the four children could agree who should apply to the Tribunal so they all consulted their own lawyer and each of them made an application in competition with each other. There

were a number of tragic consequences arising out of this imbroglio:
- The legal costs for all of them amounted to over $300,000
- None of them were appointed – the Tribunal appointed a trustee company
- None of the children can stand the sight of each other anymore.

To add insult to further injury, the trustee company determined that it was not particularly interested in managing the business, so it was sold.

While the children's inability to agree on who should be appointed was the immediate cause of this implosion, the ultimate cause was Mum's belief in a myth and the children's failure to ensure she put an appropriate document in place. It was a failure of parent planning.

Time and the Tycoon

Bill was a self-made entrepreneur, an 'A' type personality and a control freak. He was the only child of his age pensioner parents, Maud and Alex. He was also married with four children.

His success had come over many years and at a price for others, particularly for his family and his ageing parents for whom he could rarely find the time to devote to his filial duties. That wasn't a major issue for him while his parents remained independent and able to look after themselves. And, unlike the example above, Bill's lawyer had arranged for his parents to make Enduring Powers of Attorney in which they each appointed Bill to make decisions for them.

One day out of the blue, comes what we term, the 'crisis' phone call from his father to say his mother had had a fall, was in hospital and could not return home as he could not care for her and a nursing home was the only option. Bill's life now turned upside down.

In addition to managing his booming business and resentful family, he was now bestowed with the arduous task of managing his parents. He also came to a stark realisation, that he knew nothing about the lifestyle options that needed to be pursued to accommodate his mother's, let alone his father's needs.

As he grappled with these demands, he came to another red light moment – suddenly his parents, separated, as they say, by illness, would need to be able to support themselves in two homes – the home where the father lived and the nursing home where the mother was destined to go. Just to add to Bill's woes he needed to arrange for the delivery of home care services for his father who was also becoming more fragile.

Being full age pensioners, they could not finance this doubling of living costs and Bill was left to meet their financial commitments. Needless to say, this created tension with his wife as Bill needed to use some of their matrimonial assets to plug up the financial hole that his parents were in.

The other consequence was to his business. Managing his parents was almost a full-time task and the business was suffering from his many absences. Staff turnover ballooned and customers left in droves when they were constantly told that 'Bill will ring you back' but he never did.

Bill, like many in business was suffering a crisis management event in his personal life that wore away at his business and family life. The ultimate result was that Bill was forced to sell his business for a bargain basement price and is working as an employee for a former customer trying to make ends meet. Naturally, his health has suffered as well, and his marriage is teetering on the brink of destruction.

Just talk to me

As Hamlet Herd once said:
*To meet or not to meet
That is the question
Whether tis wiser for a family to suffer the slings and arrows of outrageous dysfunction or to gather and chatter in a sea of troubles or, by opposing, fan the tempest.
Aye—there's the rub!*

I descended to an adaptation of Hamlet's famous soliloquy to raise an issue that impacts on many of us in later life and bedevils our elder law practice – family disharmony and dispute.

Here is a typical scenario we confront:
- An elderly Dad has died leaving Mum at home by herself.
- She is having difficulties with everyday living activities.
- Her five adult children are, in varying degrees, concerned about her future and her needs.
- Family factions start to form with some wanting mum to stay at home and others wanting her to enter an aged care facility (ACF).
- Mum is anxious to stay home and, fortunately, in terms of her options, has significant wealth.
- Some of the children, let's call them the 'right' faction, think that the ACF is a perfect solution as it gives her 24 hour care and is cheaper than intensive in-home care.
- The 'left' faction on the other hand, are anxious that Mum's wishes be respected and anyway, it's her money and she can spend it how she likes.

Each faction has legitimate concerns although potentially different motivations. Nevertheless, Mum is usually keen to have all the children involved and to avoid making herself the cause for a holy war. What is important for all of the children to recognise is that this moment in a parent's life is the classic trigger for either bringing the family together or tearing them apart. Our experience strongly suggests that this is not a time for sibling rivalry or enmities. Instead, they need to suspend their animosities and festering resentments and acknowledge that the family is at a tipping point between unity and uproar.

They then need to go on to recognise the importance of nipping discord in the bud. In our many years on this earth being confronted by these scenarios, has given us a clear insight into the benefits of latter day 'family planning' – the crucial need for the family to meet, as a whole, with each other and Mum and discuss the issues and their concerns. In this day and age, you don't have to be physically present to 'meet' as technology enables us to do that.

Of course, all families are different, and some have regressed to a stage, regrettably, where even being in the same room together can cause them to be spiteful. If that is where your family is at then think about an alternative, a mediation.

Bringing everyone together under the guidance and impartiality of a third party such as a mediator. Mediation has been shown to be very effective in reaching consensus. While it may not mend relationships, it will enable the family to focus on the interests of the most important person – mum.

SUGGESTIONS

So, in distilling this analysis and the stories, what can you as children do to 'help' and avoid the worst of the crisis to come. Here are some thoughts and suggestions:

1. Ageing parents should not be an excuse to wage a de-facto guerrilla war with siblings – it's not about you, it's about them.
2. Take the bit by the horn and show some courage – raise the issues with your parents and your siblings.

3. It is not only 'ok' to raise good planning issues with your parents, it is critical.
4. It is not only 'ok' to discuss these with your siblings, it is crucial.
5. Be prepared to be initially rebuffed by your parents and then accused of blatant self-interest by your siblings in raising the issues.
6. It doesn't matter if you don't like, or get along with, your siblings, you have to suspend your beliefs about them and talk to them – be inclusive, not exclusive as much as it may rankle.
7. Not talking with your parents and your siblings will bring crisis followed shortly after by disaster.
8. Get help for your parents to identify what could be in store for them, and how to plan for it.
9. Help could extend across legal advice, financial advice, tax advice, counselling and mediation.
10. Be prepared to spend money (your parents) to get that help – it's money well spent.

CHAPTER 3

THE HUMAN SIDE – RELATIONSHIPS

We are about to dig deeper into your, and your parents', later lives.

THE AGEING CAULDRON

Ageing is like a large vat or cauldron into which we pour dollops of older people and their families. We then season that brew to taste with some cracked pepper from inheritance expectations, some English mustard from repressed enmities and jealousies of adult children, some jalapenos from incapacity and dependency, some chilli paste from resistant, rear guard parents, and, finally, a large squirt of wasabi paste from the law. That concoction is then heated and stirred. It slowly bubbles and ferments to produce that well-known fine vintage – the functioning family, doesn't it?

In a perfect world, parent caring is best embraced and shared amongst all the adult children. Ideally, caring should be a team task. There is much to be said for the old adage – 'the more the merrier' although, sometimes, 'the less is better' may also apply.

In your parents' generation, having lots of children may have been a prudent, albeit inadvertent, investment in the formidable and disparate needs of later life. My mother was one of five children. In her parents' later lives, those children shared the tasks and her parents even became like refugees, moving to live with various children over time.

But, with many children spread around the country, if not the world, sharing caring can sometimes be impractical. In the USA, aged care is a case of the survival of the financially fittest. But with the typical American entrepreneurial eye, businesses have cottoned on to the opportunity that absentee children represent in the context of caring for parents.

As evidence of this phenomenon, a thriving business has evolved known as 'geriatric care managers'. They are engaged by a family, not to care for an ageing parent, but to manage and coordinate those who actually provide the care and then to provide regular reports to all members of the family, for a fee. They will visit a parent in an aged care facility, for example, or review the provision of care being provided to a parent in their home as well as facilitating or coordinating, the provision of necessary health services. They add another layer to the care cake ensuring the quality of care as well as opening up a transparent and accountable regime to the family.

Family cohesion and calm can also be battered by the winds of financial demands of ageing and care, the diversity of adult children's lives, their responsibilities to their own families together with the tyranny of distance. It can give rise to tensions, demarcation disputes and, sometimes, what I call, the race to martyrdom. In many families there is usually one child who wants, or thinks they are the best, to look after, or take responsibility for, mum or dad. Alternatively, it is their life's luck to be left with the responsibility because he or she is the only one left in town. They become the martyr child either because of altruism or circumstance or even, in some cases, a dastardly, wicked plan.

While often they represent the only realistic alternative and it often works well, the situation can spur the worst features of the martyrdom leading to what I call, the Napoleonic syndrome – the 'my way', or 'I know best way', and that's because 'I know them best'. Their close and, usually, longstanding association with a parent creates a psychosis that they are the only one who knows, and can do, the job.

Having painted such an uplifting and envious landscape for our future, let's now descend to the intricacies of later life relationships most of which I have been exposed to in my practice. The fact that I have, gives some hint as to the complexities that can arise. We tend to see a lawyer's role in family relationships as limited to the traditional one – family law or the law of couples. This next section will show a new area of law which I call the 'Law of Family' and it extends beyond the troubles of a couple into the broader abyss of the extended family.

These 'family' relationships can be a spider's web of delicate connections with your parents, the spider, sitting in the middle of the web waiting for its next victim to happen along. The variety of relationships extends to not only your parents and their relationship, but to your relationship with your parents and your siblings and finally, in the context of your parents, your relationship with your partner or spouse, and not to forget, their parents.

These have been filtered from the many family dynamics that have come before me over time. They demonstrate what truly complex lives we now live and the convoluted balancing act that many of us grapple with. That task will continue to evolve even as I write. I deal with them in this chapter and I am confident some of you will identify something close to home in the words you read.

LET'S TALK ABOUT YOUR PARENTS

Not unexpectedly for a lawyer, but perhaps surprisingly for you, the first question that may need to be asked here is – *who, exactly, is a 'parent'?*

That issue is no mere technicality, particularly in the context of ageing and caring. As we will see throughout this book, longevity has a lot to answer for in terms of the permutations in relationships that it throws up.

But first, a warning – I use the term 'married' in deference to the word that most of our parents would use, rather than the more contemporary word of 'partnered' or its derivations.

THE DEMENTIA DIMENSION IN MARRIAGES

There is a famous and true story of a former judge of the United States Supreme Court, Justice Sandra Day O'Connor, the first woman to serve on that respected judicial body. For some 15 years, while she sat on the court, her husband had been suffering from Alzheimer's Disease. At some point, Sandra found that she was no longer able to undertake her judicial duties and, as well, support him in their home due to his increasing care needs.

Reluctantly, she admitted him to a nursing home – they became separated by circumstance. After some time there, he became infatuated with another resident in the facility who was suffering from the same condition and who, apparently, returned the affection. Their relationship became an escalating collage of concern for the staff at the home – whether to intervene in the relationship, what Sandra would think and whether they should tell her about it.

Eventually they plucked up the courage to tell her. Her response astonished them. She told them she was so pleased for him as he was now finally happy. Somewhat poignantly however, it was revealed last year that Sandra herself has now been diagnosed with the early stages of Alzheimer's.

On the scale of outrage, however, these not uncommon events tend to impact more on us as adult children. Burdened with the initial guilt of a parent having to be placed in aged care, the children can become overly active, and intrusive moral policemen. Not only that, some of them can be bestowed with legal powers, as they see it, to legitimately 'control' their parents' lives, for example, through the auspices of an Enduring Power of Attorney.

As it is often the case for people who suffer dementia, they can 'act out' in ways that are totally contrary to the values or standards they carried with them in their previous lives. In fear of this, I have dealt with many instances of a child who holds this power wanting to literally orchestrate minute details of their parents' lives, in order, as they would assert, to protect the moral values that their parents once had. This often leads to directions being issued to the nursing home about their parents' social interactions, who they can, or cannot be with, and even installing CCTV in the parents' room to ensure strict compliance with their commands.

This can become even more problematic where one parent has died and the surviving parent ends up in a nursing home, single. Again, the vagaries of this scenario are no better illustrated than from my own practice.

A client was one of two daughters of an elderly mother, a widow, who resided in a nursing home. The mother was suffering dementia. She was befriended by a male resident who was not afflicted by the disease. The mother had never done a Will, and, in her condition, she could not. The relevance of this will become clear shortly.

The mother was well off and the gentleman was not. Aware of this, his daughter was very encouraging of the relationship while my client was, initially at first, in a mild state of concern. That concern reached panic level when the man's daughter took them out of the facility one day, purportedly on an innocent excursion. Having done her homework to set it up, she took them to a marriage celebrant who promptly, and with no questions asked, married them. They came back to the facility that day for their honeymoon.

My client's distress at this turn of events was not so much that she had acquired an unwanted stepsister. It was the legal consequences of the event. Not having a Will, when the mother died, she would die, as the law says, intestate. Consequently, if he survived her, he would receive a large proportion of her estate thereby, ultimately, assisting the financial circumstances of her new stepsister and depriving my client of her previous reasonable expectations.

As with many stories from my archives, there is a moral in this one for adult children – make sure your parents have a Will and preferably, before any hint of dementia occurs.

LONELINESS

But, once your agitation on the story above has subsided, consider another perspective to this vexed subject. Much is said about the importance of touch in our lives. One of the more serious side effects of a lack of intimacy in our lives is loneliness. In itself, loneliness can lead to depression and, ultimately, according to the research I have seen, it can hasten death. So seriously is the subject being taken, loneliness has become a political imperative. The UK Government has established a discrete ministry known as the Ministry of Loneliness.

Adjudicating on how our parents live in later life is a tough and often, a divisive and stressful experience. As young children, our parents sought to imbue, or impose, their moral standards on us and were our moral protectors and policemen. Perhaps, not unnaturally, most of us are not comfortable in a role reversal. Of course, having to assess (decide on) your parents' choice of a new partner is not something we are that ready for, or accustomed to.

In reality, it is probably a far too simplistic analogy to compare parents as moral controllers of children with children performing the same role for parents at a later stage. The context is different and the parameters more complex. There is a lot to be said for the beneficial effects of empowerment on our parents' ability and right to lead the life they want in later life without the overbearing influence of the children. As already addressed, there is power in 'touch' as a positive force in later life and as an antidote to the scourge of loneliness. This calls for many of us to suspend our apprehensions and let go of our desire to want the best for our parents, as we see it, rather than as they see it.

On the other side of the moral ledger, lies our innate desire to protect our parents against the pervading infiltration of dementia and other mind-altering maladies. We cannot ignore the potential perverting effect of the disease on our parents' actions, which can be totally at odds with their conduct in their earlier lives.

Where parents are clinically assessed as being unable to make their own decisions, what the law calls a 'loss of capacity', the burden of our role as decision makers is exacerbated and no more so than in the crucial area of our parents' happiness. This naturally gives rise to us wanting to be more hands on, than hands off. At the same time, we want to ensure that our protective instincts and actions are not perceived as self-interest but rather, in the best interests of our parents.

As always when a tension arises between competing, but reasonable principles, the solution, is somewhere in between. It is prudent to keep a wary eye out on, and to scrutinise their activities. At the same time, we should try to avoid wrapping them in a hermetically sealed cocoon ignoring their basic human needs, if not, depriving them of their rights.

In this context, the Royal Commission into aged care has exposed the many areas of abuse of residents in nursing homes. To counter this, there will be increasing agitation and advocacy for residents to be able to install CCTV cameras in their rooms. Some could even beam pictures back to every family members' computer screen, laptop and iPhone.

On this issue, great care needs to be taken. If a resident has the necessary capacity to decide whether they want such a device in their room, so be it. But what of a resident who does not? That will leave the decision to their family and particularly, their decision maker, such as their Enduring Power of Attorney.

It would be so easy for a decision maker, conveniently removed from the situation, but concerned for a parent's welfare, to fall into the easy solution – install. But, what would that mean for the parent? It means they are the one impacted, not you. Their life would be monitored 24 hours a day as if they were on suicide watch. Their privacy would be sacrificed on the altar of protection against a real or an imagined threat to their welfare.

In a broader context, health professionals have discovered that the lifestyle transitions of older people, which are often forced upon them, are inevitably distressing and overwhelming. Moving out of their home of many years into the so-called, 'home like' environment of an aged care facility is potentially traumatising.

To meet this concern, it is now possible to obtain specialised counselling to assist in the transition. These services are available for a spouse who remains at home while the other enters aged care. They can also be provided to a widow or widower who enters aged care. I have found them to be invaluable in both addressing the complex emotions that with this life event but also as a way for a family to ease the inevitable guilt complex they live with every day – their parents' plaintiff plea – I just want to live in my own home.

In the end as well, the change in their parents' lives will challenge the cohesion of the children like no other event in their family's lives. They live on the edge and bicker and disagree about what is best for mum or dad. The assistance of an objective, professional outsider can be instrumental in maintaining that cohesion and giving a broader perspective.

THE SEVEN CLASSES OF PARENTS

Broadly speaking, each of us is unique, as are our parents. However, once you put the description 'parent' in front of them, they can take on a different persona. Experience has given me an opportunity to assess, analyse and then draw certain conclusions about, various parent categories, particularly when they put on their ageing parent badge.

The list of parent classes below is in no particular order:
- Class 1 – Biological parents married once
- Class 2 – Single surviving biological parent
- Class 3 – Biological parents married more than once
- Class 4 – 'De-facto' parents (in-laws)
- Class 5 – 'Macarthur' parents
- Class 6 – The 'I'm no martyr' parent
- Class 7 – Later LGBTI parents.

Essentially these 'classes' of parents evidence the diversity of later life relationships that have developed in response to the force of longevity mixed with increased wealth and later life diseases e.g., dementia. Unlike any previous generations, they also squarely challenge our role as dutiful and attentive children.

Class 1 – Biological parents married once

Speaking purely pragmatically, and as a matter of simplicity, for adult children, it would be infinitely preferable if our parents could live a long, happy and independent life together in retirement, untouched by the spectre of care and dependency and then, as a fitting climax, experience their transfer to heaven together, while abseiling.

As my daughter would say, that is a 'der' dream. It is, generally, inconceivable. Subconsciously, at least, you know that will not happen. The fact that it would not happen, opens up the potential alternatives and simmering realities for your elderly parents. They may want to age together and for a long time and, as most of them earnestly desire, to stay living together in their own home, a familiar and familial environment. Ignoring, for the moment, the adult children in this scenario, to achieve their goals will inevitably place enormous pressure on them, individually, and on their relationship.

They may age together but not in the same way or the same rate. They will generally have, or will acquire, a different constellation of medical conditions of varying complexities and seriousness that will eat away at their independence. Their worlds will get smaller. They won't necessarily drop dead suddenly one day. Instead they will go through a preliminary process from dependency to dying, and ultimately, death.

Nevertheless, they will usually want to care for each other. They will go from mutual lovers to mutual carers. That is both understandable and admirable but, in that desire, lurks a small, albeit well-intentioned, subterfuge. The longer they can portray an apparent ability to cope, both for themselves, and in caring for each other, the longer the discussion about 'where to next' will be avoided or delayed. That's often their plan.

Parents can be sneaky and resort to tricks or sleights of hand to mask any of their emerging deficiencies. In one example I came across, an elderly couple engaged a neighbour, sworn to secrecy, to come into their unit three times a week to provide certain domestic services for cash in hand. The ruse was only discovered when the couple's daughter became suspicious about the amount of cash her parents were getting through each week for no apparent benefit and where neither of them had a driver's licence or online accounts. The suspicion turned to alarm when it was realised the neighbour had been given the elderly couple's passbook account to also withdraw money to pay herself with pre-signed withdrawal slips.

Parents will live in denial for a while but will make at least one concession over time to avoid the spectre of the 'parent removalists'. They could do with some outside help and, with your able intervention, along comes home care to assist with their everyday living activities. This not only has the benefit of helping them, but it can actually provide a source and a sense of dignity for them in both maintaining themselves and their home. Not only that, it provides some, albeit limited, social interaction in their diminishing world.

Ultimately, in this traditional scenario, one, and then the other dies, preferably at home of course. However, events could well intervene to rupture this movie. We now delve into a number of sub species of this particular parent class.

Sub-sets of Class 1

Generally, the picture of the parental class above would be painted from an outsider's blinkered perception of the conventional path of later life and in many cases, is something we would aspire to for our parents. It represents my own parent's world (currently). But as one former, and now deceased, Prime Minister once bemoaned, *'Life wasn't meant to be easy.'* And so it is not, as the future gets closer.

The later life of your long-married parents can be affected by intervening factors in their relationship. Separation can intercede and can occur in many ways because of what I call the 4 D's of later life relationships:
- Parent Death

- Parent Divorce
- Parent Disinterest
- Parent Displacement.

Sub-set – Parent Death

As you might appreciate, as an event, there is not a lot to say in this part, apart perhaps from reminding you – it will happen. The death of one of your parents is an obvious form of permanent separation for them and I deal with the resulting single older biological parent in the Class 2 discussion below.

Sub-set – Parent Divorce

Divorce is also the death of a relationship leaving what was once your 'joined-at-the-(replacement)hips' parents, living a latter-day single life separately and, usually, apart.

Statistics suggest that while divorce in the younger generation is flatlining, it is increasing amongst the older generation. It is difficult to find any statistics in Australia. In a comparable country like America, however, it appears divorce rates for people over 50 has doubled since the 1990's and at a time when divorce rates generally have fallen.

Again, longevity has its tentacles in this development. This development creates truly daunting scenarios for the adult children. The event doubles the demands on adult children, particularly in the area of finances, as I will also discuss in the other classes below.

It also has hidden legal implications. In some States in Australia divorce will automatically revoke a Will. In other States it will have the effect of revoking the appointment of the former spouse as an Executor and any gift to them in a person's Will.

There is one further aspect in this context—the influence of dementia on our parents' relationship.

I recently read an article in *Ageing Care* entitled *I want out of my marriage!* In essence, a 68-year-old woman wrote that she couldn't say she didn't love her husband even though he was controlling, mentally abusive and cold during their 50 years of marriage. Then in later life, at the age of 79, he was diagnosed with dementia. His condition simply exacerbated his previous unsavoury personality. He no longer showered or changed his clothes, had delusions and was paranoid. She waited on him hand and foot. She ended by saying she was tired, felt unloved, used and abused. She declared 'I'm done.' She just wanted out of there.

So, is it off to the Family Court for a divorce? That's exactly where she went.

Sub-set – Parent Disinterest

Disinterest between parents is a subtle, but common outcome of a pedestrian relationship gone sour or south over a lengthy period, where routine rules, resignation pervades and inertia triumphs over action.

It leads to contorted living adaptations described in two acronyms – 'LAT' (Living apart together) or 'LTA' (Living together apart). These arrangements can have significant Centrelink implications as discussed in the *Money, Money, Money* chapter.

I recently came across an example of a LAT. An elderly female client was proud to announce to me on the day we met that, that very day, she was celebrating her 'silver separation' having been separated from her husband for 25 years even though they were still married and living together.

While your mother may try to place a fig leaf over it and explain it away as 'your father's snoring', that only purports to explain the night-time. While a single roof may lay over their heads, for some older couples it is a marriage of convenience untouched by any sense of shared time or support, let alone companionship. It is often too hard or even financially ruinous to untie the bondage of history. There can also be a certain pragmatism in the decision to let sleeping dogs lie – from an age pension point of view, it can be far more advantageous to remain married than to declare singlehood.

However, that 'put a lid-on-it' lifestyle can meet a time of reckoning when, for example, one of the spouses increasingly needs the care of the other. It is often a watershed time when a couple has to confront years of a mutual lack of desire for physical intimacy with a growing need for clinical intimacy. The 'I don't want to kiss you, but I will wipe your bottom if I have to' stage. The adult children will then have to confront the emotional stress of exacerbated parental tension.

On the other hand, the LTA (the living together apart) cohort reflects a more pro-active approach to addressing a couple's later life happiness. It can go from one simple step – sleeping in separate bedrooms for a good night's sleep to the more, new age version – physically living apart but continuing to socialise with each other and friends. The latter lifestyle probably reflects what most of us surreptitiously dream about – the best of both worlds – the comfort of the known and the thrill of the unknown.

For adult children however, separate parents often result, in a doubling of the problem of care responsibilities. When previously they could rely on each parent to provide the care to the other parent up to a point, separation often results in adult children having to divide their time between the two parents. This can also place financial pressures on those children in having to deal with the complexities of the Centrelink implications and the cost of personalised care for each of the parents.

Sub-set – Parent Dislocation

Perhaps the most poignant time for the children of Class 1 parents, however, is when one of their parents is diagnosed with dementia. Clearly, this modern-day 'plague' can severely impact on the afflicted parent and can, ultimately, be a cause of death. It is particularly insidious because it is progressively debilitating, and not a sudden, disabling condition. There is no cure all pill, injection, antidote or inoculation.

It also has serious side effects for others, most particularly for the caring spouse. Not only can the demands of care hasten a decline in their health, but it can lead, inexorably, to a separation, not so much by desire, but by circumstance. The marriage becomes lost for the afflicted spouse at best, and for the other spouse, dislocated. The affected spouse lives in another world and can often see the person they live with as a very helpful stranger or, at worst, an uninvited intruder.

When it becomes too much for the caring spouse, there may be no alternative but for the afflicted spouse to be admitted to an aged care facility. That is an historic and ground-breaking event for the current generation of older people. Their own parents' marriage was usually only ended by the death of one of them and not by the intercession of a mind-altering disease. The traditional path—from home to hospital to heaven now becomes—from home to nursing home to hospital to heaven.

That separation can also lead to downstream complications as we will see later.

Class 2 – Single surviving biological parent

Latter day singlehood brings with it some complex adjustments for an older person and a heightened sense of focus for most adult children. How an older person deals with this event gives rise to significant emotional and practical implications.

The loss of a long-term spouse usually means the loss of a joint way of life, practised and performed, if not perfected, for many years. It can result in the evaporation of the predictable reassurance that their former lives represented, replaced by the tokens and remnants of that life. One death is really like two deaths. The passing away can leave an older person bereft, not only for the loss, but for the future. The familiar sights, sounds and surroundings are but stored memories and stagnant mementos. The emotional upheaval of loss can never be underestimated and for many in the current older generation, it leads to an intense stoicism masking a troubled and delicate time. It can even challenge an older person's reason to be.

A cogent fact in this context is that statistically in Australia, overall suicide rates for men and women are higher in older age groups than any other. Indeed, men over the age of 85 suffer from the highest rate of suicide of any age group and the rate is twice that of teenagers.

A surviving parent can sometimes mutate, transforming their personalities in response to the event. Outgoing and sociable personalities can suffer a crisis of confidence and withdraw from their former way of life. Previously introverted parents can effectively retire from retirement and retreat, converting their home into an island. In one family I was involved with, the surviving wife refused to go to her late husband's funeral, not because she did not have feelings for him, but simply because she couldn't forgive him for having the temerity to die.

Retirement is often associated with the mantra 'What am I going to do now?' The death of a spouse in retirement often raises that question again and somewhat more poignantly.

Later life singlehood will befall most of us. Becoming a widow or widower is an event that at least one partner in a marriage will experience at some time. For some of us, and often suddenly, life comes a full circle. We are faced with many options we never had in our married lives – the sort we had in our late teens and twenties – opportunities to pursue, innumerable choices, things to look forward to – all propelling us into the world of the future.

Those who grasp the chance are said to be 'ageing positively'. All indications are that this approach will aid in a longer, happier life and be a countervailing factor to the common ravages of ageing. Yet despite the vistas opening up in this later life landscape, many elderly single parents, not so much by choice but more by default, retreat, or as I sometimes describe it, marinate in inertia.

There are many reasons for this:
- A permanent consuming grief at the loss of a long-term partner
- Skill sets long lost or even redundant
- Low self-esteem
- Feeling irrelevant or unwanted
- Sense of being surplus to requirements
- Physical preservation and aversion to risk.

Even rejection can play a part. A client recently told me that they had applied to volunteer for an organisation and, despite being eminently qualified, was belatedly told in a one-line email they were unwanted. There is nothing more soul destroying than being an undesirable volunteer.

One of the pervading manifestations of this inertia and the scourge of many later life singles, is the quiet and insidious malaise of loneliness. It is true that all of us can experience this emotion throughout our lives. However, as an elder lawyer, I can say that is a particularly common and virulent feeling in many of my older clients. And it is no respecter of gender – both older women and men are equally susceptible.

Once it takes hold, it can dominate our lives and thinking. It can transform our personality and test even our desire to continue on. It can cause us to do things we would never have done previously – like fall in love on-line and transfer hundreds of thousands of dollars to some love rat in the wilds of Equatorial Guinea.

For the children, it can also be a distressing time, not just for the loss of a parent but in the search to assess and minister to their surviving parent's perceived needs. Some children can tend to smother their parent while others take a hands-off approach waiting to assess the lie of the land once some time has passed. Every parent is different from my experience and the larger the family brood, the more prospect there is for stress to be overlaid on distress.

Some of us may poo poo the soft skills of counselling. But there are professionals who specialise in assisting older people adjust to this latter-day singlehood. Not only that, they can extend their services to the broader family.

Talk, it is said, is 'cheap' but in my experience there is no substitute for it. We have to develop a form of family diplomacy, a much-derided skill on the international stage but a much under-utilised art in families, especially at this crucial watershed in a parent's life. Time to adjust is initially important but a discussion soon after is vital both for the welfare of the parent and in helping them to address the future. Parents are often resistant to this preferring to stew or suffer in silence and stoicism. But the longer a discussion is left to be had, the more fraught can a parent's life become. It will also lead to rising frustration and tensions between the adult children.

But, while it is easy to say, talk, let alone diplomacy, is hard to practise. Not only that, children can often avoid collaborating and prefer the one-on-one approach with their parent. We often see this in the evolution of the 'mover and shaker' child. They're the one who will arrange to bring mum or dad in for an appointment to update their Will or Enduring Power of Attorney, for example. They will arrange any home care required, do the banking, pay the bills and generally be very 'available' for all their parent's needs (wanted or unwanted). For some it is well intentioned but, for others, malevolent.

The counter to this potentially insidious trend is for the other children to be and stay engaged with their parents, or at least as much as possible. Today, there is little practical excuse to do so although there are amongst the smorgasbord of adult children out there, the perennially disengaged.

Class 3 – Biological parents married or partnered more than once

A multiplicity of 'parents' can simply add another layer to the Neapolitan cake of later life for adult children.

The tentacles of parents can reach out to the netherworld of biological children and stepchildren. In these circumstances, death can be not just a great disruptor, it can also be a great discloser. A parent's life secrets can be unveiled on their death and the revelations can be very colourful. In one case we were involved in, much to the shock of his surviving spouse and children, the death of a particular 'socially entrepreneurial' father resulted in the revelation of two previously 'out of wedlock' adult children and an existing de-facto spouse (who was not the mother of the latter children). Indeed, in New South Wales some years ago, in a fight over a man's estate, a court determined that a man had died leaving four spouses all who were equally entitled to challenge his Will.

More common however, is the scenario of an elderly couple who have separated and one of them has subsequently established a de-facto relationship with someone else. With the current older generation, there seems to be a tendency where separation has occurred, not to go through any formal family law processes such as divorce or a property settlement dividing the assets. It's just all too much trouble and expense. For adult children, in particular, this has a number of adverse consequences when the spectre of aged care enters the imbroglio. These include:
- How will Centrelink view the situation?
- Will they be treated as still married or not?
- What do you need to establish they are not, when they are?
- How will their assets and income be treated for aged care fees?
- What does it all mean for their pension?

I will discuss these issues in a later chapter on finances.

However, this leaves the children in a divided family community which is then compounded by the subsequent need for aged care for both parents. Can I then add another complication – the de-facto partner (stepparent) also needs age care.

Picture the scene – there are now three parents to deal with. Quite apart from the financial implications, the sheer task of support and care foisted on the children is now exacerbated by the needs of a stepparent with one further twist – that stepparent also has children, the stepchildren. How will the biological children and the stepchildren demarcate their roles and what inter-play will be required or 'co-operation' will they need.

When I discussed the importance of family 'pow wows' above, when parents' emotional affairs become complicated, there can be no more important time to confront the scenarios with talk than at this moment.

Class 4 – 'De-Facto' parents (in-laws)

Notionally, many of us have four parents for a period of our lives. Our biological parents and our in-law parents.

If there ever was a reality TV show crying out for a script and production, it is the drama packed lives of adult children fortunate enough to be blessed (or cursed) with four ageing parents – their own and their partner's.

Social commentators often describe the challenge for adult children tending to the needs of their own children and their parents as being in the middle of a triple club sandwich. Add the parents in law, and it becomes a quadruple club sandwich. Oh – and did I mention the grandchildren?

As life is not one of planned, or even accidental, synchronicity, having multiple parents at various stages of ageing and frailty can be a menu for a time poor retirement for many of us. It is where your retirement meets their retirement, albeit at differing stages along the continuum.

You only have to consider the possible scenarios at even a superficial level, to realise the mess that you may have to confront. Here is one example from my practice:

- Brendan and Margaret had been retired for just 12 and 18 months respectively. They have four children.
- Brendan's parents were in their 80's, as were Margaret's. While they all still lived together in their own homes, things were starting to get a bit 'iffy' for all the parents.
- For some 6 months before they saw me, Brendan and Margaret had been in 'juggling' phase. Each day just about, Brendan would be off to check on his parents as would Margaret. It was though they hadn't retired, they'd simply changed jobs.
- The inevitable crisis crept up on them when, within 2 weeks of each other, one of their respective parents ended up in hospital as the result of a fall.

- Now they were exposed to the double whammy of what to do about four people for whom something needed to be done.
- My job was to address the various lifestyle options from home care, residential care, granny flats etc. Their job was to make it happen in the context of parental resistance, not to mention differences of opinions between Brendan and Margaret about what should happen to their respective parents.
- In many respects, my role was relatively straight forward compared to that of a financial adviser. As both sets of parents were full aged pensioners, they did not have a lot of resources to play with when it came to practical options.
- Margaret wanted her parents to move in with them and Brendan wanted his parents to move in with them.

Oh dear – it is hard to contemplate a more poignant conundrum for them. It exposed in a stark light, the pressures on boomer marriages given they were now being pulled and pushed between themselves, their parents and their other parents, not just emotionally, but financially as well.

This light becomes brighter even when one of the parents has to move into residential aged care. In trying to meet the financial obligations this imposes on the parent, sometimes the married child may be called upon to help.

Sometimes, to alleviate the necessity to sell the inheritance, their parent's 'family home', the parent's son or daughter agrees to provide some financial assistance for the move. That then potentially places a strain on the marriage. In order to do so, he or she may have to borrow money but the bank will only lend the money on the security of the couple's jointly owned home. The other member of the couple is not too happy about that given they also have ageing parents who may need financial assistance in the near future.

I have even seen an adult child draw down on their superannuation to provide this assistance or give personal guarantees for their parent's reverse mortgage both to help them out, but also to quarantine the joint assets owned with the spouse.

Needless to say, this gives rise to some tension in the couple who have invested in their relationship and finances with the intention of living a long and happy retirement and passing on the fruits of their joint enterprise to their children. The creation of a mortgage in later life is not part of that plan particularly where it is for the benefit of the in-laws.

This parent financing scenario also leads to other considerations. I have seen this development lead to a couple considering and implementing a family law financial agreement between them ('nuptial agreement'). The purpose is to ensure that the finance provided by the son or daughter to their parent is offset against their interest in the couple's assets should they subsequently separate for example. It has also given rise to the necessity for parents to reconsider their Wills where one child has provided financial assistance to them say in the form of a loan.

Quite apart from those complexities, there is the sheer weight of the practical implications of ageing parents merging, in a perfect storm, with parents-in-law. Ensuring their everyday welfare is time consuming and demanding especially where we have to take on the mantle of parent manager.

Class 5 – 'Macarthur' parents

Some of you may remember the famous cryptic phrase of General Douglas Macarthur towards the end of WWII – 'I shall return' to liberate the South Pacific.

That, indeed, is what is happening now in some later lives. A long separated or divorced spouse is moving back in to live with their former spouse, not to defrost a frozen relationship but to provide support and care for their frail former spouse. It's putting revived meaning back into 'till death do us part'. In fact, some have returned in exchange for mutual care and support.

These prodigal spouses are responding in this way, no doubt for all sorts of reasons but essentially to meet the needs of their former spouse and perhaps simply as a reflection of some repressed semblance of affection or sense of delayed duty. Be that as it may, it comes with interesting legal implications and for family dynamics generally.

Despite the fact that they may well have resolved all their property matters many years ago and gone their separate ways, technically, they could fall back into a 'legally' recognised relationship such as a de-facto relationship. Not only can this impact on Centrelink entitlements but it can then create certain legal rights for the returning spouse, both in terms of their right to challenge the frail partner's Will and even their superannuation death benefit.

Those technicalities may not please the children given the complications it poses to the enhanced inheritance expectations they acquired when their mother and father previously divorced. In other words, instead of being the only beneficiaries of their single mother or father's estate, they may have to share it with the returning parent.

Class 6 – 'I'm no martyr' parent

We all carry around a subliminal expectation that our parents will stay together through thick or thin and, ultimately, till death.

Enter dementia to interrupt this expectation. Even then we hold on to the hope that the scourge will just change the landscape of their relationship not its existence. They will each continue their devotion to each other albeit more in the form of a duty. Nothing will distract them from the needed sacrifice for their ailing spouse. They become a martyr.

But sainthood is not always the result and dementia (in a spouse) can change the other one in curious ways. They may determine that sainthood is not for them. They have for all intents and purposes lost their spouse, not to someone, but to something. They are damned if they are going to kneel and genuflect at the bed of their spouse every day in their nursing home bed.

It's time to live life not mortgage it to someone, albeit my spouse of 50 years.

I first came across this breed of later lifers at a conference on dementia in Melbourne. A particular session commenced with four people sitting side by side at a table on the podium, two men and two women probably in their 70's. Let's call them Bob and Carol, Ted and Alice. This was their story:
- Each of them was a couple currently living in a heterosexual de-facto relationship.
- Bob's wife, Cynthia, had dementia and resided in a nursing home.
- Alice lived with Ted in her home but Alice's husband, who also suffered from dementia, also lived in the home with Alice and Ted, making three altogether.

Put simply, both Bob and Alice were living with someone else who was not their matrimonial spouse. Their story essentially was that, while they still loved their respective spouses who were suffering dementia, they did not want to, as one of them put it, sacrifice their later lives by being a martyr to the cause of their dementing spouse. They did not want to divorce their spouses but just find a better way to live outside of a permanent hibernation in their marriage rather than with someone who was now a 'stranger spouse'.

I make no moral comment on this but you can guess that each of their children reached a point of dispair at their parents' actions. They had a moral outrage and a financial concern. Clearly, each of their parents could effectively die with two spouses if they died before anyone else. The financial consequences are obvious.

Class 7 – Later LGBTIQ parents

Later life 'coming out' is more common than you think. Your mum and dad can appear to have a long, faithful relationship until, that is, one of them dies. Death of a partner can have a transformative effect on a parent's personality and expose repressed feelings, if not desires.

I recently had a client who had come to see me on what appeared to be a very common request – to reconsider his Will and related documents following the death of his wife of 48 years. My expectations as to what I thought would be the usual discussion quickly did a sharp left turn.

His wife had died some 12 months previously and in a halting expose of his life since then, he ultimately revealed that as he put it, he had come to a state of self-awareness. He had repressed his growing instincts for the pleasure of male company in deference to what he perceived as the expectations others had of him during his marriage and in his wife's decline. Those standards were very much driven by his children. He recounted the words of one of his children at the celebration of his 50th wedding anniversary some two years before his wife's death. His child had fawned over the stability and solidarity that his parents presented to him and his own children. He waxed lyrical about what fantastic mentors they had been both as parents and human beings.

He had a deep sense of imminent tragedy as he was yet to tell his children something—he had found love in the arms of another man. The story was a poignant one but the task of telling still lay ahead. However, in the meantime he had determined that his new-found love was so powerful that he wanted to make provision for him in his new Will.

It was a challenging time for him and in some respects for me as his lawyer. We so often find ourselves in the role of the devil's advocate and this was a case where I had to be very devilish. I was not making any moral judgement on his decision but simply pointing out some home truths—his intentions were almost inevitably going to lead to a difficult later life with his children (not to mention his grandchildren) and ultimately, could lead to them challenging his Will.

But as I reassured him, it is mostly all about him particularly when it comes to later life. The forces of attachment and affection do not 'retire', they just tend to compete with each other – between our previous life of duties and our chosen later life of discovery.

SUGGESTIONS

In the delicate area of ageing parent/adult child relationships, there is no easy or quick fix to tensions in the respective views on how your parents should live in later life. However, many parents will cling to the desire to do what they have always done in the face of frailty. You on the other hand, will want them to avoid what you see as the clear risks of too much independence or even hedonism.

Here are a number of suggestions to walk this tightrope:

1. Accept that helping will take time and effort. It may require you to rearrange your life to some extent.
2. Put yourself in your parent's shoes as the first port of call. It is easy for you to fall into the much-maligned category of an ageist, or someone who practises ageism, if you don't start with that initial proposition.
3. Ageism will cause you to instinctively believe and act upon some common misconceptions.

The biggest of all of them is that, if your parent is old, then they are not to be believed or trusted to do anything capably or safely without someone holding their hand. It is sometimes called being 'patronising' or 'paternalistic'.

4. Subtly suggest you go with them on their next visit to their doctor just so you can see how they are going from his/her point of view. This will also create hopefully a good working relationship between you and the doctor. To that end, see if your mum or dad will sign an authority addressed to the doctor authorising him or her to discuss your parent's health.

5. Risk taking for them can be good and can even be encouraged so that they can feel, and be, in control to some extent. This will have a positive impact on their self-esteem. However, it may require compromise to ensure the risk is managed.

6. The art of compromise involves the subtle world of diplomacy. Negotiating their lives with them

is a challenge but essential. Putting in place some agreed protocols, not just with them, but with your siblings, is a useful starting point.

7. Don't be afraid to raise with them the prospect of getting help, both for you and them. Counselling in this area is a much-underutilised resource. Remember, getting old is a new experience for them and for you. Aged care counsellors or psychologists can be a powerful tool for everyone to gain insight into each other's position and find a way through the maze of emotions.

8. On a more practical level, getting financial or even legal advice about events e.g., downsizing or transitioning their lives is also helpful but they will need to spend some money to be well informed.

9. Don't take the car away until it is absolutely necessary. Just leave it in their garage and take the keys.

10. Don't be too proud to educate yourself on dementia. Many organisations provide education and training on how to understand and deal with a parent suffering from this disease.

CHAPTER 4

PARENT PERSONALITIES

Having started to dig into the intricacies of parent relationships in the last chapter, now we start mining even further into their changing personalities.

WHAT'S YOUR PARENT'S PERSONALITY?

Health, or more precisely, ill health, has a transformative effect on a person's personality. Some common, if not inevitable, truths about your parents' health might be:
- They will not usually die on the same day.
- They (one of them) will become single again.
- They will not be able to look after each other without assistance.
- They will suffer from a constellation of health issues over time.

- They will become frail and dependant, but not at the same rate.
- They will tend to develop a 'social' life centred around a stable of health professionals.
- They will have to pay something for their aged care.
- They will have a good chance of contracting Alzheimer's disease, the longer they live.

All these truisms may not befall your parents, but take it from me, some, or most will.

In many ways the dynamics of their health will seed the pressure impacting on you and your family. That pressure will build over time. Start is not the right word. It will not start one day, instead, it will creep up on you, initially, with subconscious concern about them leading to increasingly regular checks on them by phone or other technology.

Because you often don't believe what they tell you on the phone in answer to the ubiquitous question, 'How are you?', or 'What have you done today?', it will soon transition to more hands-on surveillance and domestic forensics with regular visits to their home. It will then almost inevitably move to a management role to keep them in contact with their diminishing world and to facilitate the drudgery of bills, maintenance and dealing with the outside world.

The forces of 'stay or leave' will be engaged in a guerrilla war waged between their increasingly addled aspirations of staying at home or not wanting to 'make a fuss' and your benevolent search for what is best for them, not what they think is best. In that epic encounter you will need all your powers of persuasion, cajoling and even sometimes, threats, for the ultimate victory—common sense.

It can get worse. The dominance of their health issues and their rebuffing of your advances can change their personality.

As a couple they have probably melded their personalities to form a working, serviceable operation – the old give and take ethos of a healthy relationship. Fortunately, most often their personalities complement each other's. Your mother may be an unwilling dominatrix and your father a willing supplicant who just yearns for peace or to be de-bothered. Sometimes they may have a tempestuous relationship either because of a clash of personalities or some acquired deficiencies e.g., alcoholism or gambling addiction, not to mention mental health issues.

What is certain however, is that when one of them dies or goes to another place, your single parent's personality will change. It may be in response to a number of factors including adjustment issues, relevance, loneliness, fear, 'woe is me', role deprivation or dependency.

PARENT TYPES

However, lest you think that our ageing parents represent an vague collection of clones of each other, let me break down the various types I have come across over the years and you may identify your parents.

The Middle Finger

This 'ornery' parent is at best, difficult and at worst, impossible. Initially they will delay adjusting their life to singlehood and then simply deny they need to. A lack of insight into the obvious evidence of issues affecting their independence and self-care evokes a strident response to any suggestion of limitations or of even being a danger to themselves. They will usually engage in pitch battles with any home carers brought in to assist them. They are angry at their lot and determined to make others share their misery. They are usually a crisis waiting to happen.

The Needy

They will be unable to adjust to singlehood and increasing frailty. They will yearn for company, conversation and reassurance often creating 'false friendships' with carers and constantly on the phone to family with real or imagined travails. Their emergency call button becomes a call for attention rather than for life saving measures.

The Manipulator

The image of the cardigan and cameo parent is not always what it seems. For some parents, ageing becomes a game of chess playing off one child against another like pieces on the chessboard. I was always told by my parents never to favour one child over another but to treat them equally. It has always confounded me how some elderly parents will resort to Trump-like tactics of misrepresentation, deception, and even lies about other children in some vain attempt to gain an elusive advantage. When confronted by their conduct they almost always rely on the ageing or recall defence – 'I don't remember saying that'.

Ironically, the challenge of being inconsistent and manipulative can be good for an ageing parent's mental acuity and ultimate health. The mental feat of balancing a plethora of untruths can help keep the brain active.

The 'Don't Rock the Boat'

When ageing becomes diplomacy, this parent can be the most difficult. They will repress their feelings and wishes and become supine about their wants and needs, even hiding their ill health. They will go along with every suggestion, sometimes conflicting, from their family about how to get a better life. Personal risk is for others to manage and when asked what they want will normally respond 'I don't know – what do you think?' This malaise often hides a simmering depression which can be very destructive of their happiness and frustrating for their family.

The 'Hide and Seek'

Patronising and smothering children can often be the bane of an older parent's life. In an effort to avoid the daily quiz or interrogation, and the fear of the wrong answer, some parents will resort to subterfuge or secretiveness and downright deception. Hiding something from a child's periscope is a common tactic. Even disposing of something e.g. pills, is often a preferred diversion.

To demonstrate the tricks or deceptions associated with some older people, there is a story told in a book entitled *The Longevity Economy* by Joseph Coughlin. In it he recounts the development of a 'smart scale', a machine that not only weighed people but also alerted a call centre if a person experienced any alarming weight fluctuations. It was a spin-off of the emergency call button. This is the story:

- A single elderly lady who had the machine installed, kept gaining a lot of weight in the evening when she stood on the scale, only to lose what she had gained when she stepped on the scale the next morning. It was as much as 10lbs overnight.
- An investigation revealed there was nothing wrong with the scales, the woman was healthy, eating normally and taking her medication promptly.
- They then interviewed her to get to the bottom of what seemed imponderable.

- This was the conversation:

    Interviewer: 'What is your night-time routine?'

    Woman: 'I do the same thing every single night. I make dinner, feed my cat and weigh myself.'
- It turned out, with more digging, that when she had her dinner each night so did 'Mandrake' the cat, and somewhat of a big feline feast he would have.
- She would then scoop 'Mandrake' up in her arms and stand on the scales with 'Mandrake' still in her arms.
- During the next morning weigh in, however, she did not feed 'Mandrake' or hold him when she stood on the scales.
- A light bulb moment revealed that 'Mandrake' was the cause of the dramatic fluctuations in weight.

Pillion Parents

For years, they were used to sitting in the front passenger seat of their family car. They were more important than the engine because only they could read maps and they were the driver instructor, upbraider, navigator, observer and commentator.

Now they sit in the back seat of their children's car sometimes with the pesky grandchildren or even the grocery shopping. A bit like cattle class.

It doesn't sound substantive but, to them, it is symbolic of a passing of good times and their comfortable role. It can sometimes seethe inside them.

Toxic Parents

While toxic relationships can come in many shapes and sizes, we tend to think of parents as pedestal types. But, let's not kid ourselves – some people might have been better off not having children.

Some parents cannot make the transition from 'care-free' to 'care-full' lives when they do partner and procreate. Their single personality may have been flawed and there is no evidence to suggest that parenthood is somehow a cure to those sociopathic or psychopathic features they may have evinced in their earlier lives.

These toxic parents manifest the usual traits – they find it hard to treat their children respectfully, compromise is not an acceptable solution, being responsible for their own behaviour is rejected and even the ever-present apology is hard to extract. Their unpleasant aspects of their character tend to become exaggerated in later life and, sometimes, they can use ageing as an excuse for their behaviour.

Incompetent parents inevitably feed dysfunction in families. In extreme cases, the family does not function at all because it simply does not exist as a family anymore. I recently sat next to a middle-aged woman who told me she had not seen her mother for over 30 years even though they had lived in the same town all that time. She clearly had unresolved anger and resentment from her childhood related to her liberation from an extreme religious sect to which her mother was an avid disciple. When she freed herself from both the mother's chains and that of the sect, her mother had brought down the guillotine on their relationship.

She had resigned herself and her children to never seeing her mother again. But, as life would have it, word got back to her recently that her mother was suffering from dementia and was still living in her own home alone which was causing great concern to neighbours and those trying to help her. Now the gravitational pull of dependency raised its head. She was in the agonizing position of trying to decide whether to help or not. When I met her, she was still in a catatonic state of indecision under the beguiling force of a plea for parental rescue.

If nothing else, help in the form of appropriate health professionals can be crucial in both deciding what to do and coping with both how to deal with the parent and even your siblings who may be in various stages themselves of coping with their parent. Of course, while you don't have to like your parents, there will be, in most cases, a subconscious desire to help them.

Just End it Parents

There is no doubt that acquired singlehood, when combined with frailty, is a recipe for depression which, together with loneliness, are the two prominent evils of ageing.

It is a destructive form of depression because it can be the result of a reasonable and logical assessment of your circumstances. The old retort, 'But you have your whole life to look forward to' won't cut it that much in their eyes.

These parents are also dangerous. Not only do they have the rational foundations for a pre-emptory end to their lives, they can have the convenient wherewithal to do so with all those pills that dominate their diet. They become a 'worry'.

They can also be resistant to help, even the suggestion of it.

THE RELEVANCE OF HEALTH IN PARENT PERSONALITY

However, one aspect of their lives that cannot be massaged, avoided or even delayed, is the inevitable decline of their physical or mental health.

While ill health can strike at any age, there is a uniqueness about older person's ill health that sets them apart. They tend to suffer from a galaxy of medical conditions rather than one significant malady. It can be the result of the ravages of a misspent youth, bad luck or genes, or just the body manifesting the accumulation of the forces of natural decline or wear and tear. The conditions acquired in later life can generally not be fixed by a pill or visit to a hospital. They arrive, but they don't leave and, over time, tend to make their presence more obvious.

The older person's health then begins to take over their lifestyle. It starts almost imperceptibly at first. The effort of the daily walk, the bypass of the annual holiday, the cob-webbing of domestic equipment, the withdrawal from social participation, or the dog dies and is not replaced. It begins a slow process of de-commissioning their lives motivated by de-motivation and physical disinclination. Any 'feel good' factor in making an effort starts to leak away.

Life becomes smaller and sedentary. They don't go out anymore instead, they're taken out for a glimpse of the outside world or to reminisce. The din of voices is replaced by the ding of texts or television. Their doctor summons the courage to say what they never want to hear – I'm afraid you can't drive any more.

The Big 'D'

Dementia is the ultimate elephant in the home. It is not an infection but an affliction robbing an older person of their dignity, character and personality, and, ultimately, health. It can lead to death.

In the meantime, it can also be an infliction on the broader family. Fathers and mothers become strangers to each other and their families. They also lose their innate sense of risk meaning they become dangerous to themselves and others, not necessarily because of any recklessness tendencies, but because of a lack of perception of danger. There is no other disease in my experience that so challenges relationships or family units than this one.

Before a parent suffering this disease ends up in a secure aged care facility, the sheer time, effort and energy to be on a constant welfare watch for a parent in this situation takes a toll on the adult children. Plans involving care rosters are often drawn up including some respite for the other partner. But with so many children spread over the world, it often falls to the local martyr child to be the 'gentle organiser'. For those children living elsewhere, direct conventional communications with the parent is no longer possible meaning that local child, in similar vein to the old 'town crier', then becomes also the 'parent crier' loading more responsibility on them.

People rarely end up in a hospital because of this disease. The condition is not necessarily life threatening at first, but more a behaviour control or management issue. That leaves families and spouses with some invidious and limited choices – manage at home or be managed in a nursing home?

But first, let's consider the position of the other spouse. The afflicted spouse will test the vows, physical prowess, stamina and mental health of the other spouse. It will force them to convert their home into a locked facility and all eyes and ears will focus on the afflicted one. It is like being a sentry walking on eggshells. That can have significant downside effects on their health. Loaded on top of the anguish and anxiety is the practical task of caring which will then be lumbered with a further responsibility – the legal task of making decisions for their spouse. One of those almost inevitably will be whether to admit the other spouse to a nursing home.

Adult children need to be conscious, on an ongoing basis, of this quiet strain being experienced by their mum or dad who are generally reluctant to complain. There can be a tendency to focus on the needs of the afflicted spouse and to make unthinking assumptions about the coping abilities of the other parent. Nevertheless, appreciation must always be had to what is best for both of them. In some cases, this can be what appears to be the worst for one of them. As a cynic once said to me – perhaps in light of demographic developments, we should change the marriage vow to '...till death or dementia do us part'.

And in the shroud of dementia, lies another tributary that lawyers are particularly aware of and which impacts significantly on the quality of later life. We call it in the law of capacity – the ability of a person to make their own decisions.

While I discuss in more detail the legal aspects of this concept later, in the context of health, the mental ability to decide about our health is something which most of us take for granted. Children often tend to pre-judge their parents on this aspect because they know what's best, don't they? What children often have to grapple with is the parent who decides to do, or not to do, something which the children disagree with. What makes good sense to some is bad karma to others.

By itself, being diagnosed with dementia is not a penal sentence of decisional servitude to the whims of others nor, indeed, a declaration that you have lost the ability to make your own decisions. The ability to decide for ourselves is integral to our human essence, our self-esteem and, thereby, our mental health. The law is loath to take away that right, as we will see, and children should be equally conscious and careful not to do so, even where they consider their parent's decision to be silly.

FRAMING THEIR FUN AND THEIR FRAILTY

Is there room for fun in your parents' frailty?

We tend to have a clinical view generated by that big 'F' word, 'Frailty'. Perhaps this is nowhere better demonstrated than in the breathless celebration and collaboration of marketers and techno geeks who see the aged as a market for the expropriation of frailty. Their inventiveness has produced such remarkable achievements as care robots or sensors placed under a mattress or in walls or floors, that can send night-time heart rates, and breathing and movement rates direct to your doctor or your family. Just add a CCTV camera in every room just to ensure that no one misses a thing and there you have it, parents, cling wrapped.

As an age agnostic, I ask – where does the other big 'F' word, 'Fun', fit in our parents' later lives? Can frailty come with fun or are they are bit like pineapple and pizza? What if we started with the idea of fun and see where frailty takes it?

As we get older, the tendency towards isolation inevitably leads to a loss of identity mixed with a certain aimlessness, if not idleness. Try asking your parents what they look forward to most and then wait and wait for their answer after the 'ums'.

Meeting fellow travellers in later life becomes not just difficult, but daunting, especially after becoming single again. How difficult would it be for your widowed father, in his 80's, to ask a woman at line dancing 'Would you care to dance?' He may not have used that phrase for a very, very long time.

Familiar places of interest, such as clubs or interest groups, may appeal to the particular interests of an older person. Clubs, however, don't cover all human interests or meet all their needs. But, venturing further requires effort, a curiosity, a sense of enquiry and a regular commitment.

While I deal with the vexed subject of sexual expression in a separate chapter, no discussion about fun can ignore the joy of heart palpitations.

Admittedly, if your parent is a 'middle finger up' parent, they may prefer to brood in a cupboard on a desert island. There is no denying, however, the health and mood benefits of company in whatever form it takes in later life.

As with all things good, however, come what most of us would perceive as bad things. I give a presentation to older groups entitled *Is it Love or Larceny?* addressing the older financial victims of the virtual world. Companionship for some older people can be miniaturised down to their computer desk. Hucksters will pray on the downsides of isolation through the ubiquitous online scam. When combined with online banking, the virtual relationship carries with it an intimacy and privacy often valued by older people. Even when confronted with an obvious financial fraud on them, some older people will dismiss it in a so what moment – it's my money to do with as I want. It still makes them feel better even though it is a fairy tale.

So, where does this leave you, the attentive, caring adult child? You can perhaps accept at a rational level, the importance of company in whatever form it may take for your parent. Emotionally however, it does come with fear. Our protective instincts, sometimes characterised as moral policemen or a parent 'health and safety officer', can too easily kick in. It may be well and good to monitor your parent's conduct, but to orchestrate it, is another thing.

The answer may be to encourage them to involve themselves while maintaining an inconspicuous oversight. In this, online banking is a boon for parent overseers. Having access to their accounts is not only prudent but enables you to avoid that deathly problem that many of us have – no one else knowing what our online passwords are when we die!

LUI – LOVE UNDER THE INFLUENCE

According to a research paper produced by the University of Leicester *The Psychology of the Online Dating Romance Scam,* flattery, affection and the discovery of common interests are some of the techniques that psychology-savvy scammers use to start the flare of romance. Once the romance has started, the victims become obligingly complicit in their own exploitation. Despite all the signs that they are being financially and emotionally abused, the victims scoff at any doubts expressed by others and allow the delicious self-delusion of love and commitment to carry them away.

As we all know, life is full of harmless self-delusions. My personal favourites are that the more chocolate I eat, the healthier I become, and that coffee is the elixir of youth.

But, for some people, their delusions are so powerful and compelling that their flawed thinking distorts their view of the world including how they make their decisions. Being able to make rational decisions is the cornerstone of good decision making and when our decisions are based on false and fanciful ideas, it's likely that our decisions will be at best quirky or odd, and at worse downright damaging.

But for a person who is otherwise well and with it, at what point do these delusions warrant the removal of the person's ability to look after their own affairs?

In a 2013 case, a Tribunal had to grapple with just that question. 'Faye' was an elderly woman who fell in love, via her computer monitor, with a man who described himself as a retired US criminal lawyer.

Like most victims of romance internet fraud, following the death of her husband, Faye had been leading a comfortable and well-ordered life until the day, with a click of her mouse, she entered the world of internet scamming.

Her family and friends became worried for Faye. She could think and talk of nothing other than this so-called retired lawyer who, it appeared, just like her, was alone, lonely and emotionally needy.

Faye, like so many of these victims, was fixated by the belief that she and this man were going to marry and spend the rest of their lives together. She rejected any suggestion that, in sending him large sums of money, she was being ripped-off. The sad truth was that the scammer was a gambling addict and ex-criminal who was bleeding Faye's financial security away while living with his wife in Illinois.

Faye's case was challenging for the Tribunal because she didn't fit into the usual mould of incapacity.

Two psychiatrists had found her to be cognitively intact. Apart from her General Practitioner who assessed her as being depressed and having lost touch with reality, there was simply no medical explanation, such as dementia, to explain her delusional behaviour.

However, in finding that Faye lacked capacity to manage her financial and personal affairs, the Tribunal said:

> *This case is unusual as there is no underlying broad category of disability which explains FAJ's lack of capacity ... the three health professionals support that FAJ is not suffering from any recognisable psychotic illness, a major psychiatric illness, any cognitive impairment or dementing process.*

The Tribunal found that not only did Faye lack capacity to understand the nature and effect of her decisions but that the scammer was 'exerting *control over and influencing FAJ to the extent that he is preventing her from freely and voluntarily making decisions.*'

Faye's case is insightful in relation to the issue of a person's capacity. Despite the fact that she apparently understood the nature and effect of what she was doing, the Tribunal found that she was not making these decisions freely and voluntarily and that was enough to determine that she did not have capacity to make her own decisions.

TAKING THE STUBBORN OUT OF YOUR PARENTS

For all you adult children out there, in respect to your ageing parents, do these little epithets ring a familiar bell?
- They say they'll let you know when they need help.
- They ignore doctors' advice.
- They want to do things their own way.

One adult child lamented to me that their parent told them they had 'the right to fall', after the parent's third visit to hospital following another fall and after the parent had read a social media post on the importance of self-empowerment for the elderly.

You may not be surprised to know that a recent Penn State University report on stubbornness amongst ageing parents found almost 80% of adult children said their parents were guilty of stubborn behaviour. But here's the real rub – almost 70% of those parents also described themselves as stubborn. That is a dynamite combination for frustration, if not, screaming matches.

The family Mexican standoff may be familiar to you. It's a titanic clash of expectations between what we need, what we want and what's good for us. Everyone comes at it from different and understandable perspectives:
- For parents, what is important to them is being able to do what they have always done or wanted to do. Social scientists call it 'autonomy', or we would call it, self-control. A parent's insistence, persistence or resistance is their attempt to avoid being thwarted from their desires and habits. As they see it, they may have been integral to your growing up, but they don't need you in their going down.
- For children, the old shibboleth that 'with age comes wisdom' is poppycock. Age brings with it a loss of reason, insight or even a failure by parents to remember their own experiences e.g., when they had to care for their parents.

Needless to say, there is no quick fix to this 'war of wants'. For one thing, a frontal attack on your parents with a string of expletives will not usually bring a light bulb moment for them. It could just encourage more parental trench digging and construction of firewalls. But one thing is certain – the art of negotiation becomes the secret to success. Successful negotiation is often described as a 'win/win' outcome. The real art in negotiation, however, is persuasion.

While there is no secret formula to persuasion, here are some techniques that have been used as an antidote to stubbornness:

- There is power in numbers. If you are one of five children, it can be very helpful if you, and all your siblings, are on the same page in terms of your desires for your parents.
- While that, in itself, may represent another element in negotiations i.e., with your siblings, the force of the combined family front can never be underestimated in a parent's eyes.
- If you happen to have a health professional in the family e.g., your daughter or son is an occupational therapist or physiotherapist, get them on board. Many parents

regard their children and their motives with scepticism. But, when it comes to their grandchildren, they can have a special place in the grandparents' eyes.

- Target your parents' subliminal guilt complex. They often don't appreciate the hurt and distress caused to you and other members of the family when you are rebuffed. The more you are rejected by your parents the less likely you are to persist in getting them to seek enlightenment. Indeed, adult children often report a lingering depression as a result of their parents' inflexibility.
- Find a compromise. There is usually a middle ground that gives the appearance of success to a parent but, in reality, hides a small portion of success for the concerned children. It is elusive, but often attainable.

Finally, and perhaps not surprisingly, the Penn State research also found that the stubbornness index rises as a parent's frailty increases and even more so, if a child lives with a parent. As frailty has an inexorably upward trajectory in the ageing journey, and as more and more children are starting to care for their parents, there is a forewarning, if not foreboding, for adult children.

It may be time to prepare for this later life battle or even to consider upskilling your negotiating skills to be better prepared.

THE PARENT WHO JUST WANTS TO GO HOME

Very few people want to stay in a hospital or an aged care facility.

However, we often hear of hospitals complaining about 'bed blockers' – they're usually referring to older patients for which the hospital says they can do no more, but the patient won't, or can't, leave the hospital. This arises usually where, for example, the patient is not able to go home and the family needs to frantically find some aged care facility or respite care as an alternative.

I have sympathy for the hospital and the patient in this situation. I do find it difficult to sympathise as much with the family who have usually done nothing to anticipate this event.

There is a concerning variation on this theme developing—where a hospital does not want an older patient to leave and go home even though the patient wants to, as do their family. The hospital strongly believes that, while the patient can leave, they can only go to one place – a nursing home.

I had a recent example of just this scenario. A hospital, in effect, would not let a patient leave unless it was in the back of ambulance on its way to an aged care facility. What's more, they told the patient and their family that if they did attempt to 'retrieve' the patient from his bed and take him home, they would call the police. As both the patient and his family, including his Enduring Power of Attorney, were adamant that he would be leaving, I am not sure what offence either the patient, or his family, were allegedly committing.

I have no doubt the hospital was well intentioned and truly believed that their duty of care to the patient not only applied in the hospital but outside the hospital as well.

Regrettably, I call this an emerging 'clash of the titans' issue in ageing – what's good clinical care may not actually be what the patient wants nor, indeed, what the law prescribes.

So, what does the law say? It says:
- If a person has the capacity to make their own decisions, they are entitled to do so and that could includes leaving a hospital even where the clinical indicators suggest they should not.
- If a person does not have the capacity to make their own decisions, whether the patient stays or goes, becomes a decision for their substitute decision maker, such as their Enduring Power of Attorney.
- A hospital has no power to restrain or prevent a patient from leaving. To do so against the patient's wish or that of their Enduring Power of Attorney, could well result in the hospital committing an offence e.g., assault or deprivation of liberty.
- If a hospital has significant concerns about a patient leaving or the

appropriateness of a decision by their Enduring Power of Attorney to take the patient home, it can raise its concerns with the appropriate authorities in a State or Territory such as a Public Guardian or Guardianship Tribunal.

This is not a simple case of 'goodies and baddies'. It is more complex. While the law may be counter-intuitive to what we think is best for someone and their decision to leave their hospital bed and go home might be silly, the law says most of us are entitled to be silly.

SUGGESTIONS

In the process of ageing, your parent's personality can change and become more difficult. Think about these suggestions in coping with their transformation:

1. Stay calm and try to understand the personal effects of their health and ageing and not treat them as an errant child because of their 'bad behaviour' or 'acting out'.
2. At some stage, your parents will imperceptibly mutate from the

generic image, a 'parent' to a discrete reality, a 'person' with all their foibles and idiosyncrasies.
3. Be a benign monitor of their activities and emphasise the importance of ensuring that they have you on their side when it comes to looking out for them.
4. Be on the lookout for loneliness and depression. It will show up in a transformation in their personality or acting starkly out of character. Get their doctor on side.
5. Sadly, you may have to devote your time to spending your time in keeping them active and engaged.
6. Don't be patronising or paternalistic – parents hate being treated like children.
7. Share the load with your siblings (or try to).
8. Reminiscing is important as we get older but get help if this translates into hoarding.

CHAPTER 5

YOU AND YOUR SIBLINGS

THE SIBLING WORLD

Your relationship with your siblings is usually an evolving journey, the complexity of which is not restricted to large families, although many baby boomers have many siblings.

As young children, our relationships were child-like, infused with innocence, discovery and playtime. Adolescence brought new pre-adult tensions complicated by intrusive social forces, attractions and relationships outside the confines of the family. We garnered friends, usually from our school and tertiary days. Family became a part of our world as opposed to our only world.

As we rose through adulthood, the simplicity soon transitioned to more complex elements of sibling relationships some of which were attributable to repressed and unpleasant experiences with our siblings.

Marriage and children gave us an outlet to further suppress those anxieties as our attention and focus were now on other more important things or relationships. A ritualistic civility usually prevailed in our sibling relationships. As well, our parents were often the cause for maintaining peace and tranquillity. They were usually the glue that kept us all together, on the surface at least.

In the golden olden days, dysfunction between siblings usually only erupted when the parents were no longer here – they died. Now the seeds are sown much earlier, when the parents are still here but, having lived so much longer, become dependant and even lose their capacity. Now your relationships will be tested like never before.

It can start quite innocuously. Your mum is in her 90's and lives alone in her own home. She is relatively healthy except for some hearing loss. She has all her marbles, has had no falls and still gardens. All seems well in parent land.

Your sister is very proactive and protective, calls your mum every day, takes her to appointments and is generally closer to your mum than you are. But you have been happy to accept that.

Recently, unbeknown to you, your sister had taken mum to have a look at a retirement village unit with a view to selling her home and moving into it. That home is very valuable and, on its sale, may leave your mum with a problem in relation to her age pension given that she would be left with a large amount of the equity even after purchasing the retirement village unit.

When you do find out, you raise some concerns with your sister (not to mention that she didn't tell you what she was doing) namely that, at your mum's age, maybe the independent lifestyle is not the appropriate place for a 93-year-old and the effect it might have on her pension. Your sister won't engage in discussion about it saying simply that she has discussed it with your mum, and this is what she wants to do which is all that matters anyway.

Now where do you go? On the family thermometer, the mercury is rising. You and your sister are in parallel universes and probably not even at a stage of being able to compromise. Time to bring in the experts, me thinks, because they can be a circuit breaker and you should never be ashamed to suggest it given your concerns are serious and could severely impact on your mum and her finances.

Your sister is revealing all the traits of the benevolent manipulator and ensconcing herself as irreplaceable in your mother's eyes. You can quickly become a bit player in the saga as you don't have the 'caring' runs on the board.

Time to get involved and bring in some circuit breakers before you end up at 10 paces with your sister. The best approach at this stage is information. Your sister is acting out of a limited view of the world – where is it best for mum to live? But there are implications and tributaries to know about in such a move. Gather your information in terms of what it means to her pension, the change in her lifestyle and life in a retirement village. Then sit down with both of them and convey the information. It might just pull them back from the brink.

SIBLING CONFLICT OVER PARENTS – IT'S A KILLER

To you adult children out there, as an Elder Lawyer, there is one thing I have learnt in dealing with conflict in families over the interests of mum or dad – sibling conflict is a killer.

While such conflict will not normally result in a death *in* the family, there will be a death *of* the family.

High need, dependant parents can expose a combination of terminal conditions in siblings – arrogance, self-righteousness, repressed enmities and jealousies, machinations, manipulations and the, 'I know what's best' syndrome. Together, they plant the seeds of family ruination. It leaves mum and dad in desolate despair, implodes sibling relationships, infects even the relationships between nephews and nieces and ultimately, the indignity of the intrusion of benevolent bureaucrats into the family's life.

The rumbling usually begins when a parent's incapacity requires decisions to be made for them. Dementia demands decisions and those decisions have to be made by someone.

The rumblings spur the first signs of bumbling in the children especially when decisions have to be made in a time of crisis. They tend to frantically search for answers as to who can make decisions, especially if mum or dad haven't made an Enduring Power of Attorney.

The bumbling then feeds the crumbling of relationships in a cesspool of disagreement and inertia. Conflict is the inevitable result.

Regrettably, few children in this situation realise the calamitous consequences of conflict, not just in terms of relationships and the best interests of mum or dad, but in who will actually end up making decisions for them—it won't be the family.

I have repeatedly witnessed in the Queensland Civil and Administrative

Tribunal (QCAT), siblings competing with each other to be appointed their mum or dad's decision maker. Perhaps the most dramatic I was ever involved in concerned an 83-year-old matriarch of a large family, multi-million dollar, company. Her husband had died many years ago. She had four adult children, three of whom were lawyers. The mother was the sole director and shareholder of the family company and was a controlling type. She was the sole signatory for all company cheques.

One day, she was sitting at her desk singing cheques when, suddenly, her head fell heavily onto the desk after suffering a massive stroke. She ended up in hospital in a vegetative state. The problems had just begun. She had never made an Enduring Power of Attorney believing (if she ever thought about it), that her next of kin, her children, particularly those lawyers, could make decisions for her if it became necessary. Regrettably, that was an urban myth and the reality was no one could make financial decisions for her. The company came to a grinding halt.

The solution was to apply to QCAT to be appointed her Administrator. Problem—none of the children could agree who should do that. So, they all applied in competition with each other. The tragic consequences were many – none of the children were appointed, the Public Trustee was. The legal costs totalled over $400,000. Worst of all, those children do not talk to each other anymore – their relationships are toxic and will remain so probably for the rest of their lives.

While competition as a concept is generally healthy, it is certainly not in QCAT. It tends to have an aversion to appointing competing family members. Competition is just another word for conflict, and it will not usually appoint any conflicting parties because it will invariably exacerbate the conflict.

Instead it will usually appoint a bureaucrat such as the Public Trustee or Public Guardian. What was once a private 'family business' now becomes a very 'public business'. Ponder the thought of that on your family. The word frustration, amongst many other less polite feelings, comes to mind.

When you feel the gestation of conflict simmering in your family, ask yourself a question – do you want to kill the conflict or kill the family? If the former, don't be too proud to ask for help which may be as simple as – how do we communicate better? Without that, family conflict will remain a killer.

SIBLINGS GONE BAD

Regrettably, the best laid plans of siblings will come asunder, and often spectacularly, where some siblings just won't come on board. They see the effort of coming together as more of an opportunity for revenge or righting a perceived sleight from some 30 years ago.

Their warped agenda is often encouraged by parents who have no insight into the failings and flaws of that much-loved son or daughter. They are usually the ones who excelled at something in their earlier life. It gave inestimable pride to the parent at some stage and which is forever banked and brought out by the parent whenever their shining son or daughter is rightfully criticised for some transgression, or arrogance.

On the other hand, the parental bias may be the result of pity. One of the children was the 'runt' of the litter and never quite reached the dizzy heights of the other siblings. As a result, the parents may have sought to compensate that child by being overly protective either emotionally or even financially even throughout that child's adult life. This is usually the child that has live with or close by to their parents and can take on the bragging rights of being more 'familiar' with the parents' needs than the other siblings.

STAY PUT OR BOOMERANG SIBLINGS

Some adult children are like boomerangs – they may have been politely thrown out of home many years ago but now, they're back!

We call it the 'Rodney' scenario. 'Rodney', or it could just as easily be a 'Rachel', is the proverbial or prodigal adult son or daughter who has come back home to live with their elderly parent/s and just won't leave.

For some parents, their 'Rodney' may have been a fixture in the home since birth and has become rusted on to the furniture. Another type of Rodney may have moved out of home many years ago but been driven back by life's tribulations – marital break-down, bankruptcy, or just an inability to cope in the world due to mental illness or a personality disorder.

Every day with these 'Rodneys' can be like walking on glass and they can make a parent's life hell – emboldened by a sense of entitlement (after all they are your flesh and blood), they usually refuse to help around the home or contribute to the cost of living, they can be obnoxious or worse, they could be financially, physically and emotionally abusive.

Confronted by the nightmare, the solution seems obvious, just ask Rodney to leave. But what if he thumbs his nose at your polite request or pulls on your heart strings with the wailing mantra, 'Do you want to see me living on the streets?'

A parent will have to confront some conflicting forces:
- A natural parental protective instinct not to see a child on the streets
- Coping with the stress and anxiety of their presence
- Exacerbating the situation by requiring the child to leave
- Wondering who else in the family you can call upon for help without creating another family fire
- Wondering should they suffer in silence?

The biggest challenge will come when a parent decides to bite the bullet and resort to the law for help. Unfortunately, the law does not usually provide any quick, easily accessible and cost-effective way to resolve the imbroglio not to mention the effort in resorting to the law can simply accentuate the anxiety and distress.

What may be an appropriate legal recourse will, as usual, depend on the circumstances. Generally, the recourse could range across criminal law (trespass), civil law (court ordered injunctions), domestic violence law or even residential tenancies law.

THE SIBLING WHO IS A NUT

These are the words a client recently said to me, 'My sister is a nut and is married to a nut and now she's turning me into a nutcase!'

Some years ago, in what was a large and dysfunctional family, her mother had appointed the 'nutty' sister as her Enduring Power of Attorney (EPOA). No doubt, in a family of seven children and knowing the state of her family, the mum would have approached the task of making the EPOA with some trepidation. She would probably have earnestly hoped as well that the power she was giving to her daughter would never have to be used. As events unfolded however, her hopes were to be dashed.

Two years ago, having experienced a stroke at the age of 82, the mum was in need of fulltime care and support. For reasons that became clear later, the sister was more than willing to take on this task especially as none of the other children were prepared to

put up their hands. However, it what is an all too common phenomenon, within a short space of time, the sister began to assert her 'authority' under her EPOA including:
- Taking control of mum's finances and arranging to pay herself from her mum's money for her work as the EPOA and transferring a weekly amount for board from her mum's account
- Refusing the requests of the other children to take mum out for the day
- Not allowing any of the other children into her home to see their mum without the sister or her husband being present and then only for a short time
- Returning unopened letters and cards sent to the mum by the grandchildren.

Needless to say, the sister's conduct was tearing the family even further apart and exacerbating their pervading concerns about their mum.

We have struggled for years to understand the psychology and motivation behind this type of conduct by an adult child. It can be the blossoming of years of resentment for whatever past or perceived injustices. Alternatively, it can be a latent desire to simply take advantage of the situation to their own financial benefit especially if they have been bestowed with the power of an EPOA.

From our years of experience with this conduct, what we do know is this:
- Parent isolation is one of the favourite techniques of a child who is embarking on nefarious activities with a parent's affairs.
- The Enduring Power of Attorney is the favourite tool for this purpose.
- Few of these 'no-gooders' appreciate that an EPOA is not a blank piece of paper, a power without strings attached or worse, a blank cheque – it comes with responsibilities, duties and obligations of transparency not to mention penalties for doing the wrong thing.
- When children are conducting themselves this way it is crucial for the other members of the family to act quickly.

There are various options available to quickly address these concerns which can be so important in protecting the rights and interests of parents in this situation. See some suggestions below.

THE PARENT SHUT OUT

There is nothing like an ageing, frail and dependent parent to bring out family factions most notably, the 'caring child' who shuts out the 'concerned child'.

Sometimes, the role of the caring child is a function of luck or logistics. They happen to live near mum or dad and are, consequently, conveniently able to provide the hands-on care so often required. Meantime, the other children are spread all over the country, if not the world, anxiously awaiting reports from the caring front.

At other times however, as luck would have it, the most available child can be the worst candidate for this crucial role. They may not be well suited for the role emotionally, or even financially. They can also feel emboldened, for example, by the knowledge that their parent has actually chosen to bestow upon them legal responsibility when the parent appoints them as their Enduring Power of Attorney. They can also believe, both because of the power they have and because of a certain martyrdom syndrome, that they are entitled, occasionally, if not regularly, to take advantage of the situation.

Because the law does not create a regime requiring transparency and accountability for the conduct of Enduring Powers of Attorney and because our whistle-blowing laws are so inept, what was once, perhaps, a noble commitment by the caring child becomes a tool of enrichment and a weapon of exclusion.

From our extensive experience in later life family dynamics, there is one pervasive technique that distinguishes the gestation of an abusive child and raises alarm bells – isolating or shutting out other naturally interested people. Keeping mum or dad hermetically sealed from the outside world is the obvious way to avoid scrutiny and accountability.

A particularly poignant case of this practice was recently exposed in Tasmania where a daughter (and the son-in-law) had kept her mother in a shipping container without necessary care locked away from 'interfering biddy bodies'. The trail of tragedy revealed in this case was truly inhuman and inhumane. It contained, however, the familiar prevailing theme – isolation.

To be fair however, some caring children will engage in what they perceive as well-intentioned isolation. Away from prying eyes, they can enjoy the sympathy and admiration of outsiders for the herculean task they have assumed. They can want to avoid the input or offers of help from their siblings because, in their eyes, it can only complicate or disrupt the carefully crafted routine they have established for their parent.

Be that as it may, excluding or orchestrating a parent's contact with the outside world does nothing positive for the quality of life of that parent. It exacerbates an already divided family and can create a maelstrom of negative emotions for the parent who can often feel hapless – like a ventriloquist's doll.

While it is easy to say, caring for an ageing parent should be a collaborative not a divisive exercise. Where it is difficult, strained, or made impossible, it can be hard to find a way to retrieve the situation. Again, see some suggestions below.

SUGGESTIONS

Fractious sibling relationships have the ability to destroy the happiness of older parents. They can quickly descend into acrimony and destruction.

A number of solutions come to mind, including:
- Agreeing on protocols between the children, or
- Family mediation.

Where any of these are spurned, or where the relationships are too poisonous, there may be no other option but the legal system in which, regrettably, we are so often involved but which can often provide some recourse, if not repair.

As a final suggestion, it is paramount that, where the 'outside' children start to observe the tell-tale signs of isolation of their parent, advice is sought promptly. Delay will only encourage and validate the conduct and make it harder (and more expensive) to resolve or unravel.

Properly caring for your parent may mean doing what is necessary to ensure someone else is properly caring for them.

There are, possibly, four additional recourses that, with 'grown up' families who are well intentioned, but divergent in views, could actually make a difference in confronting disputes:

1. Parent Counselling

The factors above give rise to significant emotional trauma making many older people feel like refugees floating like flotsam on a sea of stress.

For example, a common issue being confronted by an older person is the transition to aged care. This is a 'loud' and confronting experience for someone whose brain screams 'not in your life' but whose body yells out for it.

A referral to a suitably qualified aged care counsellor may well assist a family to cross the psychological gap of how best to address a parent's changing circumstances.

2. Family Harmony Agreements

As a way of improving or laying a foundation for an ongoing calm as opposed to a developing storm, why not have the members of the family attempt to 'harmonise' their aspirations and even honour their parents' wishes, dare I say, at this formative time in a family's history? It won't work in every family but bringing everyone together to harvest some harmony may just go some way to avoiding the inevitable implosion.

Why not compose a written 'Family Harmony Agreement' where everyone records their, hopefully, mutual desires for mum and dad? It won't be a legally enforceable agreement but there is something powerful and morally persuasive about written shared goals and aspirations in a family.

* A Family Harmony Agreement might include the following:
* Why do we need to discuss mum and dad?
* What are our concerns about them?
* What do we all want for them in later life?
* Should we have shared or allocated responsibilities for their needs?
* Who is best at doing what?
* Can we afford the time to devote to our roles?
* Can our spouses or partners contribute?
* Will we have our own children contributing?
* Where do we want to see mum and dad in 1, 2 or 3 years time?
* Who's best to keep records and communicate with them?

In the end, a parent is always concerned about the legacy they leave to their family. We all tend to see that more as a legacy on death. In our experience, parents should also consider their legacy in life.

3. Elder Mediation

Our cultural avoidance of family dissent and disharmony, not to mention any minimal insight into the calamitous consequences, has spurred a new service offering for families, known as Elder Mediation.

Mediation, or as it is also known more generically, alternative dispute resolution, has evolved not just in the legal space but across a broad spectrum of life. It is not only a way of resolving disputes relatively informally but, most significantly, a way of preserving relationships in the process. Litigation rarely encourages friendliness between warring and sparring opponents.

As mediation has a high success rate, there is no doubt, in my extensive experience, that such a resolution option is vital to consider for any family dispute and well before the 'no talkies' stage in the children's' relationships.

Apart from the sooner the better, in most cases however, it is when your parents are running out of options and/or money. It is definitely not when they are in hospital and you're told that they can't go home. That's too late, at least to do it well.

4. Legal Recourses

If all else fails in confronting or resolving the unresolvable, then legal recourses need to get a mention. Without them, there would be no end in sight for some family disputes.

Bear in mind that if the law has to be resorted to, the prospects of redemption in any family are doomed forever. There is no coming back. But there may be no alternative, particularly because people who have done the wrong thing usually don't want to discuss it let alone mediate it.

The recourses are many, varied and expensive. Nobody in their right mind would want to take this path given its inevitable outcomes – traditionally in this space there are winners and losers. In reality, everyone loses.

Here are just some of the potential, and actual legal actions, we have taken or are available:

* Suing an adult child for unconscionable conduct in selling a parent's assets to feed a gambling debt.

* Taking action against a child for trespass in refusing to leave his parents' home.

* Actions for an injunction to stop a child from removing a parent and taking them to another state.

* Action for deprivation of liberty where an adult child kept their parent isolated behind locked doors and windows in their own home.

* Seeking to sack an Enduring Power of Attorney for misconduct and obtaining compensation for monies taken.

* Winding up a family company to prevent a child from assuming control.

* Suing a child for negligence in failing to obtain financial advice

before making decisions for a parent under an Enduring Power of Attorney which resulted in the loss of the age pension.

* Stopping a child from transferring a parent's home to themselves when the parent was in residential aged care.

The list goes on.

CHAPTER 6

TALES FROM THE FAMILY TRENCHES

This chapter will bring together a potpourri of issues that I have faced over the years of my experience – tall tales and true from within the denizens of families.

LIVING WITH YOUR MOTHER-IN-LAW

Here is Barry's story. There wasn't much time for pleasantries with him. He put it quickly and directly to me in the first few minutes of our discussion – 'I just want to get my life and my marriage back and I want my mother-in-law out and I want her out now!' The apparent simplicity of his request could not mask a very distressed man.

In her late 80's, his mother-in-law, Muriel, had been living with him and his wife, Madeline, on and off, for about three years. For the last 6 months, however, she had been living permanently with them.

Muriel suffered from a constellation of health issues including early onset dementia. For Barry however, her most frustrating feature was her severe deafness for which she refused to wear her two hearing aids. He was tired of repeatedly exchanging yells with her and explaining to neighbours that he was not berating or arguing with her, just 'communicating'. He believed Madeline was equally at her wits end but chose not to do or say anything because, well, she was Muriel's daughter and where else could mum go.

The situation reached new depths when, just last week, their daughter rang to say that she would not be coming over to stay on the following weekend because her children (Barry's grandchildren) found it too distressing with all the noise, tension and yelling particularly at night when the kids were trying to sleep.

Barry had discussed the matter with Madeline. She had finally agreed that he would raise with Muriel the prospect of moving out and into some form of aged care. When he finally plucked up the courage to talk to Muriel, it was an unmitigated disaster. The yelling reached new heights not because of a lack of hearing but, rather, a surplus of haranguing. Muriel said there was no way she would go to one of those 'waiting rooms' and any way, she said, they had agreed that she could stay as long as she liked or needed to.

Barry was in a state of revolt and was done with caring. He forgot about the 'for better or worse' promise he made many years ago to Madeleine and had even contemplated moving out himself and leaving his wife to tend to her mother alone. So now, here he sits in his lawyer's office seeking what most clients do from us – help. In his almost semi-crazed state, Barry probably needed more than just legal assistance.

When he confirmed that they had told Muriel she could stay as long as she liked, I knew I had no alternative but to add to his layers of anguish. From a legal perspective, Muriel was not a tenant and, as such, she could not simply be evicted using the residential tenancy laws. Worse than that, the only way to have her removed was with a Supreme Court injunction. Alternatively, I told him, Muriel was probably a trespasser under the Criminal law, and he could go down to the local police station and lodge a complaint and see if they would assist in removing her. I reassured Barry that his technique had worked for us on a previous occasion but, mind you, to have a 49-year-old son removed from his parent's home.

The law is a blunt instrument in disintegrating family situations and is best avoided if discussion or even mediation can work. Here, the alternative dispute resolution horse had long bolted and the law was left holding the only solution.

I won't recount the miasma that we then descended into, suffice to say that Barry found his ultimate solution in the law – family law – he left the home and ultimately began divorce and property proceedings against Madeline.

This may appear an extreme case of family caring gone wrong but, from our legal experience as Elder Lawyers, the seeds of this family destruction are festering in more and more homes.

When the initial discussion is had about mum or dad moving in, most of us wear rose coloured glasses. We don't really think about, let alone discuss, what that means or its implications. Caring for a relative or family member may be the only alternative in many cases but that should not stop us engaging in a bit of a 'what if' conversation about the impact it will have.

While it may be anathema to some, documenting the arrangement is also crucial for a number of reasons. It creates an open transparent record of what has been agreed and who will do what. This can appease the other members of the family as well who may have some suspicions about what is really going on.

Quite apart from that, documenting can also ensure that, if appropriate, you can comply with the granny flat arrangements prescribed by Centrelink so that no one's pension entitlements are adversely affected if possible.

We predict that the sort of family tensions recounted above will increase in frequency in the near future. As the Arnott's Biscuit mantra says, however – 'There is no substitute for quality' – the inevitable stress and anxiety can be reduced if there is a bit of quality discussion and documentation of the arrangement at the outset so that relationships, including your own marriage, can be maintained not destroyed.

In experiencing my own ageing, and working as a lawyer in elder law, there are a number of less manifest features of ageing that we either avoid confronting or dismiss as inconsequential or intractable.

MUM IS 78 AND IN LOVE AGAIN

We're not a 'Dear Dorothy' service but, believe it or not, as elder lawyers, we have distilled this title from our experience of an increasing trend in later life – love (or variations of it) and its complex legal consequences.

Apparently, at least in America, over 52% of people over 65 live alone and this percentage is growing. Not surprisingly, after experiencing, for them, the relatively unique solo scene in later life, single mature types often go looking for someone or something to fill their emotional banks.

The styles of relationships they are forming in later life don't necessarily reflect our ageist notions of older people as the 'cardigan and cameo' set. It can often reflect a melange of re-kindled passion and potent pragmatism – a desire for their new 'friend' and a practical way of providing company, if not care, in later life. What they often don't consider however, is the impact of later events and the legal implications in these creative combinations.

Here's what some single, savvy septuagenarians are doing to fill their need for human contact on a regular basis:

- Re-marrying
    * See the story below.
- Moving back in with the spouse they previously divorced many years

ago to provide care for that spouse in their later life
  * Action replay can be complicated legally speaking.
- Share House arrangements
  * Something like our own younger days, where we shared house for the cost savings. Now older people are doing it to share the care they need.
- Becoming 'compactos'
  * Older people becoming companions – a derivative of the de-facto relationship – a compacto relationship.
- Maintaining 2 (or more) relationships
  * Remaining married to their spouse of many years who has had to go into aged care and, at the same time, forming and maintaining a new relationship with someone else.
- Moving in with their new partner to a granny flat at their adult child's home
  * Imagine what could happen if the parent dies leaving the 'partner'

living in the granny flat in the stepchild's home.
- Coming out
    * Later life sexual declarations, reorientation or liberation can give rise to convoluted later life issues.

As well, they are doing it in all sorts of places – from their own homes, in retirement villages or even in aged care facilities. Amongst the many examples we have dealt with, here is one to illustrate the legal morass these new-found relationships can give rise to:
- Bob and Molly remarried in later life, he was 73 and she was 75.
- They both had children from their previous marriages.
- He was rich and she was poor.
- They both agreed to keep their finances separate and had made Wills giving everything to their respective children.
- After 10 years of marriage, Molly was diagnosed with dementia.
- Shortly after that she entered an aged care facility as Bob couldn't provide her with the care she

needed any more and it was affecting his health.
- Molly was required to pay an Accommodation Bond to the aged care facility of $300,000.
- Bob, being the dutiful spouse, was prepared to pay this for her from his own resources.
- Before he did so, one of his daughters brought Bob to see me to discuss the legal implications.
- Much to his surprise and the daughter's alarm, we told them that, if Bob paid the Bond, under the law, when Molly died it would be repaid to her estate not to him.

Bob was then left with an invidious dilemma – a cleavage between his marital vows, 'for better or for worse' and his aspirations for his children – by paying the Bond he would effectively, and ultimately, be giving it to Molly's children not his own.

Bob did make a decision. I won't tell you what it was but will leave this scenario hanging so you can think about what you would do. Of course, if curiosity gets the better of you, feel free to contact me to find out what happened.

This is just one, but a significant example of the complexities that later life relationships can bring with them. Our experience suggests that, as with so many things in life, forearmed is forewarned. Before jumping heart first, let your head get in the way and seek some good legal and financial advice. Believe it or not the law can really help, either by just giving you some information about what it means to 'jump' or even better, doing things to protect you and your family after you've jumped.

Best to be sensual and sensible.

BEING A PARENT TO YOUR PARENT

Having been a heavy drinker for most of his adult life, at 82 and with his brain irrevocably altered and addled by alcohol, Cyril had reached that twilight zone where the experts believed other people could make better decisions for him than he could.

His long-suffering daughter, Prunella (a retired nurse) applied to be appointed his guardian, someone to make personal and health decisions for him. A Tribunal duly found he was incapable of making these decisions for himself and appointed Prunella as his guardian. By this time, Cyril was also residing in an aged care facility.

Armed with her new-found power as Cyril's decision maker or, as she perceived it, more his 'lifestyle and event manager', Prunella wasted no time in asserting herself. This wasn't so much an obligation but more, an opportunity. She immediately decided that she should (and could) introduce a long overdue and healthy regime for her father. She instructed the facility management, in writing, that these would be the new rules for Cyril:

- He was to have no access to alcohol.
- No one (particularly her father's sister and his old drinking mates) could visit or even telephone him without her prior approval.
- Any approved visitors were to have their bags searched for contraband.

- All mail delivered to the nursing home addressed to her father was to be given to her and not to her father.
- No residents were to share any time with him in his room.
- Staff were to report to her whether her father was fraternising with any other residents, particularly female residents.

The nursing home were initially reluctant to accede to these requests but quickly succumbed when Prunella happened to mention *A Current Affair*. In any event, as the guardian, she had the legal right to make these decisions for Cyril, didn't she?

Cyril understood enough to know that things had changed. Some of his small but regular pleasures – afternoon aperitifs with 'the girls' on the smoking balcony and the cavalcade of friends bearing gifts that clinked, not to mention the sharing of old times, had quickly faded away. The phone hardly ever rang. For him, it didn't feel like a home anymore but more a gerontological gulag where his happiness had been hijacked.

Cryril's objections to the new world order fell on deaf, albeit empathetic, ears. He told anyone who would listen that he could make his own decisions now because he wasn't drinking any more.

One person who did listen and take up his cause was a representative from a local aged care advocacy group who, at the secret request of the nursing home, had furtively visited Cyril one day in flagrant breach of the rules of 'she who must be obeyed'.

Concerned by the restrictions placed on Cyril and with his consent, the advocate lodged an application to the Tribunal for it to declare that Cyril's capacity had been restored and that he should be entitled to make his own decisions or, if that was not successful, that his daughter be sacked as his guardian and replaced by someone else.

The Tribunal would not come to the party. It declared that he had not rediscovered his capacity to make his own decisions and confirmed his daughter should stay in place as his guardian.

Before deciding what you think about that decision, it is important to understand what the decision actually was. It was not about whether Prunella was a good guardian or whether she was managing her father's affairs well. Rather, as the law stands, it was about whether her actions were so clearly wrong that she was not acting in his best interests and she should not continue to be his guardian.

It does not mean that the Tribunal thought that Prunella was doing the best job possible and you should not read the decision as in any way ratifying the prudence of the restrictions she had placed on Cyril. However, that's probably exactly how Prunella would have interpreted the decision.

From a distance, many of us might be instinctively offended by Prunella's paternalism and, even for some of us, the apparent deprivation of Cyril's human rights and liberties.

Aged care facilities are constantly confronted by well-intentioned and sometimes obsessively protective adult children who seek to control their parents' lives and even their loves in the cause of parent safety and well-being. Often, parents' rights can be sacrificed on the altar of risk management especially where those parents have reached a stage of vulnerability or fragility.

As with much of the essence of our human condition, however, finding the balance between competing epithets – *safe but sad* or *hazardous but happy* is the key.

Here are some pointers I think would be useful both for aged care providers and the Cyril's and Prunella's of this world:

- Cyril's wishes must (not should) be taken into account – his personal desires are a valid part of the decision mix.
- The role reversal and passion of children for their ageing parents can know no bounds and my experience indicates that a little bit of suggested counselling for Prunella may provide some insight for her in getting the mix right.
- The prevailing theme for managing real personal risk in Cyril's circumstance should not be

paternalistic prohibition but rather reasonable restriction. This would helpfully entail conversations and discussions between management, Prunella and other interested parties such as Cyril's old drinking mates.
- Happiness can be just as important as safety for a resident and finding the balance is the essence of good caring for a facility and good management for a guardian.
- The balance will never be static and must be adjusted over time and as circumstances change.

Sitting in my office, it all sounds pretty straight forward doesn't it?

It's not, but it's well worth a try.

YOUR PARENTS' SEPARATION

As an indication of changing social patterns in our older community, I have two clients at the moment who have just reached their 'silver separation' moment:
- Aged 78, Dorothy (not her real name) has lived separately (and apart) from her spouse for 25 years

- Aged 72, Delma (not her real name) has lived separately (but under the same roof) with her spouse for 25 years.

As a lawyer, I tend to want to delicately enquire of clients in this situation why they have never divorced. I know, for example, some of the issues arising from not divorcing include:

- They do not want to give their estate to their estranged spouse and make a Will, say, giving everything directly to their children. However, their spouse will still be eligible to challenge their Will. Their spouse would not be eligible if they had divorced.
- They may have appointed their estranged spouse as their Enduring Power of Attorney and never changed it after separation not realising that separation does not revoke the document, only divorce.
- They don't change the way they own their property from joint tenants to tenants in common.
- They don't change their Superannuation Death Benefit Nomination.

- Some perceived advantage in staying married from a Centrelink perspective.

Quite apart from any moral or cultural objections to divorce, in their own way, each of them represents an abiding feature of older failed marriages that is not shared by the younger generation of married couples.

Put bluntly, ageing brings an additional dynamic – the potential for one of the spouses to fall victim to dementia and become dependent on others for care. Who better to provide that familiar care than their estranged spouse of over 25 years. Both Dorothy and Delma shared this concern. So significant was it, they chose not to divorce but, instead, to devote their time and efforts to supporting someone they no longer loved but felt obliged to care for.

Far be it for me to pass judgement on their decision. It does behove me, however, to raise with them the longer-term legal consequences of not making a complete break.

Divorce does not prevent you from caring for your former spouse. In the legal space, however, not divorcing may have consequences you never knew or wanted.

SO, YOU WANT TO BE YOUR PARENT'S CARER?

We do a lot of work in the area of family arrangements involving adult children providing care to, or for, their parent/s. It is on the rise and likely to exponentially increase as we live longer and residential age care becomes more expensive.

If you're thinking of doing it, here are six factors you might want to consider:

- It could cost you money

    In the USA they found recently that family caregivers spend the equivalent of over AUS$9,000 a year of their own money towards their caring role which is not reimbursed.

    You may have to do the same. However, you should not be backward in coming forward in being reimbursed for legitimate expenses you pay for in relation to

the care (but see point below regarding retirement). Even if you are entitled to a carer's allowance or payment, it may not cover the costs you incur.
- Quit your job?

    It might seem like the logical and rational thing to do in order to provide the care your parent needs but, can you afford to and what are the potential downsides for you if you do?

    Keeping your job (if possible) would give you some form of safety net, in the event that your caring role came to an end. If you gave up your job, it may be difficult to go back into the workforce particularly if you are an older adult.
- Men delegate – Women do

    Traditionally, men don't seem to be comfortable with the 'hands on' demands of caring. They tend to prefer to delegate the task to paid help. Women, on the other hand, tend to get in and do it. That's why, I suspect, there are more women carers than men. How can

you achieve a better balance in the family?
- A Perfect Carer?

    You will be criticised by other family members for the care you provide even if, on any objective standard, it is very good. You may have to be prepared not only for the work of caring but the slings and arrows of discontent from your siblings (and your parent/s).
- Retirement – What Retirement?

    Many family carers are in the cohort of about to be, or recent, retirees. Those plans hatched for your retirement may have to take second fiddle to the demands of caring and for an unknown period of time.
- Get it in writing

    It might sound anathema to many families, but our experience tells us that having a written agreement in place about the roles and responsibilities of everyone goes a long way to ensuring the arrangement is transparent and in reducing the potential for dispute. No agreement, or an oral agreement, does little to achieve these ends.

The reality of the need for family caring is rising like a wave in a high swell approaching the shoreline. At least have a discussion with the family if you are thinking of entering this caring space – it will either ensure that everyone is on the same page or it may even convince you not to do it.

WHEN YOUR RETIREMENT MEETS YOUR PARENTS' RETIREMENT

We adult children can be so lucky. Longevity means you can now be in retirement at the same time as your parents. You might have less experience in this phase of life but what the heck – isn't it great to think that you and your parents can now share something in common in those later mature years. But is it?

Applying the old adage – facts tell but stories sell, here's a salutary saga on the downside of retirement synchronisation.

Alex and Eloise were looking forward to their retirement (as most do). They had 'plans' that involved significant periods of away time exploring the planet. Bob had even saved up for a single ticket on Richard Branson's spaceship. He called it his celestial respite or a nearer to God experience. Surprisingly, they had been assiduous in obtaining the best financial advice they could on their retirement years – they had a plan for themselves.

Both of them had other siblings spread all over the country but they were generally disconnected or disinterested. They each had a retired widowed parent aged in their mid-80's and were 'fortunate' enough to live in the same town as their respective parents. As children of the Great Depression, the parents had the usual bounty from their frugality and long working lives – a home, a pension and a passport account with the CBA. They still lived in their own homes, but frailty was creeping up and they were each becoming more dependent on Alex and Eloise. The parents had each made Wills giving everything equally, including their homes, to their children.

Just before their latest sojourn to Tuscany, Eloise's mum has a medical event ending up in hospital and unable to return home. Aged care now beckoned. Remarkably, almost as if it was an subconscious attempt to 'go out in sympathy' with Eloise's mum, Alex's mum suffers a similar event and can't go home.

All their meticulous planning for their own retirement years now came crashing down in the face of their parental crises. They had to confront:
- With their limited financial resources, how were their parents going to pay for aged care?
- Would it mean selling their homes?
- Would Alex and Eloise have to contribute themselves to assist their respective parents e.g., drawing down on their hard-earned superannuation?
- Would the other siblings contribute and, if so, how?
- How would this affect the relationship between Alex and Eloise when the 'matrimonial assets' may

have to be called upon to help their parents?

And so, the list goes on.

Without descending into the complex issues we had to address, it raised a number of telling features and revealed a number of unanticipated stress points about their retirement:

- As part of their financial plan for their own retirement should Alex and Eloise have included some aspect of financial planning for their parents?
- Would it be necessary for Alex and Eloise to enter into a Family Law Financial Agreement to ensure that a fair component of the matrimonial assets was allocated between their respective parents?
- Should their parents consider doing new Wills (if they could) especially if their homes had to be sold?

From my experience, this scenario is not unusual. However, very few financial planners ask their clients to consider, and plan for, the potential filial and financial responsibilities for their ageing parents as part of their own retirement plans.

Perhaps it's time to do so. Alternatively, we could all just keep working, never retire and drop dead at our desk. Now that's a tempting choice.

IS YOUR PARENT SLIDING FROM A COMPACTO TO A DE-FACTO?

I have often written about being, and have many elderly clients who are, alone.

They are not necessarily lonely but more, lonesome. They may have lost their spouse or partner through death or divorce. They may have intentionally misplaced them through what I call, disinterest. Alternatively, they may live in a parallel universe through the ravages of dementia.

In later life, they may still want to be involved rather than to retreat. They may also not want the potential personal (and family) complications of another formal marriage or even a de-facto relationship. They may have also heeded their lawyer's advice that the transition into another relationship can really leave you in a legal pickle when it comes to who pays for what or worse, who gets what when you die.

Is there an alternative which doesn't create a legal commitment (and thereby a minefield) and at the same time, satisfies our needs for involvement, social stimulation, or company. There is, and we call them 'compactos' – people in later life who just want an antidote to social isolation and some companions for the sharing of good times but not necessarily a home or a bed.

But for people whose partner may have contracted dementia and who, as a consequence, are separated, not necessarily by desire, but by circumstance – there is a particular poignancy. Some may be committed to their original marriage vow – 'till death do us part'. For others however, especially where the separation comes at a relatively early stage in their retirement, it may be more a case of 'till dementia do us part'.

I recently came across an example of this latter development. A husband and his wife were in their early 70's and, after a long marriage, she had recently had to move into aged care in the relatively advanced stages of Alzheimer's disease. She no longer recognised him or anyone else in her family. Her life expectancy was uncertain – it could be long or short.

He was a dutiful husband in every sense of the word until, that is, he met a woman who was also visiting her husband in the same facility and in similar circumstances to him. As they say, one thing led to another and before long they were 'compactos' socialising together and sharing each other's company outside the aged care facility.

They irrevocably and irresistibly moved to a moral and, as it turned out, a legal crossroads. They were both adamant that neither of them wanted to divorce their respective spouses. They were, however, contemplating moving in together and sharing their lives outside the facility visiting hours. They were about to mutate from compactos to de-factos.

Lawyers are not trained, or required, to make moral judgements about their client's life choices. We are attuned to advise on legal implications and consequences of those choices.

Put succinctly:
- You can have more than one 'spouse' simultaneously (I believe the record in Australia was four).
- For most legal purposes, 'de-facto' spouses are the same as 'married' spouses.
- Having more than one creates a legal minefield, particularly on your death, as each are entitled to challenge your Will (not to mention as are the children from both sides of the family).
- Even 'compactos' can slide inadvertently into the 'de-facto' definition and thereby create the same minefield.

Of course, there are legal devices and techniques to address these festering issues.

However, in the end, from my experience, the scourge of loneliness and the resulting search for later life happiness will usually outweigh what one client described as these 'other annoying issues'.

The best advice in these circumstances is to make your life decisions with eyes wide open and bearing in mind the potential panic attack or moral outrage of your children.

KEEP YOUR SPOUSE CLOSE BUT YOUR PARENTS CLOSER

For all those adult children embarking on a long and sustained period of well-deserved and well-saved for later life pleasure (also known as 'retiring', 'withdrawing', 'going away', 'leaving' or 'retreating'), – stop – think again – your parents need you!

Bernie and Bernice had only recently retired. Being newly hatched retirees, they were champing at the bit to take off and explore. Bernie had three siblings spread all over the world. Bernice had no siblings and had lost her parents many years ago.

Bernie's surviving parent, his father Cyril, was 83 and Bernie was also his Enduring Power of Attorney. Having just come out of hospital and in fragile health, the writing was on the wall – Cyril needed high care in a residential aged care facility. Along with his other siblings, Bernie thought that Cyril's move to aged care would be good for Cyril. It would also loosen the shackles of having to 'be around' and enable Bernie and Bernice to fire up that new Winnebago and explore this large brown land.

Cyril was a full age pensioner with not a lot in assets except for his now very valuable old Queenslander in a leafy inner suburb of Brisbane. Figures of over $1.5million were bandied about as the market value of the home.

Being the dutiful son, Bernie had found the perfect aged care facility only some 10 minutes away from his and Bernice's home. Trouble was they wanted Cyril to pay some $450,000 by way of an upfront Refundable Accommodation Deposit (RAD). Cyril didn't have that sort of money but he did own that very valuable piece of property.

Bernie and his siblings didn't often see eye to eye but, on one issue, for once, they were determined and agreed – they didn't want that home sold in order to meet the RAD payment. Besides, keeping it in his dad's name would have certain benefits for Cyril as well (so Bernie's research told him).

That Winnebago was baying for action. Bernice had set her heart on adventure and that didn't involve tending to the physical and financial needs of her frail father-in-law. They had assiduously saved all their lives for this moment but now, enter Cyril, stage left, to squash those dreams.

As usual, they briefly regretted they had not confronted Cyril's situation earlier and at least planned for it. They were now in crisis mode and had to do something about Cyril right now as the facility told him they needed a decision immediately and if not, they would have to offer the place to someone else.

Bernie was desperate. Cyril had about $100,000 in cash but where was the balance of the RAD of $350,000 to come from? While there were other options, given that time was pressing and the opportunity could be lost, Bernie decided he would provide the

$350,000 for Cyril and he would have to raid his superannuation to do that.

Bernice was none too pleased – that money was their running away money and now they would be tied down to both a financial and a 'being around' commitment for Cyril and, by the way, where were Bernie's siblings to lend a hand!

By the time Bernie and Bernice got to see me, the money had been paid and Cyril had moved into the facility. Bernie and Cyril were relatively happy. Bernice, on the other hand, wasn't really talking to either of them.

Bernie, Bernie, Bernie', were some of my first words to him as he and Bernice slid into their hot seats in our interview room. Did you know:

- As the Enduring Power of Attorney (EPOA) for Cyril, by advancing the $350,000 you may have breached your duties as the EPOA, namely, entering into a conflict transaction with Cyril?
- As you haven't documented the basis upon which you have provided the funds for Cyril, there could be a barney with your siblings about

getting it back when Cyril dies e.g., interest on the money?

- The law requires that, no matter who provides the RAD payment, it must be repaid to the resident or their estate when they leave the facility (not Bernie)?

Bernie's complexion turned white and Bernice's red – they found it difficult to look at each other – awkward.

Without boring you with the next exciting instalment in the Cyril saga, needless to say, Bernie had to expend some more hard-earned retirement savings on me and my very reasonable fees. Bernice, I understand, may have also sought some separate family law advice on her situation.

The impact of the aged care needs of our ageing parents is like a multi headed hydra – it can permeate every aspect of our lives and our families. It can even affect relationships between previously long and happily married children.

CHAPTER 7

WHERE AND HOW WILL THEY LIVE?

BUT FIRST – THE TRIPLE GUILT TRIP

Have you ever sat down and thought about how much your parents can rely (willingly or unwillingly) on you, their children, in later life, particularly when it comes to where and how they will live?

This came home to me recently when I was perusing a report which was a spreadsheet summary of details of all the people who had come and inspected units in a Retirement Village in a particular month. What initially struck me was one of the columns in the report which was headed 'With Family'. It required the salesperson to note whether a prospective resident who came to inspect the village, did so with a member of their family. What was even more revealing was that, of the 22 prospective residents who inspected that village that month, 14 of them were noted as being there with a member of their family.

What does it tell you? Probably a few things we already knew such as:
- Salespeople appreciate that, in the retirement living and aged care space, family members are just as important to target in the sales pitch as their respective mums or dads.
- Older people, particularly if they are single, will naturally rely on, and resort to, their children for advice and usually before anybody else (it's free advice).
- Older people often feel that it is just as important for their family to support their decision as it is to make their own decision. This can lead to trouble for example, where the children don't agree on mum or dad's proposed decision.

Having to make formative decisions in later life can be a regular event and the decisions themselves are often complex. Relying on our family is entirely natural and understandable.

Can you feel a 'BUT' coming on?

You're right. Initially, you might expect me to say that not even family members should advise their mum or dad on complex decision making without obtaining professional advice. That should be the first piece of family advice they give to their mum or dad – let's go and get some advice. As I bang on about the importance of this all the time, you will probably brush over this paragraph.

But here's another BUT. We're starting to discern another effect of not following our mantra – we call it the 'triple guilt trip':

Guilt 1

- Most children feel a real remorse about, as they say, 'having to put' mum or dad into an aged care facility.
- This guilt can be even worse where it is mum, for example, having to put dad (her husband) into aged care.

- As with most families, they don't obtain good professional advice about the decision, the transition and its implications.

Guilt 2

- They proceed along their chosen pathway of blissful ignorance until one day, they are hit by a clanger. A letter arrives from some authority advising that, for example, as mum's house has been sold, the proceeds of sale will now be an assessable asset and her aged care fees will increase substantially and their pension is in danger.
- The family now faces the second regret, the consequences of which are mum will have to pay more in aged care fees than they had bargained for because the family didn't realise what the implications would be in selling her home.

Guilt 3

- It's at this point it gets personal.
- The regret festers to resentment because the adult children now

realise their expected inheritance is going to be reduced by the substantial aged care fees.

This scenario is played out every day in our nation. It's usually because families focus on the price of doing something (getting advice), as opposed to the cost of doing nothing (not getting advice). Even more significant than the financial consequences, is the effect on relationships. As you can imagine, when the proverbial hits the fan, many families engage in the blame game – whose fault was it that we are now in this situation? The culprit culture leads almost inevitably to the implosion of the family.

One of our other abiding mantras is – live life with no regrets. It sounds trite to say but making decisions based on good advice will significantly reduce the potential for regret. It may even keep your family together as they confront the later life demands and needs of parents.

TRENDS IN AGEING LIVING

In the days of yore, before the War, in a comparative age of simplicity, when a parent needed to be supported in their ageing, there was really only one solution – move in with the family. This was before women started to enter the job market in any numbers and when adult daughters were 'free' to be the ultimate home makers – making a home for their spouse and children and then for their parents. It was the progenitor of 'blending', albeit of generations.

In the 1970's, along with their siblings, my parents housed my mother's parents in their later lives. They did it, not for pleasure, but out of a sense of duty and they did it for free. Still to this day, women make up the vast majority of informal care givers for their parents who may be still living at home. They also predominate in the paid home care services sector – caring is a very feminine business.

There is now a complex array of factors dissipating that single, simple solution including, the elongation of our lives, the generally slow downward spiral of our health in later life peaking with that new age dimension, dementia, increased wealth providing increased living choices thereby enabling us to pay for customised care, increased feminisation of later life, Government accepting the political imperative to subsidise our later life costs and hospitals not wanting to be de-facto aged care facilities.

A decreasing number of us will die in our own home. Rather, it will be somewhere else and that somewhere else could be more than one place. If you accept your parents' health will cascade downwards (which it will), how are you and your siblings going to address the effect of this on their lifestyle (and yours)?

You might want to sit on your hands and wait for that wakeup call conversation mentioned at the start of this book – the 'C' change. Others are not. In the last 20 years, the irrevocable forces of retirement, ageing and downsizing, have seen the development of a range of diverse and, in some cases, novel solutions to the phalanx of accommodation needs for older people, spurred on by a demographic demand and the property development industry's eye for an opportunity.

Let me start with a roll call of current options for older people:
- Home
- Home with benefits – Home support and care
- Retirement villages (with or without Home Support and Care)
- Manufactured home parks (with or without Home Support and Care)
- Other ageing lifestyles
- Residential aged care
- Family care
- Granny flats
- Tiny houses
- NORC'S
- Shared houses
- 'Hotel de Park'.

Let's undertake a brief analysis of each one to understand what they mean for your parents in terms of lifestyle. I will deal separately with the relevant financial issues in a later chapter.

STAYING AT HOME

It seems that, from everything I have read and experienced as a son and a lawyer, this option is THE preferred one – 'der Dad', as my daughter would again say.

For most of us, our home defines us. This is particularly so for older people whose home becomes their last vestige of life as they reminisce. It is a symbol of their receding personal identity and a memorial to their former lives. It is also a haven, a refuge and a place of respite.

Your parents tread those repetitive paths through their home, follow the age-old domestic routines, sleep with that long-term, before and after dark companion – their bed and its accessories and are surrounded by comforting memorabilia from the past. They awaken to familiar sounds and are reassured by the idea that their neighbours will always help. The car gathering dust in the garage is a painful memory of what once was. They fraternise with pesky pets, the African Love Birds, furry felines or lazy

Labradors. Their fate is as important as their own.

When in need, their home is a friend, indeed. I am happy to accept that as aspirational, but when does that mutate from utopia to dystopia?

As your parents may live in a state of increasing introversion, their home will become a refuge, the proverbial castle, a bit like Mont St Michel, untouched by the lapping tides of change or the dark scudding clouds above. They will cling to mutual self-sufficiency but, eventually, reality will climb the ramparts, lower the drawbridge and drain the moat.

The reality is the changing of the guard of responsibility. They are, and wish to remain, responsible for each other, their mutual guardians. At some stage, however, that will not be possible. The responsibility will then have to be delegated to the 'serfs', the adult children with a little bit of hired help from home carers. The breakdown of the aspiration evolves from the onset of physical reality – they can't look after the other anymore. The first sign, usually, is the ubiquitous fall – another big 'F' word. They are no longer impregnable, they are now vulnerable. Your will have to carefully unpick their dream weaving.

For the adult children these events come with a test of their devotional duty. As their parents' needs grow, the children are engaged in an increasingly stressful balancing act – their parents' fragility and fanatical desire to stay and the looming reality of the home becoming a disaster zone or, at least, one waiting to happen.

Discussing the 'birds and the bees' with your teenage children is a parental discomfort which many parents avoid. It is nothing compared to the unavoidable and uncomfortable 'It's time' discussion with your parents.

Be prepared for some renovations as well. They will not be the result of an interior designers' views on how to improve the delight to the eye of the spaces in the home but in response to the grim reaper safety consultant on how to decrease the risks of the space.

It is also difficult to avoid one ephemeral benefit of staying at home – the parents' ability to socialise and keep in contact with the extended family, such as the grandchildren. Their home is a meeting place, or a coming together, and they are a fulcrum for family life. I think it would be a very stoic grandchild who would prefer to see grandpa or grandma in a nursing home rather than in their own home.

However, perhaps not surprisingly, some children will avoid the subject, not out of timidity or not wanting to be the disruptor, but out of a more pragmatic motivation. Any suggestion that a parent should move from their home to somewhere more appropriate comes with a collateral question – what to do with the family home? Preserving the castle, and thereby the inheritance, can be a subliminal, but powerful motivation for some children.

They may well want to see a return on their investment in their parents in a more utilitarian sense. I have seen some children dress up this issue as a so-called honourable one – a desire to reflect, initially, their parents' wish to call somewhere 'home' but, subsequently, for it to be preserved for them and their children. It is a tangible connection to the family history and needs to be vouchsafed as a monument. Hmmm.

If, as it should be, the first question is – what is best for my parents? – your expectations for your future may need to be sublimated to theirs. The second question is – how realistically can I support them to stay at home?

A Warning

Before delving into the aged care system, let me make a salutary point. As a government regulated and, mostly, a taxpayer financed sector, the rules and regulations will naturally churn over time. Indeed, I know of no other sector where the hand of government intrudes as much.

Of course, it has taxpayer accountability to consider (some $20billion currently) and the aspiration for the bureaucratic mantra – outcomes, or bang for bucks, not to mention that elusive shibboleth, quality care. Much of what I write may well be stimulated and then superseded by more change, particularly in light of the current Royal

Commission. As such, your knowledge and information gathering task will be a constant one as much as change in the sector is constant.

STAYING AT HOME WITH SUPPORT AND CARE

If a person is eligible, the Federal Government currently offers two types of subsidised home assistance or packages:

Commonwealth Home Support Packages

These are often described as entry level assistance for eligible people over the age of 65 and over 50 for Aboriginal or Torres Strait Islander people.

They are not designed to provide complex personal care services but more to support older people with maintaining their home, independence, safety and lifestyle. As such, the services offered by this type of package includes cleaning, gardening, home maintenance and modifications, shopping, meals, social activities and transport.

Your parents will need to be assessed for their eligibility for the programme which you can do through the My Aged Care website or by contacting a service provider direct.

However, if a parent's needs are higher than the basic services provided by this package, they may have to look to obtaining a home care package referred to below.

Commonwealth Home Care Packages

In this newish living/caring offering we see the development of the hip trend in ageing – 'ageing in place'—enabling people to stay at home and 'age' when, before, that may not have been possible.

There is no doubt that the advent of the burgeoning business of home care – carers hired to enter your parents' home to assist them in what are known as 'daily living activities', has been a fillip to their pervading desire to stay at home, or at least lengthen their time at home. It has been significantly stimulated by governments of all persuasions prepared to invest billions of dollars to subsidise this assistance care.

While I will deal with the finances associated with home care later, there is an expectation that home care performs more than a physical service, albeit for a cost, it also potentially offers a another benefit – socialisation, sometimes called, conversation, a sharing of stories or a connection to the outside world beyond the television, computer, wireless and you, the parent assessors. Regrettably however, this may not be as helpful as it appears.

As their business is financially supine to the almighty government dollar, and as there are 'butchers, bakers and candlestick makers' jumping on the bandwagon, a profligacy of people are establishing home care businesses. For this and other reasons, there are looming threats to the survivability, let alone profitability, of home care organisations. In response, they have had to take a 'slash and burn' approach to their business model. The first victim is time. Many organisations are now having to ration both the time carers spend with clients and the time for individual tasks. The 'cuppa tea' ceremony is now an optional extra in the drive for efficiency and ROI – return on investment.

Home care is generally provided by Commonwealth Government approved home care providers i.e., businesses (for profit and not for profit) and there are many of them. Depending on their financial circumstances and needs, their approval entitles a parent to have the cost of their home care subsidised (not paid for completely) by the government.

Currently, the type and extent of care comes in 4 'Packages':
- Home Care Level 1 – for people with basic care needs
- Home Care Level 2 – for people with low level care needs
- Home Care Level 3 – for people with intermediate care needs
- Home Care Level 4 – for people with high care needs.

The packages are rationed and allocated by the government reflecting, supposedly, the particular, and expected, human demand and needs of a geographic area. The waiting list to receive a package currently exceeds 100,000 older people and can be more difficult to obtain in regional and rural areas. The poignant consequence of this inordinate number is that many older people will either have to transition to residential aged care or indeed, will die, before a home carer turns up at their doorstep. In that, lies a message for adult children – get in quick! However, as part of its 2020/2021 Budget, the Commonwealth Government announced the release of a further 23,000 home care packages. That would still leave some 77,000 waiting

It doesn't take much evidence of a need for assistance to obtain a package. If you notice increasing limitations or, as an occupational therapist once described it to me, a 'fall off in standards' in your parents' home – from something as simple as a disinterest in things they used to enjoy (sometimes due to increasing loss of sight or hearing), delegation of tasks to you that they used to perform e.g., banking, or other more basic manifestations such as a lack of hygiene, trouble showering, changing beds, washing, cooking or even getting out of bed or into the world, the word is – act now.

Acting now requires you to access the information and action website, 'My Aged Care' and arrange for two essential processes to be undertaken – an ACAT (Aged Care Assessment Team) assessment, a government team of people who visit your parent to assess their needs and certify them for a particular package, and an assessment by Centrelink of their assets and income to determine how much your parents will have to pay in addition to the subsidy from the government.

Be wary of home care 'privateers' – business who are not government approved and which, therefore, do not attract government subsidies. They are also not subject to the regulations and laws applying to approved home care providers and, while they are not a law free zone, you need to tread carefully. However, in cases of urgent need, they may represent the only viable alternative. Beware however, you will be paying full tariff, as they say. What could that mean? You need to read the next section on 'Finances' to appreciate the cost.

For more motivation on the importance of home care remember a few things:
- It will take a certain load off you although there are some children who will forever be described as anal and will always check on the checkers.
- It could be good for your parents.
- It could keep them at home or, at least for a little bit longer.

RETIREMENT LIVING GENERALLY

This is the 'out of home' sector where your parents may choose to go after leaving their home. That choice may have nothing to do with their care needs but a desire to simply downsize and reduce the constant call of ladders and lawnmowers.

Retirement living, is, in its array of alternative structures, the most expansive in choice and living options. It is also complicated by a divide between how the law describes them and how operators choose to brand them.

So, we have retirement communities presented or marketed in various ways:
- Retirement Village
- Over 50's Lifestyle Resort
- Serviced apartment
- Supported living unit
- Seniors Rental Village
- Manufactured Home Park or Land Lease Communities.

There are additional confusing elements:
- An Over 50's lifestyle resort may, legally speaking, be a manufactured home park.
- A supported or serviced apartment may be part of a retirement village.
- Some communities can a mixture of different types of legal structures e.g., a retirement village next to an aged care facility.
- From a legal perspective, the same type of lifestyle can be described differently e.g., in Queensland we have a Manufactured Home Park but in New South Wales they are called Land Lease Communities.

How it is described by its operator should not steer you away from what it actually is, from a legal perspective. That perspective will enable you to determine what are the rights and obligations in a particular type of community.

Apart from whether the lifestyle of a community may appeal to your parents, it is absolutely crucial to understand the underlying legal structure because, only then, will you know what law applies and how it impacts on their rights and obligations.

RETIREMENT VILLAGES

When she was in her 80's, the recently deceased and acidic American comedienne, Joan Rivers, wrote a book entitled *Don't Count the Candles: Just keep the fire lit.* In many ways it was, albeit satirically, a war cry or a call to action for people to age positively.

In it, however, she devoted an entire chapter to the subject of Retirement Villages and, in her inimitable style, was absolutely venomous about them. Joan never lived

in a retirement village but that didn't stop her from delivering a ferocious appraisal of them. She variously described them as:
- Minimum security prisons with palms
- Gerontological gulags full of sunny sterility and mind-numbing architectural sameness
- Places where every day is Sunday, and where people stare at the sprinklers and have dinner at 5.

Much of her destructive derision may have been fuelled by that infamous retirement village in Florida, 'The Villages'. It is truly a breathtaking place. In addition to being the biggest retirement village in the world, it is a gated community some of the features of which are:
- Spread over 32 square miles
- Some 128,000 residents over 55 years of age
- 2,400 special interest clubs or groups
- Some 30 golf courses
- Over 60,000 golf carts
- A 200 bed hospital.

I have sometimes described them as one of the last vestiges of apartheid – age apartheid – older people restricted to living with older people. Be that as it may, they have a long waiting list.

In Australia, the recent 'bad news' focus on retirement village living by the media (ABC) has undoubtedly shed, at best, a poor light on some of them and tarnished their reputation more broadly. But, do the words of a few disenchanted residents, no doubt exacerbated by insensitive operators, represent the broader truth?

If research and focus groups are to be believed, a significant majority of village residents are happy in a retirement village and their choice of lifestyle. They appreciate the freedom from maintenance, the sense of community, the social opportunities, engagement and connection, not to mention, security. As it invariably involves downsizing for many, it can release equity (money) from the sale of the family home leading to, money to play with or dare I mention the word, fun. Neither this cohort, or their experiences, get a mention in the media because good news doesn't sell.

So, what is the trouble with, or for, some residents of Retirement Villages and what gives rise to their angst? In a phrase – parsimony which begets ignorance which begets regret.

Before I elaborate on that cryptically provocative statement, let's understand a few essential aspects of a retirement village. As with so many things in our redoubtable federal system of government, there is little uniformity of law across this country and, historically, it has proved almost impossible to achieve with one recent remarkable exception. After many years of failure, the elusive quest for uniformity was at last achieved in 2015 when all the States and Territories agreed with the Commonwealth on a uniform definition of a 'free range egg'.

For now, however, the law on Retirement Villages is different between each State and Territory. However, to generalise:
- In most cases, you don't 'own' a retirement village unit. With some exceptions, you acquire a right to

live in your unit which is generally by way of a 99 year lease i.e., you acquire a long-term lease of the unit, but you will not doubt be in heaven by the time it expires. You are not the 'registered proprietor' of the unit, you are the 'registered lessee' of the unit.
- You pay to 'buy' your lease or right to live in the unit, you pay further when you are living in the unit and you pay again when you leave the unit.
- Operators of a Retirement Village are allowed to discriminate on the basis of age. As a consequence, most of them set a minimum age for every resident.
- The current average age of residents in all villages is 80. Interestingly that age has consistently risen over the last few years. When retirement villages were the flavour of the month their target market were the youngish retirees in the 65 to 70 age bracket.
- In many ways the arrangement is not only unique as a property

transaction, it is verging on counter intuitive:

* You pay a capital sum to buy in, sometimes called an Ingoing Contribution (on average $398,000) as if you were buying the freehold which you are usually not and then

* You pay a regular monthly amount while you are living there, sometimes called a General Services Charge (on average $200 per week), as if you were a tenant paying rent to a landlord and then

* To add a further unusual layer, you pay an amount to the operator when you leave sometimes called a Deferred Management Fee or an Exit Fee (on average the highest would be about 40% of what they paid to move in).

- With some exceptions involving compulsory buy back, if you leave, you have to wait for another person to 'buy' the unit before you get back the money you are entitled to.
- Some villages allow you to share in the capital gain on the resale of the unit, but some do not.

- The retirement village operator must approve any proposed purchaser of a unit to ensure they are 'appropriate'.
- If you die while living in the unit, the only asset you will have to give away in your Will is not the unit, but what is known as the Exit Entitlement – the amount owing to you on the subsequent resale of the unit after deducting other fees and costs such as the exit fee.

The law on retirement villages across the States and Territories is different and in a constant state of flux. For example, some States have recently changed their law to provide for what is known as a 'compulsory buy back' which requires the operator to buy back your unit if it has not been sold within a specified time. I have neither the patience, time or desire to expostulate on the different retirement village laws between states and territories. That's your job or your job to get advice on.

Social Observations on Retirement Villages

One element of the decision to move into a retirement village should also include the 'soft' features. By that I mean – what's it like to live in one?

It is hard to be alone, or even, be left alone, in a village. Your life can be under a microscope or scrutiny from resident 'rubber-neckers', 'gossip mongers' or a 'them's the rules' management. In the gated, semi-detached and Lilliputian world, your happiness may be the result of the luck of the draw:

- Who will your close neighbours be and what are they like?
- Will they live on your doorstep, always short on sugar?
- What if just don't like them and they are obsessively well intentioned?

These are just a few of the soft questions and remember, it is not that easy to just move from a unit to another in a frantic attempt to rid yourself of the pesky ones.

As with any walled community of similar backgrounds, the atmosphere can be thick with sparks. The seemingly smallest trigger can provoke the largest chain reaction in confined communities where many residents search for something to do each day. Left unaddressed, these 'things' can turn a Village into factional warfare.

Having been involved in many retirement village disputes, here are just some of those 'things' that I have had to deal with or have come across.

Sign of the Times

A feature of many retirement villages is the Residents' Committee, a representative body of residents designed to collaborate with the village operator to address and improve the lives of village residents. One of the downsides of democracy is that small, democratically elected micro bodies, such as a village residents' committee, can wield disproportional power in small places over big things.

There is an apocryphal story from America of a resident's committee in a retirement village which placed a sign on the village's front gate which read 'No children (including grandchildren) beyond this point'.

It is evidence of a subliminal tension in the retirement village world around the concept of a community – is it restricted to the residents or should the village be like a melting pot for the broader family community. Something akin to the remaking of public libraries from being exclusive clubs for readers and borrowers to a gathering place for the local community.

Flocking Cockatoos

Perhaps she was pining for her previous much loved and missed, semi-rural lifestyle, when a female resident succumbed one day to the plaintiff pleas of a lone cockatoo that had landed on her backyard clothesline. It may have landed there, an outcast from its flock and friendless, in search of a friend. As it transpired, the resident's actions soon had it gleefully accepted back into its tribe.

She began feeding it. The good news soon percolated far and wide over the bird telegraph and, you guessed it, the flock and sundry others began arriving in plague proportions, at precisely 4pm each day in her backyard. Other residents were, understandably, outraged by the transformation of their symphonic lives into cacophonic ones. There was talk of sheriffs, posses and shot guns.

The effect spread further. There was a rumour that the nearby Bird Sanctuary, where tourists gathered each afternoon to feed the wild flocks, had complained to the village management. The resident, they said, was disappointing their tourists and affecting their business by luring 'their' birds, as she was, to the resident's backyard, and bypassing the Sanctuary.

So began a slow and painful weaning of cockatoos from her backyard. Initially resistant, after an exhaustive process of mediation, she agreed to stop feeding them only after the offer of an inducement from the operator—the installation of a communal bird pen for her budgerigars near the community centre. Perhaps a win for budgies and a loss for cockies.

What Tripe

Currently, kale, quinoa and quark are the trending and emerging choice of foods of the Gods. In my younger days, when Gods were less financially endowed, that award went to tripe and chokos. Not even a rudimentary blandishment of white sauce could raise their status, or taste, from the depths of bland, but, in deference to my family's circumstances, they were cheap.

If there is one special aspect of tripe, however, that has been stored in my smell bank and lingered with me to this day, it is the aroma emanating from the its lengthy cooking – boiled till it was almost unrecognisable from the remnants of a sheep's stomach. It has the ability to infect, if not pollute, the air inside, and out, for miles.

And so it was, in one village, two single residents living side by side in semi-detached units. Their respective kitchens were located at the rear of their units which also fronted a covered and shared outdoor living area separated only by a lattice screen. It was summer and one of them had just moved in bringing with her a life-long lust for tripe. Not only was it delectable, but tripe also allowed her to keep to the careful budget her assiduous financial planner had devised for her.

Day after day, the pungent aroma swirled around the village. It was most intense just outside her kitchen window where her neighbour liked to enjoy some outdoor pastimes such as sitting in her outdoor area reflecting on life as it once was and waiting for something.

Polite remonstrations by the victim with the perpetrator came to no avail and only led to the production line intensifying. Threats by the victim to retaliate and plant a durian tree came to nothing.

The lawyers were called in. After a 'site' inspection and demonstration, the nostrils of all were called upon to adjudge whether the aroma was a 'nuisance' under the Village By-Laws. As perhaps could have been anticipated, the tripe got the thumbs down. But, in a victory for common sense, agreement was reached between the residents – the tripe lover agreed to cook it only on a limited number of days each week and to keep her doors and windows closed during the process.

Flying the Flag

A village may have been the wrong choice for her because Beryl had the reputation for being the resident 'troublemaker'. She preferred to see herself as the resident 'provocateur', challenging what she described as the 'stuffys' in the Village.

In what was later seen as the ultimate test of what real trouble can be in a Village, Beryl decided to do something she'd never done before. It was the dawning of World Aids Day and the other residents woke to discover that Beryl had erected a flagpole in her postage stamp sized back yard. At the top of it flapped a multi-coloured flag, with all the colours of the rainbow.

Initially, the residents, ignorant about its significance, were just quietly quizzical but mostly dismissive, seeing it as one of Beryl's little flights of fancy.

Having googled 'Flags of the World', it was still a mystery to one resident. It took three days before he plucked up the courage to ask her what the flag stood for. When told it was the flag of the LGBTI community and that she had put it up in support of their cause and the fight against AIDS, pandemonium swept like wildfire through the length and breadth of the village. An emergency meeting of the Residents' Committee was convened.

Some of the residents formed a small posse and decided to confront her at her front door. She was, as usual, defiant. Off they went to the hapless manager of the Village who had not faced such an issue before in her extensive time in retirement villages. Promising to address the issue, the manager combed the By-Laws and in a 'hah-hah' moment realised that Beryl had erected an unauthorised structure in her backyard, namely, the flagpole. While the flag itself was the cause celebre for the residents, it mattered little once the pole became the offender.

Confronted by the reality that it was 'agin' the law, Beryl decided she had made her point and down came the flag and flagpole. Her flag however now hangs proudly in the entry way to her unit.

OCDM – 'Older Chicks Dig Me'

Longevity and one of its consequences are often exposed in the hallowed laneways of the retirement village landscape.

A demographic fact is that, over the age of 80, the number of single women will far outnumber the number of single men. That represents potentially good news for elderly single gentlemen and, conversely, some challenging times for elderly single ladies.

I was once involved in a dispute in a retirement village involving a '*menage a trots'*, a single man and two single women, all aged over 80, and living in their own separate units in the village.

The two women were engaged in an initial light-hearted competition for the gentleman's affections, spurred on by the lothario's subtle encouragement. Soon, however, it turned into a full-blooded survival of the lustiest, if not, the fittest. From a 'cease and desist' note left by one of the women on the other woman's front door, to a shouting match between the two women at the indoor bowls tournament, and finally, a hot chip thrown by one of them at the other as a lethal projectile at the monthly residents' dinner when the police were called.

Other residents demanded action from the operator before indignity led to bloodshed. A mediation was arranged between all three of them. I was representing, as he perceived it, the innocent victim, the gentleman. At one point in the mediation, we had a break and I was sitting outside with him. He very quietly turned to me at one stage and said, 'Brian, you know what this is all about don't you?' Shaking my head in feigned ignorance, he went on 'I'm an OCDM!' To which I finally spoke, 'What's that?' Quick as a flash and with a slight supercilious splaying of his lips, he replied 'It's an acronym – OCDM—*Older Chicks Dig Me!*'

While the aim of mediation is to produce a 'win/win' for all parties, on this occasion, it was a win/lose, probably inevitable in affairs of the heart. Regrettably, one of the women conceded, said you can have him and promptly left the village.

While none of these examples are unique in the broader urban landscape, they take on increased significance in the confined cocoon of a retirement village. They can have serious consequences both in terms of the larger picture, the morale of the village and the smaller picture, a resident's individual happiness.

Manufactured Home Parks and Land Lease Communities

Time never stands still in meeting the accommodation needs of older people.

In the golden olden days, the Caravan Park was a temporary home for travellers or the holiday home for the working class. It subsequently mutated to permit permanent residency in the Mobile Home Park. Now, at least in Queensland, they have evolved again to what is known as a Manufactured Home Park (the 'MHP') – such a beguiling and evocative name. In New South Wales, they are known as Lend Lease Communities and, in the rest of Australia, by other different phrases.

For all intents and purposes, from the outside looking in, a modern MHP has all the look and appearance of a retirement village – purchase prices similar to a retirement village, detached or semi-detached units, often gated, a community centre, and caravan and boat parking bays etc. But, just like a retirement village, an MHP is communal living with all the 'soft' issues recounted under the retirement villages section above.

However, in terms of legal and financial comparisons, they are fundamentally different to, and in many ways, simpler than a retirement village. In an MHP:
- You buy an existing unit or pay to have it built on a plot in the park (current average price about $250,000).

- You own the unit but not the dirt underneath it.
- You pay to rent the land underneath the unit from the park operator and that rent can increase over time (current average about $150 per week).
- Depending on the actual MHP set up, you will have to pay individually, or through the park operator, for services such as electricity, telephone, gas and wate.
- You can sell your unit and receive the full purchase price and don't have to pay anything to the operator apart from marketing costs to sell the unit.
- Technically, although this is rarely done, you can remove the unit from the site and transport it to another property.
- There is no age limitation of who can buy into an MHP but the park operator is able to refuse to consent to a new owner provided that refusal is reasonable.
- If you die while owning an MHP unit, you can bequeath it to anyone in your Will.

While there is no age restriction or discrimination permitted, practically speaking, most residents of an MHP are elderly people.

On the face of it then, the MHP is an attractive alternative to retirement villages. It has the same community and social benefits and the structure is simpler. They are cheaper to buy into, to live in and to leave. You also get a sense of ownership.

The added advantage is that they are often developed on old caravan parks, some of which are well located near those prized areas close to the sea. However, as with all things in life, there can be complications. Some of the most common ones involve the death of a resident, the blended couple residing in an MHP or a child moving in.

I deal with these in more detail below.

Death

When a single resident in an MHP dies, they can bequeath their unit to someone in their Will. If that 'someone' happens to be their adult children, 'issues' can arise not just between the children as to what to do with the unit but more particularly with the operator of the park.

As a result of the bequest, the four adult children of the deceased can end up owning the unit. If, as is often the case, the MHP is located in a prime spot close to the sea, the children are usually keen to keep the unit as a holiday home for their respective families.

This creates tensions given that the park will then be descended upon by families and young children. This can change the whole social landscape of the park and is often anathema to the other elderly residents. Operators are then inclined to refuse to consent to the transfer of the unit to the children which, if that is accepted by them, will result in the forced sale of the unit.

Blendeds

When a couple in a second relationship buy into an MHP unit, they need to carefully consider up front what the effect will be if one of them dies while they both own the unit. Because ownership of the unit by two or more people creates effectively a tenancy in common, each of them can bequeath their share of the ownership of the unit to someone else in their Will, such as their own family. This would result in the surviving partner becoming a part owner with his former partner's family. This is not usually desirable.

So it is that, when this scenario arises, both partners are strongly advised to make a new Will in which it would be prudent to do something different. Instead of giving their share in the unit to their family when they die, they give a right to reside to their surviving partner until his or her death or departure from the unit. Upon the latter's death or departure from the unit, the families of each of them would then normally end up owning the unit in the same shares as their respective parents had when they were alive. This device in a Will is a simple process to ensure that there is no difficulty or disruption to the surviving partner continuing to live in the unit.

Children Moving in

While it is not necessarily peculiar to MHP's, my experience is that they seem to be a magnet for adult children who may have some personal issues and can conveniently submerge them in their apparent generous offer to move in with mum or dad in their new MHP unit. MHP's seem to be more accommodating for this development because, unlike retirement villages, the operator has far less control over who lives in a particular unit.

We have had a number of these types of cases, which, in my line of work means only one thing – they have gone bad.

In one case, a mum and one of her children, a single adult daughter bought the MHP unit together and so both were the owners of the unit. The daughter, as a result of a lifelong psychiatric disorder, had led a dissolute and itinerant life. The proposal germinated almost as a mutual, but implied, pact – Mum saw it as an opportunity to be, once again, a good parent to her disadvantaged daughter and to give her a place to call home.

The daughter saw it as a base to pursue her dubious relationships but under the guise of being able to say to the other members of the family that she would care for mum when needed.

It soon became clear that the aspirations would, almost inevitably, clash and spectacularly so. The daughter started to have all her old cronies come and 'stay awhile' and to stay up late or to put it succinctly, to take over. The unit soon turned to semi squalor. Mum was made to feel like a boarder in her own home, assigned to the back blocks of the unit. It was a poisonous atmosphere by the time one of her other children brought the mum to see me.

Complicating any resolution was the fact that they both owned the unit. That was mum's big mistake because, as you would appreciate, they both had a right of possession, as the lawyers would say. Without transcribing the distressing and costly course of events, suffice to say that the only resolution turned out to be to force the sale of the unit. That left mum with another disruptive transition in her life which she had little ability to finance, let alone find suitable alternatives. Needless to say, as well, as is often the case, her health suffered significantly, and she ultimately ended up in an aged care facility.

OTHER AGEING LIFESTYLES

Space and disinclination prevent me from exploring the other types of retirement living that, in some ways, are derivatives of the above styles.

In summary, however, they are:
- Rental Villages
    * They are communities specifically designed for older people with limited financial means. The person simply rents a unit and the rent is usually set at 85% of the full age pension.
    * Meals and domestic services can be supplied for additional fees and, of course, legally, they would be governed by the law on residential tenancies in the relevant state or territory.
- Serviced Apartments/Supported Accommodation

* They first emerged in the retirement village space believe it or not as a mixture of independent and dependent living.

* Far cheaper than a conventional retirement village unit, the accommodation is usually much smaller than a retirement village unit and tends to be more in the style of a bedsitter (to suit one person) albeit under the relevant retirement villages law.

* As with any retirement village a resident would pay to buy the right to live there, pay fees while living there and pay an exit fee when they leave.

* The operator can and usually does, provide domestic or care services as well.

RESIDENTIAL AGED CARE

The Setting

If there is one later life option that nobody wants, let alone contemplates as ever being necessary – the older person and their families, it's residential aged care.

First developed in the 1950's by the church and charitable sector, they started off known as 'Convalescent Homes', which as the name suggests, was where you convalesced or recovered from old age. When I was growing up in the 1950's and 1960's, there was one located just near our family home (and it's still there providing convalescence). I always wondered what went on in that walled, enclave except for my parents' entreaty that you don't want to go there. It was not till much later in life that I was to find out what it was and why I would prefer not to go there.

Later, in the last century, they became known as 'Nursing Homes' where convalescence progressed to nursing the aged and infirmed. Even then, the homes were broken down into two types, Nursing Homes and Hostels. The former being for high care and the latter for low care. They were all very much designed on a 'medical model' where ageing was a medical condition to be treated rather than a lifestyle to be supported. A facility was really a de-facto hospital from which no one exited vertically.

Now, at least for the moment, they operate under the description, 'Aged Care Facilities' (ACF).

Their development and expansion is in response to that familiar bogey, longevity. It also evidences our social compact in Australia. As a society, we are great adherents to the safety net role of government. This philosophy is nowhere better demonstrated than in our collective desire to look after our elderly and frail citizens.

To that end, governments of all persuasions, have determined that it should financially assist its citizens to obtain the necessary care in later life according to their needs and, generally speaking, their financial status. Once government starts funding what I call a 'care security program', it also leads to the creation of a mesmerising morass of regulation and control to ensure that the taxpayers' largesse (last year some $20billion) can be properly accounted for, or to put it more elegantly, we are getting what taxpayers would want for their parents.

Today we have an aged care system that is comparatively one of the most extensive, generous and complex in the world. It also operates in a landscape of relentless scrutiny governed mostly by a piece of Commonwealth legislation – the Aged Care Act.

If you believe the barrage of bad news surrounding the sector, numerous government enquiries, 'papers' with all the colours of the rainbow, 'white papers', 'green papers' and 'black papers', not to forget, the Productivity Commission and now, a Royal Commission, it is one of the great under achievers. In the game of 'Unders and Overs', it suffers from inherent under-funding and under-staffing leading, inevitably, to under-caring and under-performing.

It also suffers from a media addicted to the old adage – the only good news is bad news. The trouble with good news in aged care (and there's lots of it) is that it is no news.

Indeed, our general aversion to nursing homes (a bit like prisons) simply causes us to avert our gaze about a place we simply don't want to think about. It reminds me of what an advertising executive in the retirement market once told me – it is all well and good to sell the dream of retirement nirvana by throwing up images of retirees frolicking and kicking up the sand on a beach but, if the image does not show them wearing hats, the retiree reader will just turn away.

Apart from aged care providers websites and social media posts, there are few feel good stories about the happy aged care resident (and their families). Those that appear from time to time veer on the side of the kitsch (although some may see it as one small step against the forces of ageism). In 2018, it was reported by a news centre that Annie Avery, an 80-year-old resident of an Alabama Nursing Home was crowned 'Ms Alabama Nursing Home 2018'. It depicted Annie, in her wheelchair, adorned with her crown complemented by her winner's sash, beaming and remarking '...to be a part of this at 80 years old is wonderful...'

However, for all the foreboding that some of us may have about this later life option, either for ourselves or our parents, the reality is that families will, in many cases, need to address the issue of residential aged care for their parent/s. There are clear and present dangers that should alert us, in advance, to the need to address it including:

- Where one parent has died and the other is left to live alone in their home. This is often, naturally, a destabilising influence on the surviving parent leading to increased social isolation. Research has clearly shown that the top two causes of depression leading to death is a lack of a close relationship with someone and lack of social connections.
- Significant clinical diagnoses that foreshadow the inevitable increase in dependency such as Alzheimer's. Without a cure and with no known remission, the reality is that it will just become more debilitating and potentially, dangerous.

- Increased risk taking or adverse events in your parents' lives.
- Consistent lack of compliance with medications, either intentionally or inadvertently.
- The fatal fall.
- Inability to obtain, or to afford, increasing home care needs.

All of this gives rise to a potential conflagration in a closely related area – the relationships between, and contributions by, the adult children.

Children usually bend over backwards to keep parents at home. You, and perhaps your siblings have shared, in varying degrees, the increasing load along with a smattering of home carers. Your parents continuing decline is inevitable and their accentuating needs are looming. Your work life balance is shot, your personal care leave is exhausted, (as are you), your children and your partner keep asking where you are, and your siblings are occupied with other more pressing demands.

If there is one aspect of our families lives that has the probable, and sometimes, inevitable implosive effect, it is the attempt, collectively, to answer that big question – what are we going to do about mum or dad? There is no doubt that the later this question is addressed, the more pyrotechnical will be the consequences. In the heat of sibling disagreement, it is often overlooked that the effect is broader than on just their relationships. Disputes in this area have an inexorable impact as well on the relationships between the siblings' children i.e., the cousins and nephews. It seeps through the family tree and infects them causing them to declare, by default, support for their respective parent.

What's it like in residential aged care?

As I write this, the Royal Commission into Aged Care has just issued its Interim Report. It does paint a woeful tale of poor care and worse. Having worked in and around the sector for many years, I do know that there are many stories of satisfied residents and families. Satisfaction is a relative experience in aged care when you consider the context of ageing and dying. Indeed, a Commission, by its nature, is not looking for the best or most heart-warming stories. In some ways that would make their work superfluous.

While I may have become innocently and subconsciously aware of it almost 60 years ago, since then, my vast exposure to the insides and outsides of aged care as a lawyer allows me, I believe, to make some general observations or give some insights particularly for families who are exploring, or experiencing it for the first time:

- Once you become a resident of an ACF, you will probably never leave except to go to another ACF, or that 'other place'. Very few people will return home.
- You can try before you buy. Known as 'respite care', you can currently have up to 62 days per year living temporarily in an aged care facility both to meet some immediate and more intensive care needs and to assess what life is like in a facility.

- Some people can live in residential aged care for varying periods. The shortest time I have known, before the resident suddenly died, was 2 days. The longest time I am aware of was 12 years. The average is 2.5 years.
- There are twice as many women in aged care as men.
- It is not free – everyone has to pay to reside in an ACF. In fact, it can be a very expensive place to live although it does operate on the safety net ethos – each person pays according to their capacity to pay, generally speaking (at least for a limited time).
- The aged care sector attempts to portray the so-called 'home like' environment of its ACF's but, while things are improving, they come in all shapes and sizes. Many, (particularly the older ones) still have a more clinical or hospital feel. Some, just like economy seats in an aircraft, still compress the residents in 4-bed rooms.
- Its overriding advantage is that it offers 24 hour care, something

which many children are attracted to, given the often, precarious state of affairs for their parents who may still be living at home.
- There is an underlying sense of guilt, if not, fear and loathing experienced by children who confront the task of 'putting' their mum or dad into aged care. These suppressed emotions can percolate to the surface and the staff become the butt of the anger and disenchantment because no care is ever good enough.
- As children, you may be classified in hushed whispers by the facility under various rubrics – 'a lovely family' (no complainers), the 'AWOL family' (no visitors), 'helicopter families' (hovering with malevolent intent waiting for any opportunity to land and blast away with their AK47's), 'obsessive disordered families' (impossible to deal with or satisfy), 'ageing deniers' (mum is not really dying) or 'trouble makers' (nothing better to do than complain).

- On the other hand, you will find facilities where children aren't regarded as the sworn enemy but as crucial allies. There are places where staff are truly herculean in performing the twin tasks of aged care – caring for the resident and caring for their families.
- An ACF is a place full of people coming and going, strange noises at all times of the day and night and some who act strangely (officially described as 'acting out') affected, as they are, by their clinical conditions.
- There are two countervailing care themes running through the notion of 'care' in residential aged care – on the one hand there is the prevailing presumption that 'care' is the traditional task of managing someone's decline and making them comfortable. It is sometimes called 'protection' because it involves as little risk as possible. On the other hand, there is 'empowerment' – giving residents choices, some involving risk, in an effort to simply have a reason to continue to be.

- Understaffing leads to another insidious fallout on this aspect. Given the pressure on caring, many residents are left in their rooms or beds as long as possible and not encouraged or assisted to ambulate. With that policy at least you know where many residents are at all times. As a consequence, their usually already wasted muscles emaciate further and, ultimately, they are simply unable to move either in or out of their bed, on their own legs (even with a walker) or by self-propelling their own wheelchair. This sedentary theme enables staff to cope in their straitened situation as it frees up their time from having to assist a resident to move.
- Despite the appeal and seeming reassurance of 24-hour care in a caring facility, if you are the dutiful child, you will be amazed, nonetheless, how much time you will need to devote to your parent when they are in the facility. This is because you implicitly are concerned about the upheaval in

their life and what is happening to them. It can assuage your guilt to be a constant companion for your parent in this artificial environment.
- Your circumstances may be disrupted by one of the biggest subliminal fears of adult children – their parents being separated by circumstance. Where one can no longer look after the other and one has to go into residential care leaving the other to stay at home. The workload literally doubles.
- Some 50% of residents in residential aged care suffer from depression. In this context, your parent can be frustrated and ultimately depressed in residential care where, perhaps, their mind doesn't deserve to be, but their bodies need to be. They are mentally capable but physically frail. Their brains are fine, but their bodies have been left behind.
- Perspective can be tested. There is often a different perception or disjunct between families and staff on what is serious and what is trivial in the lexicon of good care.

I once had to mediate a dispute between a facility and the daughter of a resident (a nurse) over the daily opening and closing of a window in the resident's room. This was the same daughter who wanted to take her mum on 'outings' when she was bed bound with the bed rails down.
- Beware of gender dynamics also known as bias. I once went to a physiotherapist practice for the first time for a therapeutic massage. In their induction questionnaire I was asked if I preferred a male or female masseur. To that point I had, by chance, not by design, always been assigned a female in the various places I had been to. Being the new age aged man that I am, I answered 'No preference'. I was allocated a male masseur. To this day, I am not sure if I was really comfortable with that answer.

In the care space, some raw figures might shed a more relevant light on this issue:
- Only 1 in 10 nurses in aged care are men.

- Of the 96% of people providing informal care to someone, two thirds are women.

Those figures give you some broad insight into the feminisation of care where the vast majority of care is provided by women.

This then flows on to the family dynamics. Reflected in the saying 'Men don't buy bras', men have, and continue to have, a relatively minor role in the soft tasks of caring. This extends to all elements of the caring process including the finding and getting of care for a parent. The brothers tend to take a back seat to their sisters either in subconscious compliance with perceived societal norms i.e., it's women's' work, or because they really don't fancy buying bras. This can have a fragmenting effect on family harmony when the load is not shared equally.

Boys, you need to step up. Besides, with online shopping, what can your excuse be now – bras are just a click away? Sure, there are bad stories. One, in particular has stuck with me over the years. A male resident of a facility suffered from a medical condition known as priapism – a constant erection. It can be fatal. Care staff were flummoxed about how to deal with him. The DON was quoted one day as saying, 'Just tap it with a cold spoon – that should fix the bugger'.

Parenting to your parents' needs will expose you and your siblings to the full force of collective wisdom or individual fragmentation. You could unite and forge a path together. If you don't, your parents (who will inevitably be relying on you) will be like hapless spectators at a tennis match, on clay, at the French Open – interminable baseline rallies between sworn enemies.

If there is one overwhelming lesson, I have learnt in the maelstrom created by the aged care expedition, you and your siblings might be the centre of the action, but you are not the centre of attention. This may be good to keep in mind as you hang up on that last conversation with your irritable sister who just doesn't get it.

THE RESIDENTIAL AGED CARE SYSTEM

It is often a fruitless task to address, in any detail, this notorious system. There is one thing that has consistently characterised the sector – the constant churning of rules and regulations. As such, any static summary of it in these written words can be redundant, if not misleading, after their writing.

What does it look like inside?

Residential aged care consists of purpose-built buildings (facilities) also known as the 'built environment', in which are housed, usually, elderly people in need of 24-hour care.

The buildings are staffed by admin/management staff and care staff who can be nurses, AIN's (assistants in nursing) or carers. There will also be support staff in the form of kitchen staff, cleaners and grounds staff. They can often be co-located with associated lifestyle accommodation or a 'feeder', such as a retirement village, helping to make any subsequent transition to aged care a small amble across the road.

The residents will present in various ways – walking, shuffling, sitting, talking, not talking, being talked to or with, being visited or not being visited, lying down, semi-reclining in oversized lounge chairs, laughing, crying, dying, 'secured', looking quizzical, bored, animated or being asleep.

Inside the buildings there are rooms where people 'reside'. These rooms can vary from single rooms with ensuites to adjoining single rooms with a shared facility and sometimes, four bedrooms with shared facilities. Older ones can have both an institutional look and feel with standalone, bland brick buildings, or as Joan Rivers described them, 'mind-numbing architectural sameness'. They are, usually, no more than two stories high with long, foreboding corridors and many doors. A hospital, they would appear, by any other name.

Enter, however, the modern age of aged care. In response to the sterile, clinical tone and the God's waiting room theme, aged care providers have embarked on the innovative design and development of newer facilities that attract the eye and the hippocket. A hotel, they would appear, by any other name.

Some of these are addressed below.

High Rise Care (or 'Care in the Air')

Given the increasing dearth of good quality, well located real estate, some providers are opting to go up and not out. This can even mean demolishing old facilities and building high rise edifices in their place.

Some have even resorted to a mix use development with commercial or retail facilities on the lower floors, further up, a few floors of a retirement village with the final floors at the top devoted to an aged care facility. Some see it as a way of easing our transitions in later life by reducing them to the convenience of one building and, ultimately, facilitating closer proximity to our final destination (for most of us).

Comfort Caves

I devote a whole chapter later in this book to the dynamics of relationships in the ageing area. However, at least in the USA, developers have identified the distress and dislocation that can arise for older people who may have had to leave their partner of many years to take up a place in a facility.

Their previous life where, usually, they slept together in the one bed, is now permanently disrupted by the change. In response to the ongoing need for intimacy and privacy, some newer facilities are incorporating 'Conjugal Caves' where couples can retreat to a specially designed room for some private time. They even include a 'Do Not Disturb' sign where you can also insert the relevant times for no interruptions with a texter pen.

Care Cruising

If he ever had need for it, Kerry Packer may have chosen this option. Alternatively, he may have just converted his 'big boat' into his own private one.

While floating hotels may have come and gone, consider ocean cruise liners converted into aged care facilities either exploring the high seas or permanently docked at a port. This style of care may appeal to those who were addicted to cruising in their retirement years and yearn for at least the sense of it again when they need care.

Be aware however, that you will not find a full aged pensioner in this facility (unless their children can afford, and are inclined, to reward their parent in their later life).

Getting your Youth Fix

In her book, referred to previously, Joan Rivers devotes some pages to the need for older people to have their 'Youth Fix' – a desire to spend some time around younger people and to break away from the constant company of their peers.

To address that, some aged care providers in the USA are developing new facilities and incorporating in the development a child-care centre. Indeed, I understand one particular developer adds two additional features in their age care facilities – a viewing platform and a kinder cam.

The viewing platform is a raised platform where the residents can sit and watch the children frolicking in the adjoining childcare playground. The kinder cam is a strategically position video camera in the playground which beams pictures of the children playing back to every television screen in the facility.

Clayton's Aged Care Facilities

Some facilities have all the look and feel of an aged care facility but are not or alternatively, are not within the approval requirements of the Aged Care Act.

I have referred to them previously and they are described in many ways, but the most common are 'serviced apartments' or 'supported accommodation'. In many cases, they are not regulated by the Commonwealth legislation but rather by a relevant piece of State legislation. In Queensland, for example, some are governed by the Retirement Villages Act.

Some facilities are effectively unregulated and are known as 'unfunded facilities'. These are normally private facilities where the residents will pay dearly for their care and will not receive any government subsidy.

Clearly, understanding where a facility fits in the scheme of the law, can be crucial in your trawling and searching because it may well have a substantial impact on the cost of the care and the security of government regulation.

OTHER TYPES OF AGED CARE

Respite Care

Caring can be a mix of duty and devotion, but it can also be demanding, unrelenting work. It can breed carer resentment especially as the statistical curve of care needs goes on the exponential upward trajectory. For the carer, as well, there is usually not a lot of fun involved, or even a lot of fun to look forward to.

Being cared for can also be an arduous and anxious experience. Reliance on the generosity and attention of others can, itself, breed guilt and even resentment and frustration. At its peak, spending, on average, all day every day with someone has its own statistical satisfaction curve which, at best, can have peaks and troughs but invariably, it is downwards. Through the prism of both sets of eyes, it can put the 'tough' into mutual love and devotion.

There is simply no respite.

Governments recognise this and, apart from the relatively minor taxpayers' expense of social security benefits, such as the carer's allowance and the carer's payment, informal caring has the subliminal benefits of saving consolidated revenue billions of dollars – it keeps older people out of residential aged care.

The government programme of respite care is aimed at alleviating the stress for either the carer or the cared.

The care recipient can become a temporary resident of an age care facility away from the home and the carer can have a break. A care recipient can clock up to 63 days in a financial year on respite. This period can be extended by up to twenty-one (21) days in certain circumstances. It is the cheapest form of residential care as it only costs the basic daily care fee which is 85% of the single age pension, currently $52.25 per day. Respite care is also available in the home but usually for shorter periods and the services are less intense and limited to a few hours or an overnight stay.

It is also great way of assessing whether your mum or dad is likely to adjust well to permanent residential care and for you to judge the quality of care being provided during the respite. It is strongly advised as a way of trying before you buy.

Transitional Care

This is another form of 'temporary' support in the broader context of aged care. While it is possible to extend the time, the scheme provides up to 12 weeks of care arising out of a hospital stay with the aim of assisting an older person to recover.

It can be provided in many places – a hospital, an aged care facility, a day therapy centre, or the older person's home. The services are generally aimed at assisting the older person to recover from a medical event and to provide rehabilitation.

You will need to obtain an ACAT assessment (referred to below) while still in hospital, referred to below, and if the care is to be provided in the recipient's own home, they will need to pay 17.5% of the full age pension and if it is in an aged care facility, the fee will be the usual basic daily care fee.

Multi-Purpose Services (MPS)

One of the herculean challenges in providing services in this large brown land is the delivery of those services in rural and remote areas. The communities are simply not big enough to create and sustain the usual edifices of aged care – hospitals, home and residential aged care.

The tyranny of distance and small communities mean that services have to be aggregated into a holistic health service, including aged care. Aged care can be obtained through the MPS which are usually run out of a local or nearby hospital. Some of these hospitals even have residential aged care places.

The Aged Care Process

Where, you might ask, to start in this complex maze of law, money, geography and quality?

The government has grappled with simplifying the puzzle and has devised a website known as 'My Aged Care'. Its role and purpose is best summarised from its own home page:

> *My Aged Care is the main entry point to the aged care system in Australia. (it) aims to make it easier for older people, their families, and carers to access information on ageing and aged care, have their needs assessed and be supported to find and access services.*

It is a bit like Caesar's wife, 'all things to all men' and, like all generous and ambitious digital offerings, it suffers from its own complexities and limited user friendliness. However, it is, and remains, the only full information offering on the system as well as being able to facilitate your navigation through the system in an attempt to suit your own circumstances.

But, if amongst your siblings, you are the retired nurse, doctor, financial adviser or lawyer, look out. Your career choice may have been good to you during your working life but now, in your much-anticipated retirement, it could come back to haunt you. Your family may well be keen to anoint you as the logical manager of this arduous process. Beware, however, your expertise may result in your exploitation (especially if you just happen to live nearby to your parents) or the chosen aged care facility.

If so, remember, there is no sleight on you or indignity to seek help—there is nothing like the reassurance of an expert's advice. Besides they can help you avoid that often tedious task for you – trying to ring a bureaucrat to clarify something and then waiting, waiting, waiting.

However, to give you some important pre-system use, I have set out below some helpful advice.

Getting In, Being In, and Getting Out of Residential Aged Care

The starting point is to understand that getting in is a menagerie, a matching of eligibility to enter the system, with financial capacity to pay and an exploration of available places in facilities to suit.

The Process – Getting In

There are a number of elements to 'getting in':
- Finding a facility
- Bureaucratic requirements
- Legals.

Finding a Facility

I loath checklists at the best of times. They seem to take away that exciting element of life, spontaneity.

On this occasion, however, whimsy is not called for, rather, a logical identification of the issues is. You are not looking for another investment property and 'position, position, position' or capital gain are not the appropriate mantras. Fortunately, at least at this stage, you won't have to attend those pesky auctions to find what you are looking for. You are looking for permanent communal accommodation for your parent/s that, perchance, may suit them, or make them happy.

Instead here are some issues for your checklist:
- What are their (or your) criteria for where they would like to live?
- Are you dealing with one parent or two?
- Can you find a 'shared room' for both of them, if necessary?
- Would they have to be separated in different facilities?

- What will you do about finding out about a facility's reputation?
- Will you be the finder alone or will it be shared with other siblings?
- What protocols should you set up with your siblings to keep them in the loop?
- Is access to their current health professionals important?
- How much money do they have to play with?
- Should you try some respite care before committing?

This is not a foolproof or comprehensive list. For example, you may want some idiosyncratic features as well – religious, cultural, or ethnic. I had one client recently who was frustrated at the difficulty of finding an LGBTIQ facility for their father who, at the age of 78, had recently 'come out'. Fear not, there are facilities that cater for these needs. It may be a question, however, of how far you are prepared to go.

DIY Finding

There is a belated, and sometimes frantic, manoeuvring in families when the dawn of realisation of 'where's the money coming from?' for your parents aged care when the time arrives.

Even worse, is the equally delayed and anxious consequence of dilatory conduct – where are mum or dad going to go and who is going to arrange that. Make no mistake, the transition of a parent/s to aged care is a major and pressing family management issue. It's not just about the finances. As they say in business, it is a human resources issue. Who does what?

There is research to do – what are the options, what will it cost, what can they afford, where would they like to go, what if we need a place for both mum and dad at the same time.

Added to that is a legal complication. Mums and dads who are pre-baby boomers, tended to have a large number of children after the second world war. That is useful if we are talking about family caring for family. But, it is a minefield when the parents have lost their capacity to make decisions and some of those children (not all) have been appointed the parents' Enduring Power of Attorney. The other children can be left out in the legal cold.

This is a tension that many families manage successfully. Some do not, simply because individual members come with agendas and differences as to 'what is best'.

Aged Care Helpers

Given its complexity in every sense of the word, private businesses have also identified later life transitions as a fruitful and useful service opportunity. Not only have they created an expertise in that jewel of good decision making, information, but also in the emerging area of aged care advice that spreads over the practical, the emotional and the financial.

We have seen collateral organisations emerging such as:
- Relocation Agents who can provide on the ground assistance for such things as de-cluttering, sorting,

packing, removing and relocating your possessions or storing unneeded ones
- Relocation and Real Estate Agents who can not only offer the above services but also act as your agent to find a buyer for your home
- Aged Care Placement Agents who offer professional services to investigate, help you understand and find a suitable aged care, including home care, retirement village or supported accommodation place
- Aged Care Counsellors who can offer psychological support and assistance in the transition for older people as well as their families
- Care Managers – a service that is big in the USA but just emerging here which addresses the problem of the far-flung children saga. When children are spread all over the world it can be hard for them to keep their finger on the pulse and welfare of mum or dad in an aged care facility. These businesses are able to visit them in the facility and

provide regular reports of how they are faring on the ground.

What will frustrate all families are particular elements of aged care – the emotions, the language and the acronyms, the decision making and the paperwork. As it represents a highly charged, and first-time experience for many, it is a major family discomfort zone.

While all the above services come with a cost, they are well worth considering on a cost/benefit basis. The sheer weight of effort, time and responsibility involved in families doing a DIY aged care move can raise temperatures and repressed enmities within families. Using professional services can alleviate (not necessarily eliminate) this destructive effect.

Bureaucratic Requirements

You may have already got the message that aged care is your introduction to a world of a vast array of bureaucratic requirements. It is a process – there are people to see, assessments to be done and forms to be completed even before your parent's feet go through the front door of a facility.

Here are those processes just in summary:

ACAT Assessment

This is your parent's entry ticket to the aged care theatre.

You will be looking for what is known as an aged care 'place' sometimes referred to, patronisingly, as a 'bed'. You are shopping for a bed apparently.

Before they enter a government funded facility i.e., where their fees are subsidised, your parent needs to be assessed by an Aged Care Assessment Team (ACAT). They are usually health professionals engaged by the government to visit your parent and assess them for the level of aged care they may require e.g., home care, respite care and/or permanent residential aged care.

The assessment can be arranged directly through My Aged Care or even through your parent's GP, or other health professional. After the assessment is completed you will receive a letter setting out the assessment and their eligibility for aged care.

Centrelink

If your parent is a full age pensioner and needs to consider moving into residential aged care, you need to move from dilly dally to action mode.

When a parent's move into aged care is imminent or, as Centrelink would say, it is 'reasonable to assume' they will need to, it can be very advisable to lodge, as soon as possible, the relevant form with Centrelink setting out your assets and income. It can take between six to eight weeks for the assessment to be issued assuming you have given them everything they need.

It is what is required for Centrelink to assess the means tested care fee that may have to be paid in aged care (more on that in the next chapter). While you do not have to lodge the form (and some people consciously decide not to), beware, if you don't, you will be required to pay the full means tested care fee, and, until the form is lodged and Centrelink assesses whether you need to pay a means tested care fee, some age care providers will charge, and are charging, the full means tested care fee, even if you are a full age pensioner. This is on an 'interim' basis until the assessment by Centrelink is done.

Regrettably, many people don't lodge the form promptly and wait till they are about to move in, or even after they have moved in, before they lodge the form.

For DVA recipients the rules are different, but time and space don't permit to explore them, regrettably.

Facility Forms

'*You ain't seen nothin yet*', as they say.

The first thing to say is that facilities don't necessarily have all the same forms. However, the list can include:
- Application for Care
- Residential Care Agreement
- Direct debit authority
- Appointment of a Representative

- Privacy Statement
- Enduring Power of Attorney and Will
- Statement of financial affairs
- Resident Personal Details, Preferences and Peccadillos
- Helpful Pamphlets or Brochures
- By laws or rules of occupancy
- Welcome message.

The Legals

There is one legal document that defines a resident's rights and obligations in aged care – the 'Residential Care Agreement'. It may also, (and usually does), incorporate another agreement known as an 'Accommodation Agreement'. Together, they deal with the care and accommodation of your parent in that aged care facility from the legal perspective.

As the cost of aged care is divided into care fees and accommodation costs, the agreement will detail the care to be provided, the cost of that care and, whether any extra services are to be provided and for what additional cost.

It will also address the cost of your parent's accommodation in the facility.

It will also deal with rights and responsibilities including the right to move you from one room to another, insurance, when they can ask you to leave and ultimately the refund of any monies such as the RAD or Refundable Accommodation Deposit. Again, this will be explored in more detail in the next chapter.

Fortunately, much of what is contained within this agreement is prescribed by the legislation. However, some provisions may not be. As a result, and here it is again – get some legal advice on it not just to determine if there is anything unusual about it, or if something is not consistent with the law or, but simply to find out what it all means. Lawyers are translators in many ways.

I recently had to advise a daughter on a stressful situation. Her mother had been admitted to a secure dementia section of a facility as she was an inveterate wanderer. She was apparently 'happy' there. One day the DON of the facility approached the daughter and advised her that they had to move her mum to the open section of the facility which was not secured. The daughter was perplexed and distressed by this news but believed the facility could do it because the DON told her their Residential Care Agreement said they could. Sure enough, so it did.

It was not until she contacted me that I told her that clause in the agreement was contrary to the law and not permitted. They had no right to move her just because they decided to. The law prescribed a process that had to be followed which the facility did not and even worse, they did not know about.

AGED CARE MISTAKES

Let me get something off my chest. Many family members who become dissatisfied with their experience of the aged care system, create and perpetuate their own frustrations. There are a number of reasons for this:

The Government will always forgive and forget

Many people assume that, because the system is designed to assist the frail and vulnerable, our benevolent government, being the foundation of the system, in both administering and funding it, will be a benign and forgiving overseer—the 'we're here to help' psychology. But, it 'ain't necessarily so'.

As previously mentioned, doing well for elderly constituents currently means spending taxpayer's money to the tune of some $20billion dollars per year to fund the system. However, they must balance that largesse against the other imperative of government, being good to the taxpayers. It's also known as being answerable and accountable. Benevolence is not an excuse for blindness.

As a result, the government has created rules and regulations of biblical proportions to ensure the system is accountable and, as with the tax industry, to ensure there are no nasty avoidance techniques which could arise.

This broadly means that it is crucial that you get it right when implementing the processes because there are no 'oops' or 'innocence' pleas accepted. If you get it wrong, you, or more particularly, your mum or dad will pay.

Adviser Aversion (or the DIY Brigade)

Picture the family cohort. You are one of four adult children and the time has come to plan for mum or dad's future (and time is pressing). You are a retired English teacher adept at reading and comprehending the vagaries of technical language and the imperialism of acronyms.

The other children are too busy, too disinterested or not up to exploring a new field of endeavour. You are nominated, and agree, to take on the role of hunter and collector of information as a precursor to important decisions to be made. You plough through the My Aged Care space, talk to some friends, the neighbour up the street and your local member of Parliament. You also explore some local facilities one of which is perfect as it will take both your mum and dad. You think you're on top of it and it's time for some decisions.

The home care provider has urged you to do something as your parents cannot get the extent of home care that their needs dictate. Residential aged care is now urgent. The most significant issue to address is payment of what is known as the Refundable Accommodation Deposit (the RAD). The facility you have chosen tells you the RAD required to be paid for your parents will be $300,000 each, that's $600,000 altogether because they have no shared rooms.

You gather the family for a pow wow and layout your plan. Their home needs to be sold to pay the RAD's and, according to the local real estate agent, it should fetch about $1.2 million. Everyone agrees that's the way to go particularly because the money will be refunded when each parent dies.

The home is put on the market and a contract signed up relatively quickly.

You time the settlement of the sale contract for the day your parents are due to move into the facility. Settlement occurs and you literally deliver the two cheques for $300,000 each to the facility and the parents move in. Hunky dory – life is good.

A few weeks later you receive a letter from Centrelink noting that your parents' financial circumstances have changed, namely, they have converted an exempt asset, their home, partly into two exempt assets, the respective RAD's. However, the balance proceeds of the sale i.e., $600,000 (i.e., cash) is now determined to be an assessable asset. Along with the balance of their remaining assets, they now exceed the assets and incomes test for an age pension and will no longer receive the pension. Oh dear!

Then you realise the other cold hard consequence of your generosity in becoming the in-house family adviser and not seeking out-house advice – your siblings turn on you and bemoan 'how could this have happened!' or worse – 'it's all your fault!'

The old adage that the cost of doing nothing will always exceed the price of doing something is revealed in the rubble of family relationships.

Few of us will have experience in aged care or accessing it and most of us have to do it for the first time. It is not a place to try the old DIY approach. It may be a repetitious and self-serving statement but, you can significantly reduce the reduction of hair on your head and the bags under your eyes by spending some money before you have to spend some money.

Many of us are quite capable of doing the research and information gathering but how many of us are able to competently take the next step with that information – reaching and making informed decisions.

There are those in the professional services sector who specialise in advising families on aged care i.e., people who know their stuff – lawyers, accountants, financial advisers, counsellors and placement agencies. They are crucial in advising on the best decisions. But hey, that would cost money and why would you spend it on them when you could save it by not spending it on them.

PS, I should mention that you would be well within your rights to use your parents' money for this advice. So, it need not hurt you financially and it may avoid the emotional trial of sibling retribution.

Parents playing Santa

It astonishes me how many mums and dads have provided enormous sums of money to their adult children to give them the proverbial 'leg up'. Apparently, the affectionately known 'Bank of Mum and Dad' is now the fifth largest lender in the Australian lending space – estimated to be some $92billion. Alarmingly, over half of them, it is said, do not expect to be repaid.

Along comes aged care and those mammoth amounts of largesse handed out previously come home to roost in a number of ways:
- If they are loans, then they remain an asset in the hands of the parents and will be assessed as such by Centrelink.

- If they are either forgiven or they were gifts, they will similarly be assessed by Centrelink under the gifting rules potentially.
- If they were loans, as most of them are, repayable on demand, then the time limit for recovering those loans is 6 years from when the loans were made, not from when the demand was made.
- That money could have been very handy to pay for their aged care.
- What's the chance of getting the money back from the kids?

Say no more.

I didn't know that

Many things we don't know can hurt us. But some things we don't know could actually have helped us.

One of those is the 'hardship' provisions associated with aged care. What does that mean? In some cases, a person, who is otherwise required to, can be approved by the government to delay payment of their aged care costs e.g., the RAD or even have it waived.

Here is an example of what is known as 'unrealisable assets'. If a person is depending on selling their property, such as their retirement village unit, to pay their RAD and, for example, it sits on the market for six months or more, without any buyers, they can apply to delay payment of it without any interest being payable, or have their obligation to pay it waived.

If only you had known that.

FAMILY AGED CARE

Looks like an unusual phrase doesn't it, with some ominous undertones. But, it has arrived on our families' doorsteps in no small or uncertain way.

Family caring for family, or specifically, children caring for parents, has a long and mostly honourable history. Irrespective of culture, creed or country, it has also been a necessity.

Indeed, in other countries, there are legal obligations on children to care for their parents. They're called, filial responsibility laws. Singapore, for example, has a law known as the Parent Responsibility Act which requires adult children to look after their parents if their parents need looking after. If they don't, they can be, and are, prosecuted and ordered to do so. Even the US State of Iowa has recently passed a law which provides that, if a child does not look after their parents when they need it, the child will be disinherited from their parents' Will.

In the microcosm of Australia, before the Second World War, it was what the vast majority of families did, or were expected to do. They were times when there was no tradition of women working outside the home, they were generally freed up to provide the care – the in-house care model. As well, we didn't have the extensive social security safety net for older people that we have today. And, as longevity had not yet raised its head in any significant way, the time required for parent caring was relatively short.

Eventually, after the war, as women started to take up work outside the home, they were ultimately unable to support the in-house model. Help was at hand with the emergence of family competitors from the church and charitable sector in the form of institutions, Convalescent Homes, as they were known, for the aged and infirmed – the out-house care model.

Pressure on the family proportionally reduced as they now had an available and secure option for elderly parents to see out their days. These options have continued to expand in type and varieties bolstered by the perceived financial return to organisations providing this service helped in no small part by significant government funding. Aged care became commercialised, a business. Indeed, while aged care was initially led by the church and charitable sectors, it is now dominated by the for-profit sector.

In the 21st century however, the worm is turning. We are moving forward to the past and, once again, the family is becoming the new home of caring. In this context, the news is not good for many baby boomers and their much anticipated prosperous, joy filled, if not carefree, retirement.

Ageing statistics clearly suggest a prolongation of our lives through the creeping life expectancy tables. Along with that comes the kissing cousin of lengthening lives, dependency. More parents than ever will live for a longer time than ever and with that comes the need to support them as their frailty turns to fragility and then to dependency.

The facts are that the majority of older people either live with their spouse or alone. However, women from 65 to over 85 are much more likely than men to live with their children or a relative.

With those statistics, this area of life becomes of real relevance for older women.

Then, we have to deal with our parents' phobias about where to live in later life in the context of:
- Our general aversion to the 'institutional' care of aged care facilities
- The lack of such facilities in convenient places e.g., near us, the children
- We are living longer with disabilities
- The fixation in later life to preserve assets e.g., the family home

- The reluctance to dissipate those assets by paying for care
- The predilection for 'impoverishing' ourselves (or trying to) in order to maintain our pension and all the accoutrements that come with it.

Overlaying these mores is their understandable preference and priority to be cared for by family (generally) rather than some unconnected albeit well-intentioned, professional care provider whenever this becomes necessary.

In this age wave, how are we, as a society, going to cope when:
- They all want to stay at home but, in doing so, will need more and more care.
- Government will never either fund, or resource us enough, to do so adequately – there is a limit to the length and breadth of the safety net.
- The only way to ever be able to stay at home until death is to use our own money to pay towards the care we need.
- They are reluctant to use their own resources (as are their families) as

it may mean reducing the inheritance pool and, ironically, having to sell the very home they want to stay in (or take out the ubiquitous reverse mortgage).

Each year the number of informal carers out there in the community (usually family members) gathers pace. The latest figure I have seen is some 2.7 million, one of whom could be you. However, there were only 200,000 people in residential aged care. There are, currently, some 100,000 people awaiting a home care package and even more waiting for a better one than they have.

When throwing these factors into a life blender, the outcome, if not the resolution, seems obvious and inevitable. It's people like you, me and, hopefully, our siblings. It becomes a simple mantra for us as families – shut up (ignore it), put up (care for our parents) or pay up (for home care or residential care for our parents).

Family Care Consequences

Being an integral facilitator for many families grappling with this subject, as an elder lawyer, I am well placed to measure, just like a barometer, the rising heat in this space of later life

We are now entering the space of family arrangements for care which, in various guises, are expanding rapidly. I call it a collision between love and the law.

Family arrangements, generally, come in four types:
1. Informal Oral Arrangements
2. Family Care Agreements
3. Granny Flat Arrangements
4. 'Backyard' Care

Informal Oral Arrangements

Culturally, we have an anathema about documenting family relationships. After all, we all know and trust each other, don't we? Parents often advance large sums of money to children without a single piece of paper as evidence, let alone any record of what the terms of the advance might be e.g., loan or gift. Hmmm.

In certain areas of close relationships, the law has attempted to intervene in this pervading informality. For example, we have had, for many years, the ability for spouses and partners to enter into legally binding 'nuptial agreements' to address the consequences of a subsequent breakdown in a relationship. These agreements can be entered into before a marriage, or the start of a relationship, during them, or at the end of them. They can be particularly helpful in avoiding that one ogre associated with divorce or separation – going to court about how to divide the property. Documenting the consequences of these events is now a standard and accepted part of family law advice.

But when it comes to the broader family edifice or agreements between siblings and parents, we are reluctant to reduce them to writing. My experience is that many such arrangements are seeded in mutual trust but fall down on two common human frailties – memory (the 'who said what') and the vagaries of human relationships (the 'what ifs').

When, usually some years later, reflections on what was agreed or understood are called up, it evokes the familiar and contrasting stories of 'he said, she said' or when asked what was the arrangement on a particular issue, the answer is 'Oh, we didn't think about that!'

An example from my own practice is best to demonstrate:

- Sylvia was 73 and had recently finalised her property settlement with her former husband from which she received $300,000 in cash. That was the sum total of her assets. She was also suffering from cancer when she came to see me.
- She was on an age pension and had been living alone in a small rented unit in Brisbane. She had three children. One of them, a daughter, suggested to her that she move in with the daughter and her family given Sylvia's circumstances and the daughter would look after Sylvia for the rest of her life. However, she also suggested that

Sylvia place the money from her property settlement in the daughter's bank account as a way of avoiding the strictures of the Centrelink assets and income tests.
- Until this apparent spontaneous act of filial generosity (which the other children were unaware of), Sylvia was significantly depressed about her future for understandable reasons. Without giving a moment's thought or considering the implications, she jumped at the opportunity, moved in and duly deposited her funds in the daughter's bank account.
- Perhaps her only subconscious concern was that she really didn't like her daughter's husband, but she would repress those feelings for the sake of harmony and a sense of security for her future.
- Within three months, however, she was left standing on the footpath outside her daughter's home with her worldly possessions evicted by her daughter at the behest of her husband who wanted 'nothing more to do with that witch'.

- After finding emergency housing, she sat in front of me shortly after. As you might expect, one of our initial and immediate tasks was to recover the money because, apart from the pension, she was destitute.
- We duly wrote to the daughter and requested she repay the $300,000 to Sylvia. Her response was, regrettably, typical and, in many ways, entirely predictable. She wrote back to say she would not return the money as it was a gift!

Sylvia's circumstances went from bad to worse resulting in us having to commence legal proceedings during which, sadly, she died. The rest is a poignant story of loss and family implosion not to mention Centrelink circling her estate in light of the fiddle with her money.

There are so many times in my professional life when I am flabbergasted by the antics of adult children. They still cause me anger and frustration. I also suffer from another condition that lawyers often quietly fume about – the '*I could have told you what was likely to happen*' syndrome. While those thoughts never translate to words in front of a client, if they did, they would have been something to this effect, 'If only you had seen me beforehand, I could have advised you on the perils of the arrangement and, if you still wanted to proceed, we would have documented the arrangement'.

Lamentably, most of the arrangements within families are in the oral space or the atmosphere. As night follows day, in many cases this will lead to a disagreement about what was agreed or, at worst, total conflagration. And, need I also add, litigation – just what you wanted in retirement to spend your retirement savings on and to fill a void in your life.

In the words of Robot in 'Lost in Space', the message is clear, *'Danger Will Robinson, danger!'* The danger is double sided. Without documentation either the parent or child may be the loser. The biggest loss, however, will be to both of them, when the lawyers are finished with them.

Written Family Care Agreements

If you accept the statistic that some 15% of women aged over 85 are currently living with their children, then you might also accept a small conjecture on my part arising from that figure, namely, that percentage will inevitably increase.

If you also accept that litigation over failed family agreements is also increasing and that most of that litigation is over the 'oral arrangement', then you might, on reflection, consider suspending your disbelief about a written agreement with your mum or dad about them living with you.

It has a number of rational persuasions that may neutralise the emotional repellent. Just getting advice on and understanding the issues that need to be addressed in, an actual and real-life document called an agreement, can have a number of beneficial effects:
- It may save you from family implosion and a breakdown in your

relationship with your parents (and siblings)
- It will record for posterity and as an anti-dispute mechanism, what the terms of the agreement are
- It will provide an open and transparent record of the agreement to the other interested siblings
- It may well force your parent to review their estate planning (as we are all inclined to avoid) because of the implications of the agreement on the terms of their Will and even their Enduring Power of Attorney
- If your parent is on an age pension, it will highlight the care that needs to be taken in putting together your arrangement to ensure it does not adversely impact on their pension
- Depending on the arrangement, it will also give you the opportunity to determine if there are any CGT consequences for you (as discussed further below)
- It may avoid later accusations against you of 'elder abuse' if your oral arrangement breaks down
- Finally, and perhaps, ironically, it may well convince you not to enter

into the arrangement because of the risks and potential consequences.

In what also can be described as a downstream disaster for both you and your parents, a failure to document that leads to litigation, will, usually, seriously erode the finances of a parent in their later life. It could also result in the parent becoming homeless. In that there is a maudlin message – your parent will be unable to fund alternative accommodation as, any resources they do have, are locked up in litigation and you may well be called upon then, for a second time, to step up to the plate to meet their needs.

Shared living within families can come in all shapes and sizes and on all sorts of terms and conditions. Essentially, they can involve:
- A parent transferring their home to a child in return for a promise that the child will give a lifetime right to the parent to continue to live in the home
- A parent will finance the construction of a flat or unit on a child's property or an extension to

the property where the parent can live
- A parent simply moves in with the child and lives in a room in the child's existing home.

Inherently, these agreements should not be discouraged. In a lot of cases, they are helpful and of real benefit to the parent for all the reasons mentioned above. They can also provide a sense of security and reassurance to a child to know that they now have the ability to oversee their parent's care and welfare. It can be an antidote to the sense of 'releasing the hounds' guilt that can invariably imbue the 'putting my parent into aged care' scenario.

But in considering entering into such an agreement, what are the issues to be conscious of? We have drafted many types of these agreements and they tend to cover the following major issues:
- Background and purpose
- Legal and financial advice
- Dealing with the property
- The loan
- The accommodation
- Licence to occupy

- Care obligations
- Payment for care
- Holidays and respite
- Security of payment
- Voluntary ending of agreement
- Involuntary ending of agreement
- Disputes
- Insurance
- Enduring Power of Attorney and Will
- Costs.

While these headings may be cryptic, they give you some insight into the breadth of issues that need to be addressed. While our philosophy is to keep it simple as much as possible, there is no substitute for ensuring the agreement can address as many contingencies as possible and to provide solutions for those contingencies.

GRANNY FLAT ARRANGEMENTS

Granny flats are springing up across Australian suburbs as property owners convert their backyards for more independent living space, additional rental income and generous tax deductions.

However, a threefold recent increase in granny flat arrangements in the past five years also creates the possibility of the decline in pension or rent assistance payments and the sales of the family home, once tax free, attracting capital gains tax. About 75% more people are building their blocks of land as subdivision or granny flats in the last five years, according to government statistics. While the statistics show that increases occur alongside a general construction boom, granny flat approvals have surged with a nation-wide growth of 10%, and an expected further 2% growth by next year.

There are a variety of reasons why the Australian population are choosing to build a granny flat on their block.

In the inner-city suburbs of Brisbane, Sydney and Melbourne, there is a higher demand for single-occupant dwellers, whether they are retirees, ageing relatives in need of care, travellers, students and more. For some, it is an opportunity to gain additional income to assist managing the high costs of living or even save for that long-awaited overseas trip. For others, it can be a great way to provide extra living space, an office or studio separate from the main house.

With the increasing cost of living, many young people are staying home with their parents and relatives longer than before, with rates of under 25-year-olds moving out falling by 20% in the last five years. It is also common for ageing relatives to remain close and involved with their families while maintaining their own independent lives. An ageing population, rising house prices and capitalising on existing land are all contributing factors to a rise in the popularity of granny flat arrangements. Undoubtedly the granny flat boom could clearly be considered an indicator of classic Australian entrepreneurship making the most out of their situation.

What is a Granny Flat Arrangement?

A granny flat arrangement is similar to a family care agreement referred to above, but it is driven and controlled by Centrelink requirements and the need to preserve age pensions.

The arrangement can be established when you exchange assets or money with someone else in return for the right to live on their property for life.

Longevity means it has taken on an increasingly relevant lifestyle significance in later life. The term has also reached the dizzying heights of a recognised legal term. The Federal Government first introduced the concept in changes to the Social Security Act in 1991 which are known, colloquially, as the 'granny flat rules'.

Before examining those rules, I have another beef with the term, 'granny flat arrangement' – the use of the word 'arrangement'. It probably represents our innate attempt to downplay the significance of it and to avoid the spectre of any legal implications. Let's be frank, however, a granny flat arrangement is more than an arrangement, it is an agreement with all the legal implications that has.

The granny flat rules have no effect on the non-age pensioner or self-funded retiree who may enter into this type of agreement. They will probably just enter a Family Care Agreement.

However, if a parent is on an age pension and is considering a living arrangement involving children or anyone else, it is vital to understand the age pension implications in doing so i.e., the granny flat rules.

It all gets a bit contorted but here is an abbreviated explanation. The necessity for the rules arises out of the impact of another social security rule – known as the 'deprivation rule' or the rule about gifting assets. Because qualification for an age pension is limited by the assets and incomes test, in the good old days, older people would often give away assets to qualify for the pension. The government got wind of this and introduced a law to address this 'avoidance' device. Put simply, the current rule is that if an age pensioner gives away assets or money of more than $10,000 in any year or an aggregate of $30,000 over five years (and up to five years before they qualified for a pension), anything above those limits will be regarded as still theirs for another five years, even though they may have given it away. It is a 'Clayton's' gift in Centrelink's eyes. You may have given something away but you still have it.

The government, through Centrelink, want to encourage them, for obvious reasons, in terms of limiting the increasing expenditure on subsidising aged care. But, because the essence of a granny flat agreement is the gifting of assets or money, the government had to create an exception and hence the granny flat rules.

So, what is a granny flat agreement? It usually involves an older person/s paying something or transferring an asset to someone in exchange for a right to live in a home for life. That home must be used as the person's principal place of residence.

They come in various shapes and sizes and here are some examples:
- Parents sell their home and pay for a granny flat to be built in the daughter's backyard.
- A parent sells their home and pays their child for the right to simply move in to a child's home.

- A parent transfers the title to their home to her son while retaining the right to live there.
- A parent sells their home and uses the proceeds towards a new home for their daughter.

All in exchange for a right to live there for life.

Any of these arrangements must satisfy certain criteria to qualify as a granny flat, namely:

- A person pays for a life interest or right to accommodation for life.
- That life interest or right to accommodation must be in a private residence that is to the person's principal home.
- The parties to the arrangement do not reasonably contemplate that it will come to an end within five years.

The amount of the payment is generally not relevant except if it exceeds what is known as the 'reasonableness test'. In a nutshell and as an example, if a person transfers not only their home to someone else but additional assets, the test will be applied and it may be that the additional amount is not covered by the exemption and will be assessed as a gift.

Regrettably, another arm of government has cast a small uncertainty over them, in terms of potential CGT consequences for the adult child involved. There is some suggestion by the ATO that certain types of granny flat agreements may activate some CGT obligations on a child involving, as some agreements do, the grant of a right to reside in the child's home which may be perceived as the creation of taxable right even though it relates to the child's principal place of residence.

Fortunately, the government has discovered this double message imbroglio and has referred the tax issue to the Board of Taxation for review and recommendations. As a result of the Board of Taxations review and recommendations, it is pleasing to note that, in its 2020/2021 Budget, the Commonwealth Government announced legislation would be introduced with effect from 1 July 2021 providing that a homeowner would no longer have to pay CGT for the creation, variation or termination of a formal written granny flat agreement providing accommodation of older Australians or people with disabilities.

The granny flat rules consist of a number of elements which all need to be satisfied before an agreement will be accepted as compliant and not result in any change to the parent's pension entitlements. Again, you are well advised to seek financial advice on the agreement, before it is signed. I also have the agreements I draft vetted by Centrelink before they are signed just to be sure, to be sure.

OTHER AGEING LIFESTYLES

How your parents will live and with whom in later life is not a static subject. It is not a snapshot in time but a moving picture full of technicolour and surround sound.

It is also the fodder for innovation in relationships, entrepreneurs in the built environment and property developers with 'vision'. It is also a challenge to that later life sloth – the law.

The conventional choices for how we live and how we can do so more happily in later life, are being challenged and disrupted like never before. Some of these are subtle.

For example, the days of the retirement village with detached or semi-detached units on a flat broadacre site on the edge of town are limited. Instead, we are now witnessing high rise retirement villages in cities – inner city retirement. It puts the 'upsizing' in 'downsizing'. Not only that, but the days of the traditional ageing pathway from home to village to aged care is becoming truncated.

Retirement villages are becoming de-facto aged are facilities. Having moved in as independent retirees, as the ravages of ageing impact, there is no need to move, just have home care delivered to your unit. Even better, have one of your children move into the unit with you (legal care is needed on this one).

Other developments are more out there.

Tiny Houses

I often get quizzical at the efforts of people to be noticed.

I have often wondered why rich moguls, popstars or movie stars feel the need to live in a 20-room mansion, most of which is just a mausoleum. It is a way of being noticed I suppose, or even just attracting attention in social media or basking in the vicarious awe and envy of starry-eyed travellers on tourist buses. Ego is not a dirty word, let alone the message, 'Look at me'.

If ageing is downsizing, then being noticed is not normally part of the process. Not that I am suggesting that we become anonymous or deny ourselves a healthy ageing ego, rather, we tend to take up living options that are more realistic and not necessarily meant to impress.

So it is, we have seen a surge of interest in the 'tiny house', a fully self-contained home. While they can vary in size, they are, as the name suggests, very small. The living area contains all the usual accoutrements for our needs albeit, in a very efficient space. One particular advantage is that many of them come on wheels. Just like a caravan or Winnebago, they can be transported from one place to another.

They create an interesting extension to the concept of family caring. Now, mum or dad can wheel their home onto the daughter's property and take up occupation knowing that daughter and family are close on hand to help when needed. When, as can often happen however, mum or dad outlive their welcome, they can simply up stumps and wheel it to the son's property up the road.

They have a lot going for them but, beware, many local councils are yet to get up to speed on this unconventional lifestyle and you may confront the typical regulatory obstacles that innovation often provokes.

Naturally Occurring Retirement Communities – NORC's

NORC is an acronym, 'Naturally Occurring Retirement Communities'. They are based on the concept of older people servicing older people – a mutual care and support arrangement.

The best example of this is a community in Beacon Hill, a suburb of Boston, USA. The idea germinated in a community where older people had long lived and who had no desire to uproot themselves in the face of the forces of ageing i.e., to move.

Neighbourhood meetings resulted in the creation of a collective or confederation of older people in the community dedicated to helping each stay in their own home as long as possible. It had a number of practical advantages. Their combined purchasing power resulted in discounts on services that may need to be brought in for members of the group. It also saved on labour costs. All the members were also volunteers mutually helping out each other in providing for their essential needs. Call it a latter-day Kibbutz, if you like.

But perhaps the most shining advantage is that it serves an essential need of many older people – socialisation, the antidote to the ravages of loneliness and isolation.

I am not aware of any similar formal type community in this country, although there are, no doubt, many examples out there of locals and local organisations helping locals that goes unheralded.

Friends with Care Benefits

As reported recently by TimeInc, Gloria Gaynor, famous for her 70's hit song, *I Will Survive*, at the age of 70, is doing just that. From being single and living alone for many years, when a friend fell on hard times following a divorce, Gloria offered for her to move in with her, which the friend duly did.

Gloria is quoted as saying it is wonderful to have the companionship and camaraderie as well as the security of having someone there if something happens to you.

Sharing a home with others might sound like a throwback to our younger student days when we each had separate vegemite and other precious items in the communal fridge, but now, life is coming a full circle for some. It is not for everyone, but it does make a lot of practical sense and again, is a useful means of sparring with that loneliness epidemic. Not only that, it may appeal to older people who cannot afford to live alone and have an aversion to family or institutions.

If your parents are interested in exploring this opportunity look at 'Speed Room Mating', a Home Sharing Program run by the New York Foundation for senior citizens.

Share Housing

In what can only be described as laying the foundations for the future, even baby boomers themselves are investing in a lifestyle in perpetuity, also known as Co-Housing.

What does that mean? It normally arises from a group of friends or acquaintances in retirement who have chatted and conversed about how they want to live in later life, now that it is getting closer. They hatch a cunning, collective plot the essence of which is that they will buy land and on it construct a home where they all can live and support each other. It will be designed so that the respective couples will have their own separate self-contained living space but there will be a communal kitchen. To address the legal and financial issues they agree as follows:

- They will form a company.
- Each member will be issued with an equal number of shares and will be a director of the company.
- The price for those shares will be an equal proportion of the overall cost of buying and constructing the home.
- With that money, the company will purchase the land and construct the home.

- Each couple agrees to contribute equally to the ongoing costs of living in the home.
- Should they have to leave, a couple's share will only be paid out to them or the last of them to die, if another outside couple is prepared to 'buy in' and purchase the then value of the shares.

It is happening even though I know it is 'out there', as they say, and would only appeal to the well-heeled, sociable retiree with a fairly large and lazy amount of cash, to afford the idea. From a lawyer's perspective it has quite a few hairs on it. No doubt, as well, the couples' children may not be too pleased with it from an inheritance point of view. However, it again makes sense in that people are contemplating and activating the future for themselves rather than reacting.

Tiny Aged Care

Also known as Aged Care Pods, this is another attempt to address the de-institutionalisation of aged care.

Essentially, they are small, detached buildings in suburban areas. Each building is a miniature, self-contained aged care facility. Around a communal dining and kitchen area are located up to 10 separate rooms where the residents can retreat.

Its aim is to take away the feeling of being a small cog in a large care machine and improve the time available for care staff and thereby, the quality of care provided to each resident. Each pod has a nurse on station and various support staff for around the clock care and support.

While this type of aged care is highly personalised and attentive, it comes at a cost. But, as one sage once said to me, 'At 86, what do I need to save for?'

Hotel de Park

Believe it or not, I once had an elderly client who was a millionaire but lived nowhere in particular. He was a 'bagman', the male equivalent of a 'bag-lady', many of whom he counted as friends. He was careful with his money and carefree with his lifestyle. Personal hygiene was over-hyped and only for 'toffees'. Cars were a poor substitute for feet. For him, parking in the city was never a problem. He just ambled from one park to the next. In one, he was known as the Mayor of the Park.

He was always on holidays. He could have been easily diagnosed with a mental illness but from his eyes, he lived the way he wanted. For all intents and purposes, he was happy living an uncomplicated life, albeit a well-worn and unconventional one. To my eyes he was just different, idiosyncratic and slightly eccentric. He was a middle finger parent to his four children.

When children see their parents this way, however, they don't usually ascribe their choice of lifestyle generously, or with any respect to the right to live the way the parent wants. Instead, it is clothed in mental illness, where he has simply lost the plot, gone haywire and balmy. He needs protection.

So it was he became my client in an attempt to resist a legal process begun by his children seeking to have two of them appointed as his Administrator and Guardian, i.e., to make decisions for him, as, on their argument, he was incapable of doing so.

It was a long, painful, and, much to his chagrin, costly process to 'prove his innocence' as he called it. But he was found 'not guilty' of having lost his capacity to make his own decisions. No one was appointed as the Tribunal determined he was quite capable of making his own decisions, even though they were lifestyle decisions others vehemently disagreed with.

Squalor and Hoarding

In America, there is an organisation devoted to upholding 'squalor rights' or, as their tag line pronounces, to 'defend the right to live in squalor'. A closely aligned set of rights are promulgated for hoarders and their right to hoard.

To most eyes of course, living in an environment, and/or personally, which does not abide by our traditional notions of cleanliness and neatness is abhorrent. Indeed, if it adversely impacts on others e.g., neighbours, it is unacceptable, if not, a health risk for the person concerned and their neighbours.

But what if it does not pose such a risk or, even if it just exposes the person to personal health risks and does not impinge on other citizens?

Families, of course, are often shocked and horrified by how their parent may have gone over to his 'dark side'. It is offensive, if not humiliating, and something has to be done about it. This often leads to legal proceedings similar to the Park man above. It is always a difficult decision for any adjudicating body to determine whether this lifestyle does indicate a mental illness which may impact on a person's decision-making capacity. Do they need intervention in the form of an appointed decision maker?

Again, it is not black and white and there may well be a place for squalor rights for parents and frustration for children.

Private Care

'A riddle wrapped in a mystery inside an enigma' so said Winston Churchill when ruminating about Russia's intentions at the start of World War 2. In today's context, he could just as easily have been describing our aged care system.

Being both a lawyer and a decision maker for a number of older people receiving care as I am, I can speak from professional and personal experience about the voyage through the murky and muddy world of caring.

The sheer volume and opaqueness of the regulation and the costs of aged care have sent me off on paths and tributaries that are just exhausting and a management challenge to say the least. I often feel like those early historical explorers embarking on their voyage of discovery across this wide brown land.

Just recently, for example, I stumbled on the Continence Aids Payment Scheme – a little known government subsidy payable (with conditions of course) to people suffering incontinence to assist in the purchase of incontinence aids. Needless to say it requires the completion of another set of forms and bureaucratic inquisitions.

I have been daunted by a ceaseless pursuit to understand the aged care systems (and there is more than one) and all that they have to offer, not to mention the strings and stings that come with the offers. With all due respect to the My Aged Care website, I have discovered reams of words and a raft of regulation that could keep me occupied for endless hours of eye glazing research, only to determine, tentatively in many cases, that my client is not eligible (until of course they change the rules again).

It got me thinking about the cost/benefit of all the effort and frustration to find the right pigeon hole for each client and whether, ultimately, it was worth it. With one of my clients, for example, some 50% of the government subsidy for her home care package is taken by the home care provider, not to pay for the cost of care but in what is describes as their 'administration fee'.

So, it was I turned to that underworld of care – private care or as cynics would describe it, backyard care. Put simply, it is care provided essentially by an unregulated and unsubsidised segment of the care community. Most of the members of this group are people we are very familiar with – informal, unpaid carers – family members, friends and neighbours providing care to people at home. There are apparently over 2,000,000 of them.

But there is another developing subset of this group – the private paid carer or, as they are sometimes called, 'support worker'. Best described as outriders in the care industry they are individuals who advertise themselves as just that, individuals, able and available to provide care for a fee outside the regulated environment of the traditional subsidised home care system.

By way of example, a support worker's internet site states that she is '...only happy if you are happy' and 'I believe I can give you a better care so you can stay in your own home as long as possible.' She states that she has a current police check in place, can work seven days a week between 9.30am and 9.30pm, has a TAFE Certificate 3 in Individual Support, intermediate cooking skills and a First Aid Certificate. Her charges are $20 per hour.

Cost Comparison

I then compared her cost with that of a home care provider. If she was to provide 24 hour 7 days a week care, it would cost $3,360 per week. If a home care provider did so, they could charge some $7,200 per week, not taking into account any government subsidies under a home care package. Even if we took into account any subsidy payable towards the home care providers cost, it would still well exceed that of the support worker.

Question – is the significant saving in money of the private support worker value for money when compared with that of the home care provider?

In pure monetary terms, the answer is obvious. Even on the measurement of what I call 'form phobia', the simplicity of the support worker compared to the bureaucracy of the home care provider is attractive. But what if we applied other criteria to the comparison? What are the risks associated with the support worker that may not apply to the home care provider and are those risks worth the savings?

Risk Comparison

With a home care provider at least, you have the protection of a government regulated and cost regulated system not to mention the onerous requirements placed on home care providers in terms of the quality of care they are obliged to provide.

With a private carer however, there are some 'issues':
- They are essentially unregulated and not subject to a quality of care regime.
- If you engage them are you employing them, or are they independent contractors.

    * This is a pregnant issue as it gives rise to questions such as, if they are your employee will you

have to ensure you meet your obligations under tax law, superannuation law, workplace health and safety law and what are your insurance obligations to cover them?
- What if they get sick?
- What sort of insurance will they need to cover the services they provide?
- Should you document your arrangement with them?

Here's a simple example of the issues. Recently, a carer/housekeeper working privately for an elderly lady received more than $7,000 in compensation after she broke her tailbone when she slipped and fell while polishing a kitchen floor in the home of an elderly lady. She was off work for four months and her WorkCover claim was more than $7,000 including a $5,500 disability settlement.

If you hire domestic help you should realise that you can be sued if a domestic helper is injured while on your premises. There is a danger as well that your current standard householder's insurance policy will not cover you against any claim for injury suffered by your home help.

For any of you who hire help such as cleaners, nannies or home carers, you can take out a Household Workers Policy with WorkCover which costs about $20 for two years.

Fortunately, the homeowner who recently engaged a cleaner aged 60 who fractured her leg when she tripped over the family dog and fell down the stairs had taken out a Household Workers Policy and was protected when the cleaner lodged the inevitable claim.

For $20, it is pretty good peace of mind.

Do you Dare with Private Care?

The world of the private carer is undoubtedly expanding especially as it offers a significant saving in cost and bureaucracy. Adult children will be attracted to it for the savings on their inheritance. It's all very tempting.

However, it comes with both risks and uncertainties that could leave you in a legal minefield if something goes wrong.

As for me, I don't have the privilege of making the decision as if it was my care that was being decided. I have to make the decision for other people and, in that respect, I cannot afford to be a risk taker. I will stick to the system for better or worse and in sickness and in health.

As for you – it's your choice (but, please, before you succumb to temptation, get some advice).

The desire for parents to live at home, the limited subsidised home care available and the cost of alternative care in residential aged care, has resulted in families taking risks.

One of those is advertising for full-time, live in carers for their mum or dad and then engaging the most likely candidate to do so. The 'carers' are often unqualified, with no experience, not subject to any police check and don't even have any first aid training. They may even be using the opportunity to just turn a page in their life to get away from some oppressive personal situation.

But, they're cheap! One I saw recently was prepared to be paid $700 per week (cash in hand) to provide live in, 24 hour, 7 days a week care. They were entitled to free board and food and up to 3 hours off on Friday between 4 and 7pm and between 2 and 5pm on Saturday.

This is riven with risk on many levels. With no qualifications, background or referee checks, dubious motivations, and derisory remuneration, it is hard to contemplate how this could not end badly. Legally, it was a simmering nightmare of issues:
- Was she an employee of the parent?
- Was she an independent contractor?
- What about tax obligations?
- What about workers compensation or insurance?
- What if she did the wrong thing?

In the case I referred to, disaster was the result. The arrangement was not documented, and the carer ended up physically abusing the older person and then skipped town having been given access to the older person's PIN number for her ATM access.

The family is now mulling in fierce remorse at their penny pinching and giving credence again to the old adage – you get what you pay for.

STORIES

If your Parents Live in a Retirement Village you need to Read this

In our relentless quest to be champion legal myth busters, here's another expose on a little sleeping, ageing myth, ripe for busting.

It relates to an increasing trend in our later lifestyles, namely, older people, usually widowed, arranging for one of their adult children to move in with them. This is, legally speaking, an 'issue' in itself. It is even more of an 'issue' when it involves a retirement village (RV).

At this point, at least in Queensland, it is important to understand some basic law about 'ownership' of a RV unit. The most common form of tenure or ownership for a resident in an RV is via a 99 year lease. When you pay for your new retirement village unit, you usually obtain a leasehold interest not a freehold interest.

Now here's the rub. When two or more people hold a leasehold interest in a RV unit, the law says they hold it as joint tenants not as tenants in common. And, as you may know, if you are a joint tenant of an interest and you die, your interest goes automatically to the survivor and does not depend on what your Will may say.

Here is a recent example that came across my desk of a family blissfully unaware of this law:

- Doris, aged 86, lived alone in a retirement village unit having lost her husband some years ago.
- She had two children, Robert and Bronwyn, both of whom were retired and single.
- Concerned about Doris' increasing frailty, Bronwyn suggested she move in with Doris in her unit to look after her.
- The village operator agreed to the proposal provided Doris and Bronwyn signed up to a new lease

of the unit together. Bronwyn didn't pay anything to Doris for her right to live in the unit with her and to become a co-lessee.
- Doris had made a conventional Will giving everything to Robert and Bronwyn equally.

Doris died recently and it came time to assess what her estate consisted of. The controversy arose in relation to Doris' interest in the retirement village unit. Robert, the son, thought the unit would be sold and he would receive half the proceeds as an equal beneficiary with Bronwyn under his mum's Will. He was in for a rude shock.

As indicated above, the law regarded Doris and Bronwyn as joint tenants and, as a result, on the death of Doris, Bronwyn was entitled to become the sole lessee (owner) of the unit by law. Doris' Will was irrelevant. Consequently, his sister would not only be entitled to remain living in the unit but, when it was sold, Bronwyn would be entitled to the entire net proceeds of sale. Alternatively, if Bronwyn died, the entire net proceeds of sale would form part of her estate.

Robert was not a happy chappy because:
- He was not aware that Bronwyn had become a joint lessee with his mum and thought she had just moved in to look after Doris.
- As things started to unravel and Robert was told that they were both lessees of the unit, he thought, briefly and wrongly, that at least he would get one half of Doris's one-half interest in the unit under her Will.
- It was not what his mum intended to happen (and somewhat bizarrely, probably not what Bronwyn intended either).
- Bronwyn had no intention of selling and moving out and was quite happy to stay in the unit until the forces of nature took her to another place.
- At its last valuation, the net sale proceeds of the unit was worth just over $400,000.

Robert's brief expectation of sharing at least in the proceeds from Doris' one half interest quickly evaporated when confronted by the harsh legal reality.

He wouldn't receive anything in relation to the unit. Bronwyn, on the other hand, couldn't believe her luck.

Sad to say but another 'ho-hum' moment for we lawyers – Doris had failed to obtain legal advice when she so gratefully accepted her daughter's offer of help. Why would she? – after all, it was family business and lawyers are only family disruptors with all their 'what ifs' and 'but did you knows'.

If Doris is looking down from above now, she may rue the legacy of her lethargy. Instead of sharing her wealth with her two children, she has left for them, a legacy of implosion.

I went to an Aged Care Facility and this is what I saw

I had been asked to see a single, elderly man who, following a fall at his home of over 30 years, had been, as they say, 'placed' in the facility, some one week before, by his energetic and attentive enduring attorneys .

At first sight, he looked remarkably well. He had, as he said, 'dressed up' for my visit and had been waiting patiently for me in the reception area. He smiled when he met me. He was 'ambulatory' and engaged. In my first discussion with him, he was clearly distressed about being where he was. His small room with a single bed and shared ensuite was a little piece of Lilliput, a universe away from the lifestyle and freedom of choice he enjoyed his own home.

His enduring attorneys, perhaps well-intentioned, decided that a fall was enough to bubble wrap and hermetically seal him in the protective micro living of the facility. He won't get up to any dangerous mischief there, such as falling, will he?

Suffice to say, after protracted negotiations, the time finally came for his release some three days later. I was there to facilitate his 'discharge' but his enduring attorneys were not. He was on his way home. I have two reflections, in particular, on my experience with him.

The right to take risks in later life is an important part of happiness – experts describe it as the dignity of risk. Sure, he may fall on his return home, but he may just as easily fall in a nursing home. When it comes to where we would all prefer to fall, the answer is almost unanimous.

But the other abiding memory of my experience was the aged care facility. It took us some 20 minutes to leave the facility. It wasn't because of any last-minute hitch or paperwork. He simply needed the time to say goodbye to the staff. The hugs, kisses and affection that flowed between him and the staff was poignant – and it was genuine. He hated being there, but he loved those who were there with him.

For all the care nightmares emanating from the Royal Commission, there are some real and endearing good news stories. Most of them will probably never be told. At least I can tell this one.

CHAPTER 8

MONEY, MONEY, MONEY

Life can be about planning to be rich in life and even to die rich. But, if you are successful in at least the first part, in later life when it comes to aged care, it may well eat away at your success.

This chapter will take up the financial implications and costs associated with the various ageing lifestyle options referred to in the previous chapter.

THE FINANCIAL DEMANDS OF CARE

The essence of the financial implications of your parents ageing and their need for care is encapsulated in a number of relevant, interconnected laws:
- Centrelink
- Aged care
- Tax

- Death.

Each of them has to be considered, individually and collectively, in making informed decisions about what to do and how to pay for it.

In this context, two things trouble me about the vexed area of money and parents' aged care:
- How few adult children or their parents, in the throes of facilitating the aged care process, give any considered thought or credence to the financial consequences or implications of the downsizing, particularly in respect to tax and social security entitlements.

    * Of course, in the proverbial 'C' change mode, silly decisions are made in haste such as selling mum's extensive share portfolio to finance the aged care costs and thereby activating a huge CGT liability for her.
- How few financial advisers, in providing that retirement plan to the newly retired couple, ever consider or advise on the issue of planning for their frailty i.e., aged care. In the vast lexicon of issues

covered in a financial planner's biblical Statement of Advice, (often designed more to appease the regulators than empower the client), I have rarely seen a heading 'Your Aged Care'. Equally, in advising adult children, I have never seen a heading, 'Your Parents' Aged Care'.

The significance of these concerns is best demonstrated by two respective examples on each:

- The only child of an elderly mother (and her Enduring Power of Attorney) came to see me with a letter from Centrelink in her trembling hands. She was a 'Mum Manager'. Up to that point, her mother had been receiving a full age pension and, as you might think, the letter dropped like a bombshell on the daughter's doorstep.

    It noted that it had come to Centrelink's attention that her mother had recently sold her inner-city home for some $2.1million dollars and had purchased an interest in a retirement village for $550,000 (don't think Centrelink doesn't know these things). They further noted, ominously, that this transaction had not been reported to them as was required by the social security rules, namely, to advise on a pensioner's change in financial circumstances. In perfunctory, but pregnant terms, it finally asked for a 'please explain' within 14 days.

Remarkably, the daughter had done no research on why the letter was sent even before she came to see me. I then had to reveal the stark truth, which was, in summary:

While she resided in her inner-city home, the home was an exempt asset under the assets and incomes test for an age pension and, based on her other assets, she qualified for the full age pension.

When she sold the home, however, she converted that exempt asset into a partial exempt asset, the retirement village unit of $550,000 and an assessable asset, being the balance of the sale proceeds of some $1.55million.

As a result, her mother was no longer eligible for any pension as she far exceeded her eligibility under the assets and incomes test. Gone also were all the other benefits that come with receiving an age pension.

It is hard to conceive that this situation could have arisen, but it is not uncommon. The old saying, 'once a pensioner, always a pensioner' can be easily dismissed by later life events and yet we children do not seem to appreciate that.

The rest of the story does not bear recounting given its inevitable outcome. Sadly, it also resulted, as is often the case, in the breakdown of the daughter's relationship with her mother who kept exhorting her daughter with the plea, 'How could this have happened?!'

- In respect to the second alarm bell concerning financial advisers, it is my view that few of them have the necessary experience, let alone expertise, to advise on financial planning for aged care. I suspect this may be the creature of historical poo pooing of older people and their placement at the bottom of the food chain compared to the more remunerative and younger target client. Curiously, however, I have observed of late, an increase in the number of advisers including aged care advice as a discrete part of their service offering. The word is getting around, me thinks.

But as an example of the disaster that can arise from poor financial advice, here is an example from my own practice:

* Bob aged 84 was married to Belinda aged 78.

* For both of them, it was their second marriage and they both had children from their first marriage.

* Bob was relatively well off and they both lived in the home owned by Bob. At the outset of their marriage they had agreed to keep their finances separate but to share equally in the daily cost of living.

* They had each made Wills giving everything to their respective children.

* After nine years of marriage, Belinda's health declined

dramatically. Bob couldn't care for Belinda anymore and she had to move into residential aged care suffering also from dementia.

* For that, the facility wanted payment of a Refundable Accommodation Deposit (RAD) of $300,000. Belinda didn't have that sort of money, but Bob did.

* Bob went to see a financial adviser who reassured Bob that, if he paid the RAD, as it was fully refundable on Belinda's departure from the facility, it would come back to him in due course.

* He duly paid the RAD from his own funds.

* Belinda subsequently died and Bob was expecting the return of the RAD to him.

* Needless to say, he was aghast when he received a letter from the facility shortly after, advising him that, under the law, the RAD had to be refunded to Belinda's estate and not to him.

* That meant it would then go to her children under her Will.

The financial adviser was clearly unaware of this hidden stonefish of a law that has stentorian consequences for the ignorant, particularly in the blended family. Again, almost inevitably, Bob is now involved in litigation against Belinda's estate and his much-maligned stepchildren.

Taking advice is always advisable but getting good advice is even more important.

CENTRELINK

Some basic Centrelink rules need to be considered in any lifestyle transitions for your parents:
- Assets test
- Incomes test
- Gifting test
- Separation test.

Again, each of them has to be considered, both individually and collectively, in assessing the impact on your parents' pension and aged care fees.

Given that some of the tests change over the course of every year, it is not prudent for me to expound in detail on each except to make some general comments in the context of aged care.

Assets and Income Tests

Generally speaking, the need for aged care, be it home care or residential care, will require the expenditure of your parents' money. In some cases, large sums of money, for example in the payment of a refundable accommodation deposit in residential aged care. That may require your parents to deal with some assets, such as selling the family home. Understanding the implications of that is crucial in determining the best options.

As a simple and common example, let's look at the sale of the family home. In most cases, that will release a large amount of equity or money. While they retain the family home, it is exempt from the Centrelink assets test. Once it is sold and converted into money, that money becomes assessable under the assets test and the incomes test, the latter being subject to the deemed interest rate on money. The test that results in the lower pension will be the one applied by Centrelink.

As we will see below, as well, the family home figures prominently in aged care costs and how they are assessed by Centrelink.

Gifting

I have already referred in a previous chapter to the gifting test applied by Centrelink and how it restricts the ability of an older person to impoverish themselves to qualify for a pension or a higher pension.

Separation

The complexity of later life relationships is no better seen than in the Centrelink rules applying to the various forms of separation that a couple may experience and the impact of those rules on the pension.

In response to these developments, Centrelink has created different classes of separation in couples and, for the purposes of assessing eligibility for the age pension and even aged care fees, have come up with different rules that apply depending on the nature of the separation.

But, before analysing those classes, it would be helpful to understand how Centrelink treats a couple for the purpose of assessing their eligibility for an age pension. A couple can be married, in a de-facto relationship or have a registered relationship (same sex couples). In those circumstances, when assessing the couple's age pension entitlements, the assets and income of the couple are combined irrespective of who owns the assets or receives the income.

However, a couple may not be treated as a couple for Centrelink purposes in the following circumstances, namely, where they:
- Live separately and apart
- Live separated by illness
- Live separated under the one roof.

Here's a brief explanation of each and the age pension implications:

Living separately and apart

The essence of this status is that a relationship has ended or ceased to exist. If so, the two people are no longer treated as a couple.

To establish this, they must show that they are living apart permanently or indefinitely, and there has been an estrangement or breakdown of their relationship. It will not apply if they are separated by illness or economic circumstances.

If a couple qualifies under these requirements, they are treated as single and their individual assets and income will not be combined.

Living separated by illness

For a couple to fall into this category, certain criteria must be met, namely:
- They are unable to live together in their home
- The inability to live together:
    * Is due to illness or infirmity of either or both of them
    * Results in their living expenses being or likely to be, greater than otherwise, and
    * Is likely to continue indefinitely.

If a couple satisfies these criteria they will be assessed against the single rate of pension even though Centrelink will combine their income and assets as if they were a couple.

Living separated under the one roof

This is by far the most complicated and personally intrusive class you could fall into. I once had a client who told me at our first meeting that she had just celebrated her 'silver separation'. She had been separated from her husband for 25 years even though they had been living in the same house the whole time.

In a nutshell, a couple's relationship will be assessed against five broad criteria:

- Financial aspects of the relationship e.g., who pays for what if anything
- Nature of the household e.g., sleeping in separate rooms
- Social aspects of the relationship e.g., do they socialise together
- Sexual relationship e.g., the presence or otherwise of intimacy

For those who may fall into any of the above categories, or feel themselves falling into one, it might be a good idea to get some good financial advice about where you stand, just to be sure, to be sure.

AGED CARE

Home Care – The Private System

The drought of subsidised home care packages will create emotional and financial stress. Your family may have to do the heavy lifting and the division of labour may not be fair for all sorts of reasons. Your conservative brothers may not be comfortable with intrusive, intimate caring for mum or dad or, helpfully, have fled the country to be simply and sadly, unavailable, but no doubt very supportive. You may also live nearby to them which makes you a sitting duck.

Financially, consider this – what would the cost of the worst-case scenario of 24 hour, 7 day a week in home care for your parents – about

- Nature of the commitment to each other e.g., do they share information and plans.

If the criteria are satisfied, i.e., they may live together but lead totally different lives, then each member of the couple will not be treated as a couple, but as an individual.

What does it all mean?

Given the fluid nature of later life relationships, the impact of these rules cannot be underestimated or understated.

However, there is one particular area that is becoming difficult if not, vexed. It relates to older people becoming 'companions' or, at least on the surface, something less than de-facto. Even companionship can push the boundaries of relationships. It might do you to check out the definition of a 'de-facto' couple to see if you are, or are becoming, more than companions.

Where these types of relationships develop, it can have interesting implications in many areas—on the age pension, on aged care fees and even on Wills.

$7,000 per week. Have your parents stashed a lazy $350,000 per year to spend on their home care and the privilege of staying at home? PS – there goes the inheritance.

Bear in mind as well that, even if they qualify for the highest level of home care package referred to below, it will only go a very small way to providing intensive care and nowhere near 24 hours 7 days a week. That would leave your parents with having to top up their care costs significantly.

Carers Financial Assistance

While your parents may have to wait interminably for a home care package, you may not have to wait for some financial assistance to care for them at home.

The government provides social security payments to people who care for frail, older people at home. They are known as the carer's payment or, a separate one, a carer's allowance together with a carer's supplement.

A carer's payment gives financial assistance to a carer who is unable to work because of the care they provide at home. A carer's allowance is an income supplement for your parents or you if you are a carer for them to assist with providing extra daily care. A carer's supplement is an annual lump sum payment to further assist in the cost of caring. A person can receive all three.

There are other forms of government assistance as well depending on the frailty of your parent. For example, the Continence Aids Payment Scheme which helps people with permanent and severe incontinence to pay for incontinence products which are very expensive.

Home Care – The Government System

Remember, there are government home care regimes that operate:
- Commonwealth Home Support Programme
- Commonwealth Home Care Packages.

Commonwealth Home Support Programme

The government describes this programme as an 'entry level' programme of support for older people in basic tasks around their home to enable them to live independently and stay at home.

The support services are provided by many organisations and are paid for partly by the older person (if they can afford it) and through government subsidies. The user pays fee varies between providers who are required to advertise their fees on their website.

The services that can be provided include, help around the house, transport, meals, personal care, home modifications and social support.

Home Care Packages

These packages are designed to provide a higher or more intense form of support or care for older people.

The cost of a home care package is part user pays and part government subsidy. The user pay component consists of a basic daily fee (which everyone pays) and an income tested fee which is payable depending on your financial circumstances. The government subsidy amount depends on which level home care package you have been allocated between 1 and 4 level. The lower the level, the lower the care and care cost and the lower the subsidy.

Basic Daily Fee

In a nutshell the current breakdown of who pays what for a home care package based on the level of the package and on a daily basis is as follows:

	User Pays ($ per day)
Level 1	9.63
Level 2	10.19
Level 3	10.48
Level 4	10.75

Income Tested Fee

In respect to the income tested fee, the current rules are:
- You can pay up to $15.43 per day if:
    * You are single and earning over $27,840.80 per year

* You are a member of a couple living together earning over $21,606.00 per year
    * If you are a member of a couple living apart due to illness and earning over $27,320.80 per year.
- You can pay between $15.25 and $30.49 per day if:
    * You are single and earning over $53,731.60 per year
    * You are a member of a couple living together earning over $41,121.60 per year
    * If you are a member of a couple living apart due to illness and earning over $53,211.60 per year.
- There are annual and lifetime limits on the payment of the income tested fee which vary over time.

Bear in mind that these figures will change over time and as well, if your parents require additional services outside those available under the package, they may well have to pay for them separately.

It is important to also understand that each home care package provider will charge different amounts for their services and they won't be limited to the basic daily fee or income tested fee. Their costs must be listed on their website so clearly it is very advisable to check that their site for the actual costs.

RESIDENTIAL AGED CARE

Like a writer sitting down on the first day to write a book and pondering that crucial first sentence – what do I say? It is now some days since I wrote that sentence and I have finally had the courage and conviction to return to it and answer the question.

If, in life, money is the root of all evil, then, in aged care, it's not quite as bad, money is just the root of exasperation. It is a morass of regulation, partial regulation, government funding, user pays, price controls, price caps, cash flow and laws of biblical proportions. Even I struggle with it most notably because it is like making butter – a constant churning of the ingredients. In the interests of brevity, however, I will attempt to keep it simple and direct.

Let's start with some fundamental financials:
- Your financial circumstances might be simple by any other standard, but not in aged care.
- Everybody, no matter how poor, will pay something for their aged care.
- To some extent, the cost is like our progressive taxation system – the more you own or earn, the more you pay.
- There are, however, limits on what everyone (rich or poor) has to pay.
- In aged care, you cannot ignore the 'kissing cousin' role of Centrelink and the effect of aged care transition on pension entitlements.
- The cost of being in aged care will increase during your time in aged care.
- It requires a major assessment of your finances and ability to pay (ongoing).
- Changing your residence from one aged care facility to another can come at an additional cost.

- Beware of planning not far enough ahead and the five year rule on gifting.
- Different rules apply to current residents of a facility who entered before 1 July 2014.
- Beware of couples entering aged care at the same time. There could be a very good case for them not to do so on the same day but rather, on different days e.g., one on a Wednesday and the other, the next day, Thursday.
- It should never, ever be done without good prior legal and financial advice.

Having got those small matters out of the way, what are the basics you need to know? Beware, you are about to enter acronym heaven. You will pay for four essential things in residential age care:
- Accommodation
- Care Services
- Extra services
- Additional services.

Accommodation

Unless you are very poor, you will have to pay a price for the right to live in your single, shared or multi-bed room in an approved aged care facility. This is known as a Refundable Accommodation Deposit (RAD). It used to be called an Accommodation Bond and continues to be for those who entered residential aged care before 1 July 2014 under what are delightfully known as 'grandfather' provisions.

There are rules about the RAD, the major ones of which are:

- A person cannot be required to pay more than the maximum (currently $550,000) unless the operator has received special approval from a government authority to charge more. In that context, the biggest one I have seen was $800,000.
- Being poor, referred to a 'low-means' can help. Below certain asset and income thresholds, a person will not be required to pay anything for their accommodation, or a means tested care fee (see below). At certain higher levels of

assets and income they may only be required to make a contribution to accommodation costs (a DAC – Daily Accommodation Contribution).
- An operator is required to set out on their website, the RAD's they charge which can vary according to the standard of accommodation in each facility.
- The amount of RAD to be paid (up to the maximum) is negotiable and a person must be left with a certain minimum asset value, despite the apparent fixed prices on the operator's website.
- A RAD is an assessable asset for the purposes of assessing aged care fees but it is an exempt asset for pension purposes. As a side comment, the RAD can be an interesting technique used by non-pensioners in order to become pensioners because the RAD is an exempt asset for pension financial tests. So, they can reduce their assessable assets by paying more of a RAD.
- Any RAD paid must be refunded in full to the resident or their estate

if they leave or die unless they owe money to the facility for other reasons – it doesn't matter if someone else has paid for it.
- A RAD can be paid in a number of different ways:
    * An up-front lump sum (RAD)
    * In instalments (also known as a DAP – a daily accommodation payment)
    * A combination of a RAD and a DAP
    * Have a DAP deducted from any part RAD you have paid.

In most cases, deciding on how much to pay, how to pay it (and that perennial issue – what to do with the family home) are complex, multifaceted and difficult financial decisions. You usually only get one chance to get it right.

The Family Home

It is an abiding issue about where the family home sits in the assessment of a person's aged care fees and pension. It is an important consideration. It is, after all, an 'asset' in common parlance but is it treated as such in assessing a person's assets for age care costs? The rules (here it is again, 'currently') are:

Effect on aged care fees

- The home is exempt if a spouse or a 'protected person' still lives there.
    * A protected person is your partner, a dependant child, an eligible carer who has been living with you in the home for the previous 2 years and an eligible close relative who has been living with you in the home for the last 5 years.
- Otherwise it is an assessable asset but is currently capped in value at $168,351.20 (currently).
- If you rent it out, the net rental income is assessable.

  Effect on the pension
- Exempt if a spouse continues to live there, or
- If no spouse is still living there, exempt for 2 years after the person leaves it, and

- After that 2 years, its net market value is an assessable asset and any rental income is assessable.

Care Services

To the cost of accommodation, you now have to add the cost of being cared for in a facility. These care costs are divided into two elements:
- Basic daily care fee
- Means tested care fee.

Everybody pays the basic daily care fee which is set at 85% of the age pension meaning the fee goes up every time the age pension is indexed i.e., goes up.

Only certain people may have to pay the means tested care fee. These people would be generally described as well off in a comparative sense to full age pensioners, such as self-funded retirees.

While you don't have to, most people will lodge a form with Centrelink, called the Form sa457, which then allows Centrelink to assess whether, and to what extent, you will need to pay this additional fee. It uses your income and assets to determine the precise amount you will need to pay.

But there are both annual and lifetime caps or limits to this fee. You cannot pay more than $28,087.41 of this fee in any one year and no more than a total of $67,409.85 over your lifetime. After that, the fee cuts out completely.

Neither of these care fees represents the total cost of your care and that's why the Government pays a subsidy to aged care providers to provide you with the care you need. How that is determined is for another day and doesn't really reflect how much you will have to pay.

PS – This book is not meant to be a research or reform agenda for aged care. However, ask yourself a question that naturally arises from this regime – should a multi-millionaire be limited to just $67,409.85 in an aged care means tested fee?

Extra Services

For parents who want a little bit extra in their life in the facility, it is possible to obtain extra services over and above the care services provided for in the fees above. These extra services usually come in a package deal and include some 'icing on the cake' offerings such as choice of meals, wine with meals and a more 'hotel' type room with special fixtures and fittings and concierge type services. They come at a cost and cannot be offered by a facility unless they are approved to do so.

Additional Services

Some personal services are not covered by the above and are provided on an as required basis. This usually includes such things as hairdressing, physio, outings, prescriptions, aids, doctors, podiatrist, dentist, and bus trips etc. It will all add up.

At the end of the investigation process and the completion of your homework, you should be able to set down on a piece of paper the individual components and total cost to your parent of living in a particular facility. If you can't do that, you haven't done your homework properly and you could be in for a rude shock. But before the shock arrives, you may (should) care to check your calculations with a financial adviser.

ALTERNATIVE WAYS TO PAY FOR AGED CARE

Confronting the prospect of aged care can be very much like 'the chicken and the egg' – which comes first? – the care or the cost?

Do we start with the chicken – the wish – where and how do you want to live? Or, do you start with the egg – the cost – 'how are we going to pay for it?

There is no doubt that we mostly start with the chicken – the pervading desire to stay at home. Staying at home can be financially cheaper and emotionally more desirable. It will still stretch our resources given the rationed government assistance and the increasing care needs (read, cost) that we will need to confront as we stay longer at home.

So how can be prepare for, and afford, the increasing cost of care at home?

Reverse Mortgages

'Investor Sentiment' or 'Consumer Sentiment' are oft used phrases to describe an elusive concept in the marketplace – what are investors or customers thinking? Or, even more unfathomable, what are they feeling? While econometricians assert that sentiment can be measured at any point in time, it remains, mostly, a fickle, unpredictable science. Indeed, since the last federal election, we could add political polling to that field of endeavour.

In the share market, investor sentiment can vary between inscrutable and irrational. It can also be imponderable such as when a company's share price falls in response to record profits. In the ageing market, however, consumer sentiment has been rock solid for years – Leave me alone to stay at home!

Building on this thinking and responding to these sentiments, what we can broadly describe as 'private equity funders' have identified increased longevity and the need for, and costs of, aged care – meet your friend – locked up equity in the family home.

They seemed to be a complementary set of factors leading, some years ago, to the development of the reverse mortgage product, even from some well-known financial institutions.

Private financiers, and even the government, have identified this cultural addiction to preserve the family home both for the older person and their successors. For financiers it is a business opportunity. For the government it can save on consolidated revenue in reducing the public cost of funding residential aged care.

The attraction for financiers lies in the huge value of the equity held by most older Australians in their own home. The Australian Securities and Investments Commission (ASIC) has estimated that more than $500billion of equity held in a consumer's home is held by people over 65 and 70% of them own their home outright. Offsetting that apparent, asset resilience however, is the gnawing statistic that only 62% of couples are able to have a comfortable retirement income. In other words, they represent the classic conundrum – asset rich but cash poor.

In focusing on our imperative to stay at home, a home, writ large with comfort, familiarity and history but which sits frozen in time engorged with value, financiers have offered a product designed to both provide financial assistance to older people for their needs on the security of their own home but with some special features. These loans and securities are known collectively as reverse mortgages. They are also known variously by other names such as a 'Lifetime Loan', 'Seniors Home Equity Release Loan', an 'Aged Care Loan' or a recent creation, the 'Household Loan'. Another significant attraction is that the home is also an exempt asset for age pension entitlement and these products allow us to retain that exempt asset albeit with a rising debt over it.

So, what are they? Most of us are familiar with the concept of a mortgage – a security we give over our home to a lender to ensure we meet our loan repayment obligations from time to time. If we do not, the lender can sell our home to obtain repayment of the loan. As we make our repayments on the loan, your equity in the home goes up and the debt does down.

The reverse mortgage is different – it works in the opposite way as the adjective suggests. Generally, instead of you making regular repayments of a loan, you don't have to make any repayments during the life of the loan but interest, of course, keeps accruing. The loan only has to be repaid when you die or sell the home. However, because you are not making repayments, the debt goes up and the equity goes down over time.

The finance can come in different types:
- You can borrow a lump sum
- You can draw-down on the total approved loan from the lender instead of taking one lump sum (similar to a line of credit)

- You can take an income stream from the lender
- A combination of all of the above.

These types of products have been used for all sorts of age care purposes including to assist in paying a RAD, for home care costs, to do renovations to the home to suit your particular ageing needs or just in living costs.

The average loan is $147,000 through brokers and $104,000 direct through lenders and average $123,000 and most loans are line of credit.

Other Financing Options

Selling a 'bit' of your home

Even managed investment schemes are getting in on the aged care scene. A recent fund was established which effectively turns the value or equity in a person's home into shares, just like shares in a company.

The fund then markets those shares to investors who can buy them and end up owning 'a bit' of the home. As one report I read about it described it, a person can 'sell the back bedroom'.

The seller, or the person who owns the home, can nominate whether they want a lump sum for the bit or a monthly payment. It comes with other detailed terms and, in the end, it is another option that may not suit everyone.

The Pension Loans Scheme

The federal government has operated this scheme for some 30 years and still does. Before recent changes, a pensioner could borrow an amount capped at the maximum age pension rate. Those on a full age pension, therefore, did not qualify for the scheme. The loan obtained can only be drawn down as an income stream and not as a lump sum. The amount was secured by a reverse mortgage over the pensioner's home.

From 1 July 2019, the scheme was expanded. Now, all age pensioners will be eligible to access the scheme to increase their income to up to 150% of the full age pension. At current rates, this means that a single age pensioner could up their income by $11,799 per year and a couple by $17,787 per year.

It can still only be taken as an income stream and not as a lump sum which differs from the private reverse mortgage market where you can drawdown a lump sum.

In addition, the assets and incomes tests will no longer apply to exclude pensioners who would otherwise be eligible for the scheme.

The increased ambit of the scheme has a number of attractions:
- Single people who have no income except the age pension can access another source of income
- It can boost savings which are depleting over time to meet ageing needs
- It could be used to pay for more home care as it becomes necessary.

Having already dealt with the first two options above in an earlier part, let's consider the other two.

Family Financing

We are familiar with the 'Bank of Mum and Dad', where parents have provided financial assistance to their children. This section is about a collateral family lender, the 'bank of son and daughter'.

I will always take with me to my own aged care, the son who brought his parents to see me one day who were in a parental pickle. The son was also quite angry. Unbeknown to him, his parents had taken out a secret reverse mortgage to meet their ongoing living costs. Not that unusual except the son, when he found out, was apoplectic.

He bemoaned that he could have given his parents the money they needed, and they didn't need to have gone through the expensive process and consequence of borrowing from a reverse mortgage provider.

One can always question the motives of a son in this situation but, financially, his concern was understandable. Going into debt late in life is anathema to many of us. We are deluged with the rhetorical question – Do you have enough to live on in retirement? Clearly, if the answer is no, taking on debt in later life is potentially a life change for the worse.

Inheritance expectations can often be a subliminal concern for children in these circumstances but being financed by your children can often be the cheapest form of finance, financially speaking. Trouble is it can lead to trouble and I don't just mean the ability to pay it back.

Apart from so-called 'low doc' loans, most arrangements with a financier are properly assessed and documented, ignoring, for the moment, the revelations in the banking Royal Commission. When it comes to families however, the arrangement is usually a 'no doc' one where there is no written record, let alone agreement, let alone a written agreement, of what the arrangement was when a son or daughter 'advances' money to their parents.

Needless to say, this creates a diverse sea of tensions:
- If a parent has died, who can verify what the arrangement was?
- What if the money from the child came from joint funds of the child and their spouse – where does that

leave the spouse in the event of a family law dispute?
- What were some essential details such as when is it to be repaid, is there interest payable, was any security given?
- Will the other children simply accept the unilateral evidence of the child who advanced the money and accept it comes out of the parent's estate first before anyone else gets their share of the estate?

And so, it goes on.

In other parts of this book I have quietly railed against our aversion to documenting family arrangements and the implosion that can cause. Perhaps for the sake of relentless repetition, I should leave it there.

TAX

I am not a tax adviser, but I am a tax identifier. That means I am familiar with potential tax issues arising out of aged care. Some of these are:
- Selling the family home to fund aged care converts a Capital Gains Tax (CGT) exempt asset into

money. If that money sits in a bank account earning interest, that interest is taxable as income.
- Selling other assets, such as shares, to fund aged care can also give rise to a CGT obligation.
- Loans made to children which provide for payment of interest will result in that interest being taxable income.
- Gifting tax assessable assets to a child may also give rise to a CGT obligation even though there is no gift duty in this country and that's why CGT is sometimes described as a hidden gift duty.

This is but a small piece of tax titillation designed to emphasise, yet again, the importance of understanding the implications of parent's financial dealings and the importance of good prior advice.

DEATH

Your parents' death is a sad event, but it may also reveal some sad financial news directly attributable to their aged care.

In their Wills, some parents give a specific asset to someone, such as their family home. What happens if that home has to be sold when the parent is still alive to fund their aged care. Generally speaking, the law says that, in relation to the Will, that asset is 'adeemed' meaning the beneficiary of the asset in the Will misses out and won't even be entitled to receive any alternative asset or compensation for losing out.

I have already alluded to the implications of someone advancing money to someone to fund the payment of that person's RAD in aged care. To remind you, the law says that RAD, when it is refunded must be refunded to the resident or their estate, not the person who paid it. That leaves that person having to seek to recover their payment from the resident's estate. That can be problematic at best.

These are but just two examples of why we always recommend that a person who enters aged care review, if they can, their Will.

STORIES

In the whirling dervish of ageing, when you overlay our complex lives with longevity, dysfunction, frailty, dependency and money, you have the makings of many sagas, rivalling that of the Forsyth's. Just add my experience to the brew and those sagas take on epic proportions.

Below are a series of such sagas. They are not meant to scare you (although some will). Rather, they serve as illustrative examples of the miasma that can arise in our, and our parents', later lives. Let me assure you – tall tales they are not. They are taken from my own experience.

Parent Poker

Two pairs are usually a winning hand in poker but not when it comes to the game of ageing parents. You may be 'blessed' to have your own parents and your spouse's parents all alive and upright at the same time. When they start moving, indefatigably at first, towards the horizontal it can be, at best, a mixed blessing.

If you removed your personal investment in your parents and were pragmatic about it, a staggering of each parent's descent into frailty would be infinitely preferable but unattainable. As if the sheer number of parents isn't tough enough, add additional factors, namely, their decline will happen at different speeds and times and in different places. This will place significant pressure on finances and most particularly on relationships, both between you and your spouse and between you and your parents and parents-in-law.

Here's how. Bob and Carol were in the early stages of their much-anticipated retirement. Bob was particularly excited about giving up work and as a springboard to their new life journey, had recently read '100 things to do before you die' which fuelled his wanderlust for the world.

Bob's parents were Brendan and Barbara. She was becoming a significant handful for Brendan as her dementia intensified. Carol's parents were Celia and Cedric, and Cedric was having constant falls at his home, and was in and out of hospital.

Bob wanted his mum, Barbara to move into aged care, both for her own well being, and that of his father Brendan. Carol wanted her parents to move in with her and Bob, so she could watch over them.

Bob's parents were not well off, but Bob had been a successful businessman and Carol had been a stay at home mum. Bob suggested to Carol that he drawdown some of his super to pay for his mum's RAD at a local aged care facility and thereby keep his parents' home for Brendan to be able to still live there. Carol was none too pleased about that nor was Bob too pleased about Carol's suggestion for her parents to move in.

The stage is now set for a saga. There was a happy (of sorts) ending but not before much angst and anxiety culminating, after 42 years of marriage, in Bob and Carol having to enter a family law financial agreement between the two of them to account for Bob's contribution of 'matrimonial assets' for his mother's RAD.

Remember, it's all true.

Blended's – What's mine's not yours!

Second marriages, or more usually, relationships are increasing amongst the elderly and so it was for Jenny aged 82 and Jeremy aged 80. They brought to their latter-day union, the usual complicating accoutrements – significant discrepancies in their respective financial resources and lots of adult children.

'Getting on', and with both having 'medical issues', one of Jenny's daughters, Julie, suggested they move out of their home (owned solely by Jenny) and move in with her and her family. For that purpose, Jenny agreed to pay for the construction of a detached granny flat. On completion, both Jenny and Jeremy moved in and life was hunky dory until, suddenly one day, Jenny had a massive stroke and promptly died.

Julie hadn't always seen eye to eye with Jeremy but suppressed her feelings in deference to her devotion to her mother. That cause had now evaporated, but, for a while, Jeremy was left to lament his loss alone in the granny flat.

However, within three months of Jenny's death, Julie 'came out', as it were, and gave a letter to Jeremy requiring him to leave the flat within 14 days.

Oh dear, I said to Jeremy, pity you didn't document the arrangement. Now we have to see what we can do, but I suspect it will be tough and costly.

Remember, it's all true.

Home Care Hopes and Dreams

Sonia, one of three children, was your typical filial, and slightly obsessively devoted daughter of Sarah. She'll never forget the words that blurted out of her mother's mouth at the last family Christmas gathering—'If you ever put me in a nursing home, I'll disinherit the lot of you.' That was no idle or baseless threat. Sarah was a woman of significant financial resources running into quite a few million dollars.

The family said nothing at the time until her words came back to haunt them later that year. After a fall at home, and an initial diagnosis of dementia, the ACAT team had been called and assessed her as needing permanent high care in a residential aged care facility.

Here was another 'oh dear' moment. Not sure whether her mum had gone through with her threat after the Christmas party and changed her Will to disinherit the children if she ended up in a nursing home, the children gathered to discuss the options.

Earnestly wanting to respect her wishes, they first made contact with a local home care provider about the prospect of obtaining 24 hour, 7 day a week care for Sarah at her home to keep her out of that dark place, a nursing home. Sure, was the response, we can do that, and by the way it will cost $7,200 per week – that's per week.

So, there they are, the 3 children sitting in front of me. What should we do, Mr Herd (remembering that one of them was also Sarah's enduring power of attorney). It was clear they were now on the horns of a dilemma. At approximately $350,000 per year for full-time in-home care, Sarah could initially afford it, but for how long? Her life expectancy was unknown.

Without overtly admitting it, on the other side of the family ledger was some simmering self-interest. At the rate of knots her money would be going out the door on home care, Sarah would also be depleting her estate at terminal velocity. As beneficiaries of her estate (or so they believed) that was not good news.

The oh dears just kept piling up on top of each other. Suffice to say that they all agreed eventually to share the load of providing care for Sarah themselves with the assistance of some occasional home care. How sacrificial and philanthropic was that, or was it?

Remember, it's all true.

Children Borrowing

Children will do things outside the lessons of their own life experience or commercial instincts when it comes to providing for their mum or dad. They will even go into debt themselves to do so.

As it was for Jason, a member of that endangered species, a suburban branch manager for a well-known bank and one of four children of Nerida, their elderly mother. Jason was also soon to retire, or more precisely, made redundant.

Unbeknown to the other children, Nerida had bequeathed her home to Jason in her Will in recompense for all that he had done for her during her life over and above the other children. Jason knew that too, but the other siblings did not.

When Nerida was asked to pay a RAD of $350,000 to go into an aged care facility, Jason knew she didn't have that sort of money. Her home was looking vulnerable as it may have to be sold to pay the RAD. Distressed by that prospect, given his inheritance expectations, Jason concluded the only way to protect his interests was for him to provide the RAD for Nerida, which he duly did by borrowing the funds from his soon to be former employer. He drew his own personal cheque to pay for it. Of course, the arrangement was not documented but, as he understood it, as the RAD was refundable, it would be refunded to him because he paid it.

On Nerida's death, some 12 months later, Jason's expectations were soon to turn to woes. His siblings discovered the gift of the home to him in Nerida's Will to which there was a pandemonic response. He then disclosed to the other siblings for the first time, the money he had advanced to the facility for Nerida's RAD. He told them that he was waiting for it to be refunded to him from the facility.

Well what do you know, when the letter from the facility arrives advising that the RAD would be refunded to Nerida's estate and not him (as required by the law), he went paler than a geisha. Suddenly, being the financial guru he believed himself to be, and expecting a refund from the facility, with the money going into his mother's estate, he would now be an unsecured creditor of his own mum's estate.

The other children were apoplectic, in a fighting mood and could smell an opportunity. As Jason hadn't documented the money he advanced for Nerida, they asserted it was a gift and not a loan and he could whistle Dixie for his money. The children also brought a family provision application challenging their mum's Will and, in particular, the gifting on the home to him.

The pantomime goes on and the rest is the proverbial lawyer's picnic.

When too Much Care is too Much Care

This story is hard to believe except, as you now know, it comes from my own experience.

I think I have more than enough experience in my professional involvement in the gyrations of later life, to make general observations about people.

In that vein, and to be honest, there is a particular breed of adult child who falls into the obsessive, compulsive spectrum. Their later lives are relentlessly and singularly devoted to pursuing their warped view about what is best for their declining parent. Their concerns are often fanciful, contrived, bordering on paranoiac or simple mental disturbance brought on by their parents' plight. They are the ultimate Armageddon experience for any aged care provider because, for this child, good is never good enough and even good itself, will always be the subject of complaint.

Bronwyn fitted the mould perfectly. After a thorough and exhausting search, she had placed her severely dementing mother in a soon to be hapless, aged care facility. That was the day the war began. I won't recount the trail of trenchant and trivial complaints she aggressively pursued with the facility about their perceived lack of care, even extending to accusations of trying to kill her mother. Bronwyn was one of two children but, regrettably, her mother had chosen her to be her sole Enduring Power of Attorney. The other daughter went into retreat in the face of Bronwyn's type A personality.

When, in Bronwyn's eyes, the situation had become intolerable, instead of finding an alternative facility that could meet her exacting standards, she did something very odd. She engaged a home care provider to provide carers to come into the facility and sit in her mother's room, 24 hours a day in three shifts. She called it necessary oversight. Remember, this is in an aged care facility which is obliged to provide 24 hour care.

Quite apart from the tension it caused with the facility, the crunch came when Bronwyn's sister found out. What alarmed her most was the fact that, using her Enduring Power of Attorney for her mother, Bronwyn was actually paying for the home care using her mother's money. At some $7,000 per week, that was no miserly sum on top of the aged care fees being paid to the facility.

From there, three legal fronts were opened—one with the home care provider and their access to the facility, the facility itself who, in response to their staff's refusal to allow the situation to continue, were threatening to evict the mother and one with the sister who brought an application to a Tribunal to have her sister sacked as the Enduring Power of Attorney.

But it's ours

I have often referred to the 'mafioso syndrome' within many Australian families of all cultural backgrounds, the 'keep it (the problems) in the family' ethos.

Nowhere is this better demonstrated than how children view their roles when acting as Enduring Powers of Attorney for a parent and the unintended consequences their actions have on their parent's affairs and, their aged care.

Three adult children were sitting in front of me one day. They had received a letter from a Public Trustee's office querying the recent sale of their mother's home. As the discussion progressed, these were the revelations from the children:
- They had recently placed their mother in an aged care facility as she was very frail and suffering

from the advance stage of Alzheimer's.
- She still owned her home which had sat idle and vacant since going into aged care.
- All three of them were her EPOA.
- Believing she had no further use for the home and knowing, in any event, that she had gifted her entire estate to them in her Will, they undertook a bit of pre-emptive estate planning for her.
- They sold her home using their EPOA and then split the total proceeds of about $950,000 equally between the three of them.

No doubt most of you could drive a D9 dozer through their shallow thinking and thoughtless conduct including:
- Their mum was still for this earth, so it wasn't theirs to have.
- They had significantly breached their duties as her EPOA in being involved in what is known as a conflict transaction i.e., preferring their own interests to their mum's.

This latter aspect was the crunch. Without realising or knowing it, by selling her home, they had converted an exempt asset for pension purposes and mostly, for aged care purposes, into an assessable asset, namely the proceeds of sale. They then caused her to breach the gifting rules by giving the money to themselves, meaning that their mum was now, and still is, attributed as having an assessable asset of $950,000 even though she doesn't actually have it and, in fact, never had it. Amongst other things, that is called a planning disaster because mum lost her pension and her aged care fees went up.

There is a poignant epilogue to this story. Mum had lived in the home for over 60 years. It was part of her fabric. It defined her and, importantly, stored her memories. One of her constant requests of her children when they come to visit her is for them to take her to see her home.

SUGGESTIONS

There is but one. Don't let your parents do anything without getting good legal and financial advice.

CHAPTER 9

THE LAW OF FAMILY

This chapter could be viewed either as the 'necessary evil' of this compendium or, from my biased stance, a vital cog in the machinations of getting things right for us and our parents. When you get things right, up front, fewer things can go wrong or as badly wrong, at the other end.

I am not intending to present the legal issues in an arid, technical light. Rather, I have chosen to relate a number of common legal scenarios as an insight, not so much into the law itself, but to the necessity to understand the importance of obtaining legal advice and what happens if you don't. You may think of your parents' affairs as simple, but, trust me, they are often like the Babushka Dolls – peel one layer away to reveal another surprising layer.

LEGAL CRINGE FACTORS

But first, on the subject of the law, we adult children can tend to suffer from a number of cringe factors:
- We often don't see any significant legal implications or needs in our parents' later lives. After all, their worlds are small, and getting smaller. In fact, the only legal thing we may associate with our parents in later life is their after-life – their Wills.
- Their lives are essentially cocooned and controlled and funded by the government, the benevolent regulator, who knows all and will ensure that they don't get ripped off or suffer from pangs of regret about some decision they made.
- We don't need advice because the internet is a treasure trove of information and we'll have no difficulty in joining the dots and applying them to our parents' circumstances.
- We are loath to raise legal things with our parents for fear of being accused of harbouring some hidden

agenda or pursuing blatant self-interest or perish the thought, influencing them to do something.

Here are the words of an article I wrote recently on the recalcitrance of adult children and their parents around later life issues. It was entitled 'I wish I'd known what I was getting myself in for!'

The language of life is becoming so lazy.

In their communication, the young prefer arid acronyms such as 'LOL' (Laugh out loud) or 'YOLO' (You only live once) particularly because they tend to be parent apprehension proof. For mature types like me, valiant attempts to interpret their hieroglyphics can result in embarrassing misunderstandings. When, in trying to be too cool, a professional friend signed off a humorous email to me with 'LOL', I was miffed. 'Lots of Love', I thought, was a bit inappropriate given the previous platonic and professional nature of our relationship. I agonised for some time about how to respond.

We adults are not far behind in mindless and meaningless mantras. Our languid language of choice tends to be the ubiquitous platitude. Think how many times you have heard:

* *At the end of the day*
* *Moving forward/going forward*
* *Sounds like a plan*
* *As night follows day*
* *Taking one day at a time*

I could just scream!

However, as an elder lawyer servicing the needs of our older population and their children, I have noticed that even that august and revered group and their families can fall into the same malady. They tend to speak in catch cries. An increasingly familiar one goes like this, 'I wish we'd known what we were getting ourselves in for!'

I was sitting in my office with my client, Bob, together with his three adult children, when those ominous words fell from his lips. In his early 80's, Bob was engaging in a bit of hand wringing as he recounted the saga. Some 10 years ago, in downsizing mode, he and his wife Beryl entered into a Retirement Village contract which, amongst other things, promised retirement nirvana and, they thought, ease of transition in later life if either of them needed to move into aged care. In fact, the operator of the village also ran an aged care facility just next door to the Village.

Bob's memory of the day and the children, who were also there, is now a bit foggy, but he distinctly remembers the sales lady who signed them up for the unit. He described her as engaging and very persuasive with a come hither look adorned by big hair, fluorescent molars and a smile that could recharge a thousand electric gophers. Even when they were presented with contract documents of biblical proportions, Bob felt so confident in the information that he had been given by 'she who cannot be resisted', he and Beryl simply signed up there and then. His three children also pleaded guilty as, at the time, they were just as anxious as their parents to find another suitable place for them to live.

Now, years later, Bob is in what we call a 'C' change. One of life's big events has arrived and he is in crisis management mode. Beryl has had a stroke and neither he nor home carers can cope with caring for her in the retirement village unit anymore. He needs to find an aged care facility for her, fast. Trouble is, despite what he thought he had signed up for so many years ago, there is no available place in the adjoining aged care facility. Oh and, by the way, the Village manager had reminded him, if you had read your documents 10 years ago, you would know we give no guarantees about a place being available. Bob now had to find a place for Beryl which could be miles away and, to make matters worse, Bob had to give up driving two years ago.

He has also started to realise that, from a financial perspective, life just got twice as expensive. Not only is he having to pay the fees *at the Village but, when he does find an aged care place for Beryl, they will need to meet those aged care costs as well. Bob realises he and Beryl will now have to support two homes, not one.*

In many ways, Bob and Beryl are the personification of a typical Australian malaise. She'll be right! If you're happy with what you hear from someone, move on and enjoy the benefits of their persuasive promises (or suffer the consequences of your naivety). Most of us just don't see the need to seek some good financial and legal advice before taking some formative life step. That would cost us money—why would we want to do that!?

Too many of us focus on the price of doing something as opposed to the cost of doing nothing. Getting good advice beforehand would cost—not getting good advice is free, isn't it? I know which is cheaper, but which is the better value?'

Say no more.

SOME LEGAL LEARNINGS

Here are some basic truths or, to use a modern expression, 'learnings', I have gathered in my many years of legal experience in the ageing sector:

- There is a dirty 'F' word (worse than the one we are used to hearing from those with a limited vocabulary) – 'FREE!' which has its usual consequence in the familiar aphorism – 'You pay nothing – you get nothing'.

Example – The 'Mum and Dad' Will

Perhaps apart from price, the aversion to seeking the assistance of lawyers is that they will just over complicate the person's circumstances or aspirations. Some may even subconsciously think that lawyers have a vested interest in doing so.

And so it is with Wills. Most people just want a simple document that reflects long held and clear aspirations – everything to my spouse and then to the children equally (the Mum and Dad Will). How complicated can that be?

The trouble is not that wants and wishes are complicated, rather it's the complexity arising from the person's circumstances that can complicate the otherwise conventional and unremarkable death desires for your family.

Bob and Beryl saw an ad in a local newspaper – a lawyer offering 'Free Wills'. Bob's mum had died recently and, naturally, one topic of Bob and Beryl's conversation after the funeral was the old shibboleth, 'we better do something about our Wills'. What really caught their attention in the ad, however, was not the second word, but the first one. Ironically, although ultimately, sadly, they jumped at the chance. The lawyer gave them a Free Mum and Dad Will. Job done.

This is what then happened:

* Bob died and everything went to Beryl.

* Beryl then died leaving 4 adult children and an estate worth about $1millon. So, each of the children could have expected to receive about $250,000 each.

* The eldest son, Barry, was an inveterate gambler and in huge hock to casinos and the white shoe brigade on the Gold Coast. His $250,000 went straight to the white shoe brigade.

* The second eldest, Barbara was married to a no-hoper who ran a no-hoper business. Just before Beryl's death, the no-hoper husband came to Barbara and said business was a bit slow and he needed to get a loan from the NAB. He extended a small document to her and asked her to sign it – a personal guarantee. Love knows no limits and Barbara duly signed. Of course, the business went belly up and in walked the NAB to Barbara with its hand out requesting that she hand over that $250,000 from her mother's estate under the personal guarantee.

* Brooke was the third child. Her marriage was on the rocks when Beryl died. Brooke and her estranged spouse were in the throes of reaching a family law property settlement when Beryl suddenly

died. Brooke's $250,000 from her mother's estate then became part of the matrimonial property pool to be shared with her loving but estranged husband.

* The youngest child, Bronte, was a GP with three young children. Like many professional people Bronte lived with tax problems. Suddenly on receiving her $250,000, what did Bronte have? – a worse tax problem.

* So, perhaps like most parents, Bob and Beryl had worked hard all their lives and saved frugally to benefit their children. But what did they actually end up doing with their free Will? – bequeathing the fruits of their labour, not to their children, but to the white shoe brigade, the NAB, loving ex-spouses and the Commissioner of Taxation.

Of course, if they'd come to see me (for a reasonable FEE!), we could have avoided this disaster with some clever legal techniques.

- Retrospective advice is always more expensive than prospective advice (and the news is generally worse)

Example – Giving things away

It was recently reported in the media that an elderly age pensioner (aged 92) had received an inheritance of some $1.2 million from a relative's estate.

Thinking that, at her age, the money could be used for other more beneficial purposes, she donated it to a charity.

Needless to say, the lady did not obtain financial or legal advice beforehand. The consequence might be obvious to many of you but for her, when Centrelink came a knocking, she was devastated to discover the realities of the 'gifting rules' and that she had kissed her pension goodbye. Not only that, she would be hard pressed to get the money back me thinks. These days, charities tend not to be that charitable.

- If you don't put some essential legal documents in place, you're mad. In fact, it's probably too late, because – you're mad!

Example – Not doing an Enduring Power of Attorney

There are many myths that swirl around our lives. One of them is the ubiquitous one about the 'next of kin'. We seem to have this amorphous, almost genetic belief that, when things go wrong for our mental faculties e.g., dementia, those family members who fall into the next of kin category (e.g., spouse or children), can make decisions for us.

Wrong! – when it comes to losing your capacity and financial decisions need to be made for you, it is a myth that the next of kin can make these decisions for you. Unless you have done an EPOA appointing someone to make financial, no one can make those decisions for us.

For the Brown family, this came as rude shock one day. They then discovered they had to go through a legal process before a Tribunal to have someone appointed to make financial decisions for their father. Trouble was to get that decision they had to show their father had lost his capacity to make those decisions. That required him to be what is known as 'compliant' or willing to be assessed by a doctor as to his capacity.

Having no insight, he point blank refused to do so as he had always had a life-long disdain for the medical profession. Now the family had to make another application to the Tribunal for it to direct the father to be medically assessed, to which he again dug his heels in. The sorry saga continued for another eight months before he relented. Can you imagine what effect this had on the family and his financial affairs?

- Doing something means not just doing it, it also means doing it well

Example – Misplaced and misguided affection

One of the delicate diplomatic demands for a parent is how to balance the interests of their children when it comes to appointing a trusted Enduring Power of Attorney.

It involves a fine balance between inclusiveness and

practicality. An elderly widow had five children. She approached a neighbour who was a Justice of the Peace. Not wanting to offend any of her children's sensitivities or be seen to be favouring any of them, she appointed all five of them as her EPOA. Not only that, she appointed them jointly i.e., all five had to agree on any decision.

All she achieved, when the document had to be used, was to exhume and exacerbate sibling tensions leading to a freezing of decision making that was lost in a blizzard of dispute.

Lawyers were warming their hands and filling their pockets in fruitless attempts to defrost the lamentable saga.

- Families that don't get advice on, or document, their financial or legal relationships are doomed to rue the day they didn't

Example – I'll look after you in your old age

I know it is anathema for parents to document their financial relationships with their children but, read on.

An elderly couple of limited means and on age pensions, had three adult children. One of the children ran a small business that was in trouble. He approached his parents on 13 different occasions seeking money from them to prop up his business (and extravagant lifestyle).

On each request he assured them he would look after them in their old age and would pay it back. He repeated this mantra word for word on 13 occasions resulting in the parents advancing in total, some $284,000 to him. It represented most of their life savings.

You guessed it, when one of the parents needed to enter residential aged care and needed the money back, he politely told them it was a gift and he would not be returning the money.

Legal proceedings ensued which gobbled up a lot of the money in legal costs. While the court decided ultimately that the son must pay the money back, by then, he was on his knees financially and went bankrupt. The money was never repaid.

Families can represent the very worst-case legal scenario – the oral arrangement leading to a disagreement about what was agreed. It is just informal. So, families often resort to the use of euphemisms to describe their financial relationships – it is not an 'agreement', but more an 'arrangement'. It suggests some informality or to use a colloquial expression, 'wriggle room'.

The law is not concerned by style, but more by substance. The 'he said, she said, no you didn't, yes I did' dispute is a legal imbroglio that inevitably, and invariably, has an uncertain and costly outcome.

- Keeping things 'in the family'

Example – 'Mum – why don't you move in with us tomorrow?'

The apparent generosity of a child to a parent can come back to bite the parent.

At the age of 74, my client was in a bad way. She had recently completed a property settlement with her former husband and received some $300,000 from the settlement. Sadly, at the same time, she had been diagnosed with the advance stages of Hodgkin's Lymphoma.

Recognising her mother's plight (or perhaps relishing an opportunity), one of her three children, a daughter, suggested to her mum that she move out of her rented bed sitter and move in with her and her family. Not only that, the daughter suggested that the mother place the $300,000 into the daughter's bank account to keep it away from the prying eyes of Centrelink and thereby not affect her pension.

As night follows day, within two months she was standing on the footpath outside her daughter's home with packed bags beside her waiting for an Uber. She had been evicted by her son-in-law.

The sequel is both tragic and pathetic in the true sense of that word. When the mum consulted me and I promptly asked the daughter for the money back, the response was entirely predictable – it was a gift! Of course, it represented mum's entire assets.

Shortly after, she died. Now the other two children are litigating to retrieve the money for their mum's estate.

I'm often called 'Brian the Badger' because I have a tendency to harp on about or badger people about the silliness and sadness of not documenting things with their children. Here is another example to ensconce the nickname.

- Influencing your parents is a bad thing – isn't it?

Example – Not all influence is undue

Most of us do it – influence our parents (or at least try to). Influence has a good side and a bad side. The law says the latter type can be very bad – it's called undue influence.

A family of five adult children came into my office one day with their ageing mother (two of them had actually travelled from their overseas homes to be at the meeting). Unusually, they were all in agreement about wanting me to convince their mother that her manic aversion to allowing home carers into her home to assist her was at best, unwise and at worst, a death wish.

They thought they could up the ante with her from the helpful cajoling strategy they had unsuccessfully employed and get a lawyer to be the grim reaper threatening hell, pestilence and damnation if she didn't succumb to their urgings.

Happy to say it worked. Perhaps you may see some irony here. Influencing children turning in desperation to the influencing lawyer. Was I guilty of undue influence?

The law describes 'undue influence' as a person taking advantage of a position of power over another person and then influencing that person to do something to benefit the influencer and which is not a reflection of the victim's own free will. There is undoubtedly a cohort of children who engage in this practice particularly with older, frail and dependent parents. The law comes down hard on such conduct and rightfully so.

But not all influence is undue. Let's call it getting involved (see below). It can be well intentioned and beneficial for a parent. Parents themselves can be the ultimate disruptors in our lives and influencing them to do what is reasonable for their own welfare (and for others) is entirely acceptable and very often, crucial.

The problem is that suspicion can arise where children do not share the same view of a parent's welfare and one of them seeks to go behind the others' backs.

Keeping other children in the loop is a great place to start in avoiding the heinous allegation of undue influence.

Avoid the 'FOGI' badge – the 'fear of getting involved' where you don't want to be seen to be disrupting your parents quiet and comfortable demise lest you be accused of selfishness at best or self-interest at worst.

- Well whadya know!

Example – Things you wouldn't believe

If you have been appointed as your parent's EPOA, you'd be surprised at some of the things you can do in that role.

As an example, EPOA's have done the following things for a parent who has lost capacity and, as it turns out, quite lawfully:

* Applied for and obtained a divorce for their parent

* Agreed to a family law property settlement on behalf of their parent

* Changed the nominee of a death benefit nomination of a parent in their superannuation fund

* Withdrawn all the funds in their parent's superannuation fund before the parent has actually died

* Taken over a family trust when a parent has lost capacity

* Assumed control of a family company when the parent has lost capacity.

Some things EPOA's are called upon to do are very difficult. The best example I have come across is where a child, who was also the EPOA for a parent, had been given the parent's home in the parent's Will. However, the parent was required to move into residential aged care when they were alive and for that purpose, the home had to be sold to pay for the aged care. In doing so, of course, he had to sell his inheritance.

While the law has ways to address this after the parent dies, it gives you some indication of the breadth of complexities that an EPOA may have to confront and

where they may have to act against their own interests.
- What you don't know won't hurt you (or anybody else)

Example – Disabled children

Many parents are naturally concerned to treat their children equally and in an even-handed way. This is not to be criticised except where equality leads to egregious results.

In the pursuit of this egalitarian legacy, a parent gave their entire estate equally amongst their five children. In an estate worth about $5million the children should have been pleased with that result. Most of them were, except for one or, at least, their decision maker.

That child was severely disabled and receiving a disability pension which, as you may know, in determining their initial and ongoing eligibility, is subject to the Centrelink assets and incomes test.

You guessed it—on receiving their $1million share of their mother's estate, that child immediately lost their disability pension and all the accoutrement benefits that come with it.

Of course, had the parent sought that recurring theme of this publication – legal and financial advice, they almost certainly would have done a Will in a different way which may well have preserved the disability pension for that child. I am thinking of what is known as a Special Disability Trust. But no, no thought was given to the old cause and effect syndrome.

A failure of parental thought (or advice) in this area of disabled children is equally applicable when parents come to do their EPOA documents. If they have been providing for and/or caring for a disabled child, what will happen to that child if that parent loses their capacity? This question can be answered with intelligent and discrete clauses in the EPOA document and may well make that unfortunate event to be more seamless for the disabled child than it would otherwise be.

- Oh dear – is that right?

Example – An EPOA is a job – right?

Having been one myself and having to use it, I can tell you that being someone's EPOA can be a responsible, relentless and stressful job. Another person's life and welfare, if not happiness, is in your hands and you are being watched.

It is easy for children who are appointed as a parent's EPOA to see the appointment not only as recognition of their talents but also as their parent, effectively, employing them to do the job. As such, they may feel entitled to a fair days pay. This belief is only exacerbated by the lack of assistance or support from the other siblings.

Wrong. Apart perhaps for professionals or organisations who perform the job, an EPOA is not entitled to be paid to do it. They are entitled to be reimbursed for any of their own money they spend for the benefit of a parent but not to make taxable income from their efforts.

- Should you tell on your parents?

Example – Being a 'snitch'

'Snitching' has traditionally been frowned upon in Australian culture (at least amongst criminals). It just ain't the right thing to do – it is a matter of honour amongst thieves.

However, in the wider world, government imposes obligations on citizens to self-snitch – to disclose changes in their circumstances to ensure that they continue to receive (or not receive) what they are entitled to. I am particularly thinking about Centrelink and social security entitlements. There is a general legal obligation on a social security recipient, such as an age pensioner, to advise Centrelink of any change in their financial circumstances within 14 days of that change occurring. Potentially, if you don't report when you should, you can be prosecuted for failing to do so.

But, what if the recipient, such as your parent, has lost capacity and is not able to notify? It would then potentially fall on their EPOA to do so. But, will they or, indeed, do they have to?

I recently had a case involving a 93-year-old, full age pensioner who, unexpectedly one day, received an inheritance of just over $500,000 from a long lost relative. She had also lost her capacity and was a resident of a nursing home. Her daughter was her EPOA and, prudently, she came to seek my advice about it.

I am always a supporter of lawyers giving simple, black and white answers to a client's question such a – yes or no. But as you may know, we prefer the murky grey world of 'it depends'.

This is how I answered her question, 'should I report this to Centrelink?':

* Your mother has an obligation to do so.
* In her condition, she is unable to do so and as such would not be prosecuted for failing to do so.
* As her EPOA, you need to consider whether, in that role, you

have taken on the obligation your mother otherwise had.

* In my view, the law is at best unclear. Having analysed the relevant law, it seems to me that it does not specifically impose an obligation on someone such as an EPOA to report to Centrelink.

* But, you may take the moral high ground and report it, if you wish, all the while understanding the adverse impact that could have on your mother's pension and aged care fees. That is not to mention, of course, the apoplectic reaction from the other less moral children who would only see the wrong in the affect on her pension and loss of their inheritance. They would not see any redeeming right in doing the right thing for the Australian taxpayer.

I do not wish to give away her decision except to say she regularly came back to see me after her siblings did go feral and sought to have her removed as the mother's EPOA.

- Failing to connect the dots in your parents' affairs

Example – Not superannuation again

If ever there was a reason to get involved in your parents' affairs it's this case involving the ignorance surrounding the interplay between the role of an Executor of a Will and the Trustee of a self-managed superannuation fund (SMSF).

Dad had two children, a son and daughter. Not surprisingly, his Will left everything to them in equal shares. Part of his wealth consisted of $1million in his Self-Managed Superannuation Fund (SMSF). He and his deceased wife had been the trustees of the SMSF but, when his wife died, he appointed one of his children, his daughter as a co-trustee with him.

Consistent with his Will, the dad had made a non-binding death benefit nomination providing that his death benefit in the SMSF, the $1million, was to be paid to his two children equally. He died and his co-trustee, his daughter then appointed her husband as a trustee.

Shortly thereafter, the daughter and son-in-law, as the trustees, and ignoring the father's nomination as they were entitled to, decided to pay the death benefit in full to the daughter, herself.

The son was suitably outraged and challenged the decision. He failed. Because the nomination was not binding, the trustees of the fund had a discretion who they should pay the benefit to. In those circumstances, there was nothing to prevent them from paying it to the daughter and not complying with her father's wishes.

Our lives are interwoven in many ways and nowhere is this better demonstrated than in this case where Dad did not understand the law let alone the intrinsic connection between his Will and SMSF. The children don't talk to each other anymore (they did before Dad died).

- The trouble with things

Example – Not the jewellery and war medals

It is perhaps not surprising and entirely predictable that sentimental things can play a large, if not a major role in the estate of a parent. They tend to be those familiar personal items — the high end, low end jewellery and the much-cherished war medals.

By their very nature, they are fraught. Pieces of jewellery tend to be of different financial value from next to nothing to thousands of dollars. Often, however, it is not their market value but their sentimental attachment where the true 'value' lies. Except perhaps for a Victoria Cross, war medals generally don't have a market value and to boot, a parent may have more than one, some of which may have been handed down from their parents.

But their monetary value (or lack of) pales into insignificance when it comes to their distribution. Who gets what and why?

Parents are the worst enemies when it comes to this crucial issue. Often times, they may have 'promised' a certain piece of jewellery to some child or the medals to another. While the so-called promise is almost always impossible to prove (beyond a reasonable doubt), the angst can then be exacerbated by interrupting factors:

A widow died with both various pieces of jewellery and her late husband's war medals. In what can only be described as a feeding frenzy, her children were swarming over her home within a day of her demise. They weren't looking for hidden treasure, only the jewellery and the medals. Low and behold their wise mother had anticipated this rush of blood and had helpfully, or so she thought, placed various items in separate envelopes addressed to various children. She didn't stick the envelopes down, however which then opened the door for skulduggery amongst the children or at least those who arrived first. Other letters then surfaced from her to her various children giving some of the items to different children to those in the envelopes. I smell a lawyer's picnic.

SUGGESTIONS

Here's some basic advice for the cost of this book:

1. Get involved in your parents' legal and financial affairs (do it sensitively and strategically and get your siblings on board).
2. Do some family planning based on the advice above.
3. Make sure they have the basics – a Will, Enduring Power of Attorney and Advance Health Directive.
4. Facilitate them getting these documents done if they haven't done them.

CHAPTER 10

ELDER ABUSE

This chapter exposes some children for what they are, or can become – parent pirates, buccaneers and brigands.

THE LANDSCAPE

In the 19th century and even for most of the 20th century, the social, or what I prefer to call it, the 'family' evil of elder abuse, was unknown, at least in public discourse. It didn't even have the interest of the law. One likely reason for that is that there were probably relatively few elders to abuse or who, at least, were worthwhile abusing financially.

In the new millennium, increased longevity begets dementia which begets dependency and, together with expanding wealth amongst the older cohort, have, in combination, led to a 'coming out' of the issue and ignited the hares of the media, if not the tortoises that are our politicians.

Arise the Enduring Power of Attorney

In some ways, legal developments have also raised the stakes and added fuel to the pyre. To understand the law's role, ask yourself, as I have often asked my friends, what does Qantas, the Commonwealth Bank and electricity supply have in common with incapacity? It may appear an obtuse question but, put simply and to put you out of your misery, they have all been privatised.

Generally, before the 1990's, if a person lost their capacity to make decisions, their welfare was often dealt with within the Dickensian mental health regime. So it was that a benevolent bureaucrat, such as the 'Legal Friend', a 'Committee' or 'the Legal Friend' would assume the decision-making role for that person. It was the state's ultimate safety net regime for an older person. Families did not get a look in. Effectively, an older member of the family became like a ward of the state as orphans once were.

Then in the late 1990's, lawmakers introduced the Enduring Power of Attorney. A document in which a person could appoint anyone as their decision maker if the person lost their capacity to do so. Suddenly, decisions for these people were able to be brought into the family fold as it were and not left in the hands of faceless bureaucrats. It was not only a privatisation, but also a very private arrangement.

There was, and still is, no regime of transparency or accountability on EPOA's requiring them to provide any information or reports on their activities to any authority. Bad conduct relies on the person being sprung or uncovered by someone else who then reports it. Any wrongdoing by EPOA's is only usually picked up if some bystander, good neighbour, concerned citizen or even a family member happened upon it and decided to disclose their concerns to an authority (discussed below). It is a bit like a citizen's arrest and comes with some dangers and limitations.

Privacy has a lot to answer for in enabling the bad EPOA to get away with it. The old mantra that our home is our castle has never had more relevant that under our privacy laws. Our humble castle has now been surrounded by an impassable moat, unscalable ramparts and a drawbridge that only those inside know how to lower. The crucial element of activating concerns about abuse, namely information, is now hidden behind an iron curtain. Many of us would have been confronted by the frustration of trying to find out information about mum or dad from an institution only to be met by the usual denial and reliance on your parents' rights to privacy.

With the rise of 'in-house' (as opposed to 'out-house') decision making, through the EPOA, it doesn't take much to imagine the sort of activity or manipulation that can go on behind the front door of an older person's home, and all apparently legitimised in the form of a legal document. What is more alarming, of course, is that much of it can be even more silent and secretive through the expansion in our digital economy and the ability, for example, to operate our finances on-line behind the anonymity of a computer screen and with no oversight by trusty bank tellers.

Ironically, however, while online banking has, on the one hand, facilitated the miscreant EPOA, on the other hand, with just access to an online password, our ability to make discoveries and obtain information is potentially just a few clicks away. That however raises one obvious imperative – gaining access to your parents' online access information by sharing passwords with you. Of course, it may be totally academic if your parent has totally delegated their financial affairs to an EPOA and can't remember passwords or, indeed, is not capable of remembering them.

THE ABUSE

Without traversing the complex and internecine nature of elder abuse or indeed, why it happens, it is happening more and more. At least, so says my instinct, gut and legal experience. Statistics are hard to come by but, even if they were available, it would not change the reality of its pernicious existence and exponential incidence.

As most abuse occurs inside families by family members, and is mostly in the form of financial abuse, what is the role of adult children if their parents are suffering from such abuse? Of course, if you, dear reader, are an abuser, you might care to look away at this stage. Your secrets are about to be unveiled.

Financial abuse stems from a variety of factors including feigned innocence, ignorance, incompetence, negligence or greed or a combination of some or all of those maladies. Here are some familiar tactics used by EPOA's with their parent's financial affairs:
- Isolating a parent so no one can get access to them or to information about their affairs
- Changing passwords and not telling anyone until another family member is denied access
- Selling assets and pocketing some, or all, of the proceeds
- Changing superannuation death benefit nominations

- Being appointed the Centrelink 'Nominee' as well as being the EPOA
- Failing to pay aged care fees or other parental debts
- Taking out reverse mortgages over assets and pocketing the advance monies
- Misusing granny flat arrangements
- Transferring ownership of property to themselves
- Gifting monies to themselves or paying themselves to be the EPOA
- Paying for their kids' education and other living expenses
- Using or transferring mum or dad's car or letting the kids use it
- Failing to ensure the parent's assets are maintained or insured
- Failing to obtain financial or legal advice about significant financial decisions for their parents
- Using parents' money for a family law property settlement with a former spouse
- 'Borrowing' in order to feed an addiction e.g. gambling or drugs (always with the intention of repaying!)

- Operating a pseudo 'Ponzi scheme' – borrowing to service personal borrowings
- Changing important positions in their parents' legal entities such as a family trust or company so that the EPOA effectively becomes the controller of these entities.

And so, the list could go on from the litany and lexicon of misdeeds that have come to my attention.

Regrettably, many of these virtually quasi-criminal offences are not discovered until after the parent has died. As beneficiaries of the parent's Will, the other children then exclaim shock and horror encapsulated in the familiar, retrospective refrain 'Where has all the money gone?!'

CONSEQUENCES

While being inquisitive or enquiring about your parents' financial affairs can seem to be overly intrusive and perceived as motivated by self-interest, that is certainly not the case in circumstances where a parent has lost capacity and one of the children is the sole EPOA. That is a 'bells and whistle' situation.

One of the alarming aspects of financial abuse is that it is often perpetrated by previously untainted, upstanding citizens e.g., your brother or sister. They may even have respectable well-paying positions or a successful business. The magnet of large sums of money marinating in a bank account to which access can be obtained by a few clicks of a keyboard can mutate even an honourable member of the family.

Let's be frank – why you would want to intervene in a situation like this. Why would you be moved to shake rattle and roll the family cage rather than just let sleeping dogs lie in a doomed attempt to maintain a veneer of family harmony just for the sake of not worrying your parents? Why make war when peace can be maintained by standing back and just wondering?

There are both principled and pragmatic reasons for having an enquiring mind. As a matter of principle, while your parents are alive it is their money, nobody else's. Too many children equate dementia with death and, when dementia strikes, they proceed to manage their parent's affairs as if they were already in heaven.

There are some good, pragmatic reasons why you should have an enquiring mind. Too many times have I seen the unintended consequences of children illicitly dealing with their parents' money. First, gifting money to children (through the auspices of an EPOA) can have calamitous downstream effects. The Centrelink gifting rules come to mind. Second, what is not often known or considered is the effect of these actions on aged care costs. The gifting rules apply equally to pension entitlements as they do to aged care fees which are assessed on similar lines. As a result, there can be the double whammy effect on both the pension and aged care fees. Not only that, it may significantly reduce the financial ability for a parent to pay accommodation costs in aged care.

From your perspective, while it is a subsidiary issue, it could have a very adverse effect on your inheritance. Not only that, it will almost certainly lead to litigation after your parents have died. In particular, at least in Queensland, there is the ability of beneficiaries of a parent's estate to sue a brother or sister who was the EPOA and who defalcated monies which would require that EPOA to pay back the money to the estate. Quite apart from the ugly, costly side of that recourse, it guarantees the implosion of the family – not a legacy your parents would have intended. I should add that often the money is gone so you can 'whistle dixie' as they say.

WHAT CAN YOU DO?

Step 1 – approaching the EPOA to obtain information

This approach is normally met with one of four responses:
- So, you're interested now eh?
- What – you don't trust your own brother/sister?
- Is this the sort of recognition I get for all the work I have to do?
- Sure – what would you like to know?

Of course, this suggestion of direct questioning is easy for me to make and often hard for you to do. Who knows what the reaction might be to the pregnant question – 'Can you let me know what's happening please?' More than likely it will be met with feigned outrage and the usual riposte that attack is the best form of defence.

Be that as it may, the ravages of abuse are inevitably exacerbated by indifference or inaction. You may want to keep it in the family, but it still doesn't justify sitting on the sidelines. Remember, bad things happen when good people do nothing.

Step 2 – taking it to the family

It may well be that other members of the family are also in the dark and at various stages of concern. At this point you may have what I call the 'fear of factions'. By raising it with them, it will crystallise a number of possible outcomes including that some of them are already 'in on it' while others may express similar concern and are happy for you to take the load of taking it further.

Whatever the reaction, this step is crucial to gauge the reactions and hopefully to ensconce your next step.

Step 3 – seek expert legal advice

I know this sounds self-serving, but it is essential.

It is relatively important that you have at least some basis for your concerns before proceeding to Step 4 below. This is particularly so given that you are potentially about to disclose some illicit, if not illegal conduct by a, member of your family. One way or the other, that will have the inevitable implosive effect that will stay with you for the rest of you and your family's life.

Seeking legal advice raises another issue for you. You will not only have to devote time to your enquiries and advice but that will also come with a personal financial cost to you. This can be relieved to some extent if other members of the family are prepared to contribute, at least to the cost of the legwork, if not the legwork itself.

Step 4 – taking it outside the family

It is probably important before this next step is taken to understand the limitations and the implications.

One of your limitations will be information. Gaining access to your parents' financial affairs or even asking them about their affairs may be met with a brick wall. Without being someone like their EPOA, you have no legal status to require anyone to tell you anything. A bank will more than likely clam up and sprout 'Privacy'. Your investigations will no doubt spread through the family and reach the ears of the offending member. Are you ready for the consequences?

To alleviate those concerns, you need an ally who does have some legal clout. Regrettably, at the moment, only Queensland has the vehicle with that chutzpah. We have an authority known as the Public Guardian who is empowered to investigate financial abuse of people who may have lost their capacity. They can require anyone to produce documents or answer questions. To date, no other State or Territory has clothed its comparable statutory authority with such power.

In other places, you are perhaps left with making a complaint to the police. For them, such a complaint raises some cultural issues. Many a time has a family member who raised such a complaint with the police been met with the familiar refrain—that's a civil matter for the family to work out. This is even the case where there is powerful evidence of criminal conduct.

While that response is unfortunate, it also leaves many families with nowhere else to turn except for civil litigation where the bogey of legal costs raises its ugly head. You are asked to answer the seminal question – how much of your own money are you prepared to spend (and lose) to pursue your parents' interests? Only you can answer that.

STORIES

Who's One of the Biggest Elder Abusers? – The Law

We've all read horror stories about bad things happening to parents who go guarantor for their children and end up losing their home.

Guarantees being called upon are the more obvious ways that things can go wrong. There are even more subtle ways that parents can get stung particularly when their children and the law form an unholy alliance. The source of the problem is the law's propensity to presume, also known as legal presumptions. One of the best-known legal presumptions is, of course, the presumption of innocence – everyone charged with a criminal offence is presumed innocent until it is proven otherwise.

But here's another one – if a parent provides money to an adult child, the law presumes the assistance to be a gift unless the parent can prove otherwise. As financial arrangements between parents and children are usually informal, undocumented and lost in the fog of time, proving otherwise can be a herculean feat. Not only that, by the time the issue explodes, the parent may well have lost their capacity or, indeed, died and have no ability to give their side of the story.

More and more cases are coming before the courts involving financial relationships between parents and adult children gone bad, usually at the hands of the children. Recently, a parent was forced to sue one of her three children who was also the parent's EPOA. Why? Because some years earlier, unbeknown to the other children, the parent had signed over the ownership of a property to him having been convinced to do so in order, as he put it at the time, to protect her from Centrelink and preserve her pension because of so-called recent changes to the law. This was codswallop but mum trusted him – after all she had appointed him as her EPOA.

There appears to be an expectation of intimacy and privacy when it comes to family financial arrangements. It is hush hush and not to be discussed especially if the other children don't know. Simmering in this cultural cauldron untouched by any legal advice let alone documents, are the seeds of family implosion.

For as long as the law clings to Dickensian notions of parent/child financial relationships through the auspices of the presumption of gifting, more and more Muriel's will suffer at the hands of their rapacious children.

The Circle of Custody and Contact in Later Life

Many of us are familiar with the term 'Family Law' either because we have been, regrettably, a party to a family law dispute ourselves or, at least, some of our children have.

Older people can become embroiled in family law disputes, not so much between themselves, but in the maelstrom that can arise from the breakdown of their children's relationships. So, for example, we often see older parents applying to the Family Court for contact with, or access to, their grandchildren or even being a party to a financial agreement between a child and their spouse to protect that child's inheritance.

In acting for older people, however, we have identified an analogous 'family' issue. It is the simmering and developing events surrounding disputes and disharmony between adult children about their ageing parents. It doesn't fit within our traditional understanding of Family Law, so we have devised a derivative – we call it the 'Law of Family'.

While the seeds of family conflict in later life can germinate from anywhere, and at any time, one that is particularly prevalent is the tendency of some older children to isolate their ageing parents from the other adult children (and their children, the grandchildren).

As a result, the usual dispute between estranged spouses about contact or custody of their children comes full circle and becomes a dispute between adult children about contact or custody of their parents.

The poignancy and pathos of this circle of family life is no better

demonstrated than in this typical scenario we recently confronted:
- Mavis is 85, having difficulty getting about and needing some daily assistance with life.
- One of her children, Murray has moved in to 'look after her' although this wasn't discussed with the other 3 adult children.
- Murray is a 'systems man' and knows the social security ropes – he's on the skids, on a disability pension and keen to be on a carer's allowance as well.
- He's also anxious to preserve the family home owned by Mavis and not to have it 'wasted', as he calls it, on aged care fees.
- Melinda is Mavis' dutiful daughter. She usually phones her mum every day and visits her at least once a week accompanied by her children who are always happy to see grandma.
- When Murray moved in he convinced his mum to put a few 'necessary things' in place such as appointing him her Enduring Power of Attorney, having signing authority

on her bank account, being her social security nominee and a secondary card holder on her Visa card – Murray took control.
- He has a subliminal fear that Melinda's regular presence will lead to a certain amount of unwanted scrutiny of his conduct.
- To limit that potential, he institutes a number of initiatives:

    * He changes the locks on the doors of the home so Melinda just can't turn up unannounced with her key.

    * He tells Melinda that she can't take Mavis on outings anymore without his approval.

    * She (and her children) can't come to see Mavis unless it is pre-arranged and only if he is there If she rings, she is only to talk to him and not Mavis.

He is engaging in a familiar pattern of deprivation done for notionally protective reasons e.g., 'Mum doesn't need the stress' or 'This is what Mum wants'. Not only that, he can feel engorged by power, namely, having the Enduring Power of Attorney for mum bestows him with power and abilities far beyond those of other mortal siblings – doesn't it?

Almost invariably this type of conduct hides a scheme of skulduggery designed to bolster their power and their pocket. What is often forgotten is the impact it has on the mum's life and her happiness. She becomes torn between being forever grateful for that son who so selflessly gave up his freedom to care for her and the natural love and affection of the other members of the family.

Allowing this situation to fester and ferment does nothing to improve mum's precarious position, her vulnerability or the broader relationships in the family. Restorative action is required not acquiescing to his requests which will just feed the power hunger and encourage him to go even further.

Our advice is never let this linger on. Getting good legal advice about your options is crucial to limiting the damage and achieving some measure of relationship retrieval. You owe it to yourself and your mum.

Parent Pirates

I often ask myself – what is it with adult children and their parents?

We have so many cases in our office involving adult children abusing their parents particularly in relation to their financial affairs. Statistics indicate that, in Queensland at least, our experience is shared by many others. It is estimated, for example, that:
- 75% of all abuse is inflicted by adult children on their parents
- 60% of the abuse is financial
- 42% of the abusers are the Enduring Power of Attorney for their parent.

These are the telling reminders of what is described as modern-day parental plunder. The 'gold in them thar hills' is a vat in which a conniving concoction is brewed and into which are poured parents who have become dependent, frail and reliant, children emboldened by having been bestowed by their parents as their EPOA's.

The skulduggery includes but not limited to:
- Stealing the parent's money

- Isolating the parent from the other siblings
- Changing the parent's bank account passwords
- Changing signatories on a parent's bank account
- Not spending money for the benefit of the parent's
- Paying themselves to be the EPOA
- Failing to get advice on important financial decisions for the parent
- Becoming the Centrelink or NDIS nominee for their parent.

This is just a series of examples of the dishonour roll of outlaw children. There are many others. Perhaps it explains why governments, both State and Federal, are now taking an interest in the subject of elder abuse although don't hold your hat on anything productive coming out of that.

For those who suspect or know that your brother, sister or friend is taking an ageing parent to the cleaners, there are things you can do – preferably sooner rather than later. Trouble is most of us won't until the parent dies and we ask the ubiquitous question – where has all the money gone?!

While for many of us there may be a tinge of self interest in pursuing 'bad' siblings, the more important motivating force should be the interests of the parent. How far does filial duty go for you? If you have concerns, maybe it's time to do something!

I Care – Therefore I am Entitled Aren't I?

What is the price for martyrdom in a family? This is becoming an increasingly common question being asked by the 'martyr' children in families.

As aged care becomes more expensive, families are internalising the caring arrangements for their ageing parents and keep it 'in house' as opposed to 'out house'. Caring for parents is becoming 'the' family business of the 21st Century.

It can take many forms – from full blown care, such as an adult child moving in with a parent to care for them, to simply taking mum or dad to medical appointments. Some children's contributions can border on the heroic.

Other children can be more bystanders. Still others, living in Dubai, just can't help.

Even though many caring children may be eligible for a carer's allowance or pension, parents are often moved to compensate their 'martyr' child for all they have done for them in their later lives. They are known to do such things as:
- Transfer assets to the child when the parent is still alive (e.g. in a granny flat arrangement)
- Promise to change their Will to give more to the caring child
- Pay a child to look after them.

But, what if the parent doesn't do any of these things (or even if they do) – does the caring child have any recourse to some compensation or better compensation after their parent has died? After all, some of these children may have to give up their job to provide the care, or worse, their marriage.

As the law currently stands, a caring child might consider, for example:
1. If the parent's Will did not compensate them but the parent

had previously promised to do so, trying to enforce that promise in a Court after the parent has died, or
2. Bringing a challenge to the parent's Will seeking better provision from the estate (over and above the entitlements of the other children), or
3. Challenging a superannuation death benefit payout or a greater share of it.

Except for lawyers, none of these options are attractive involving, as they do, potentially acrimonious legal proceedings and the implosion of the broader family unit. Not the sort of legacy a parent wants to leave.

We think that the law is starting to recognise the contributions of the caring child more and more especially where a parent has failed to do so. We may well be moving to a situation where the law will acknowledge the caring child in some form of compensation for their care.

If your family is at the caring crossroads, it can really help to be forearmed with the options available and how a parent might want to acknowledge a child's contribution (if they do). Having a meeting with us may just clear the air and avoid a future family fiasco.

Hear No Abuse, See No Abuse, Speak No Abuse?

Our media, political landscape and social networks are replete with the surging interest in, and almost daily outrage at, stories of older, vulnerable people being abused, namely, Elder Abuse.

Most of the focus is on the heinous actions of family members or caring organisations and the tragic consequences to an older member of a family. Much of the fodder for these stories comes from concerned citizens and, closer to home, even neighbours of the victims.

What is the situation out in suburbia if you as a neighbour, believe that the elderly person living next door to you is being abused, in whatever form it comes in – physical, emotional or financial? How far does being a 'good' neighbour go? Should you report your concerns and, if so, to whom and what are the potential consequences of doing so?

As the law would have it, there is no 'duty to rescue' imposed on us as citizens, generally speaking. If you see me one night in the sea with my hand frantically waving in the air and screaming 'Help, rescue me!', the law does not require you to do so or to attempt to do so. The same principle would apply to your next-door neighbour who may be in trouble.

But, as human beings, we are often moved not by our immediate legal obligations but more our underlying and instinctive moral beliefs to do the right thing by someone else in need.

Where we are moved to do something, as opposed to doing nothing, what should we do? It is very much a personal decision to do anything understanding that, simply reporting it will probably not be the end of your involvement in the matter.

In cases of criminal conduct, you could report to it to the police. If the neighbour has lost their capacity to make decisions through dementia, for example, you may also be able to report your concerns to a government protective agency such as, in Queensland, the Public Guardian.

What if your neighbour asks you not to do anything – are you obliged to respect their wish? The ubiquitous law of privacy now regulates much of our relationships with organisations and bureaucracies. Again, however, it does not apply to relationships between us as citizens generally. You would be able to go against your neighbour's request and report it without any breach of their privacy.

If you are motivated to report, are there any other potential implications? Provided you had a reasonable basis to report your concerns, the answer is generally no. Bear in mind however, if your reasonable suspicions turn out to be baseless, you could find yourself in some legal hot water. I don't need to remind you of the serious nature of an allegation that someone is abusing their mother or father. If that turns out to be untrue, the law would say that you have defamed that person and quite badly to boot.

Fortunately, at least in Queensland, to address this danger and to encourage people to report their legitimate concerns, the law does provide what is known as 'Whistle-blowing' protection for people who do report. This protection applies, in particular, to reporting on illicit conduct of an Enduring Power of Attorney. Its protection is limited and not as expansive as it should be.

Needless to say, as well, pragmatically speaking, reporting your concerns may give rise to some tension between you and your neighbour, if not their family.

In the end, there would be little legal downside for you to remain like the three monkeys – hear no abuse, see no abuse, speak no abuse. It is also known as apathy.

But if your morality or standards are more active and human, and ensuring you appreciated the implications beforehand, you may still want to do the right thing and the law would generally support you. It's up to you.

We're Watching You

Lawyers (like other professionals) are traditionally seen as delivering a service to meet a need for a reasonable price and then saying goodbye to the client – the one-off transaction. But, should we be doing more, especially for our older clients?

In recent times particularly, we've had occasions to be concerned about the welfare of an older client owing to the dubious conduct of other people. We've then had to consider what we should do about it that doesn't involve restricting our role to the standard service module above. In other words, should we 'blow the whistle' on someone.

For a lawyer that can be an ethical challenge given our obligations of client privacy and confidentiality. Fortunately, we are assisted in this conundrum with very helpful ethical guidelines issued by our Law Societies.

I then started to wonder about how this issue might be dealt with in other professions such as accountants and financial advisers. In many ways they are similar to lawyers in the delivery of a service to a client. However, they are also different in that they can often have an ongoing relationship with a client that does not involve a simple one-off transaction as is the case for most legal services. I see my accountant and financial adviser at least once a year.

As such, over time, they can be even better placed to discern adverse changes in their clients' circumstances. In other words, they can feel, suspect or even know there is potentially something that is not right.

But what assistance do they have in determining what to do about a client they may be concerned about who is being taken advantage of or where things about the client just don't seem right anymore? Very little, it seems, from my examination of the websites of such august peak bodies as the Financial Planning Association of Australia (FDA), CPA Australia (CPA) or the Insurance Council Australia (ICA).

That's odd particularly because, in America, there are significant steps being taken to address financial advisors' duties in these circumstances.

For example, the US Financial Industry Regulatory Authority (FINRA) issued a ruling to all its 632,000 financial adviser members, approved by the US Securities and Exchange Commission (SEC), which provides that:

- A financial adviser who reasonably believes that 'financial exploitation' of a 'specified adult' has occurred or is occurring, may place a temporary hold on the disbursement of funds or securities from the account of the specified adult.
- 'Financial exploitation' means wrongly taking or withholding an adult's funds, any act or omission by an EPOA or obtaining control of funds through undue influence.
- A 'specified adult' is a natural person aged 65 and older who the adviser reasonably believes has a mental or physical impairment that renders the individual unable to protect his or her own interests.

This Ruling commenced on 5 February 2018.

I wonder what the FPA, CPA or ICA thinks about that? Perhaps you should ask your accountant or financial adviser what they think.

Abuse Now – Lose Later

Our politicians are Claytons like – the lawmakers you have when you don't have lawmakers.

They are very good at appearing to do something when they're really not – they are always first past the post in the rhetoric stakes but bring up the rear in the action stakes.

A more subtle variation has developed as well – actually passing reforming laws but delaying their commencement – sometimes for a very long time. Bit like the tortoise and the hare really – race through the law impressing the constituents but then wait forever to have the law actually come into force while the 'system' and the bureaucrats try to play catch up.

Generally, however, if you raise an important issue for much needed reform, it will be shuffled off to the avoidance factories – an inter-departmental committee, a law reform commission, a panel of experts, a working group, a parliamentary committee, a task force or a 'take your time' request for a ministerial briefing.

Fortunately, when the stakes are high involving usually social evils and threats to the vulnerable, they are prone to act remarkably expeditiously – it's their mantra – 'we're listening to the people and we hear what you say!' Take the recent changes to law in relation to paedophilia and social media bullying and harassment.

But, at other end of the lexicon of social evil, the elderly, it seems they adopt the same pace as their ageing constituents – slow. We are awash with plans, working groups and other beneficent movers and shakers on tackling elder abuse – we have lots of aspiration but little action.

They're not waiting in the US State of Illinois.

Just this month it was reported that the State legislature had passed a law providing that if a person is convicted of financial exploitation, abuse or neglect of an elderly person, the convicted person will lose any benefit or entitlements under the elderly person's Will. Ouch. I'd call that going for the inheritance jugular.

In Australia, we already have what is known as the law of forfeiture – if you are responsible for the death of someone you will lose your inheritance from that person. Now, Illinois has extended that punishment to encompass a person's conduct that does not amount to murder, but simply, abuse.

For me it is an attractive disincentive to an abuser – let me know your thoughts.

Stealing a Parent's Feelings

We rarely hear of children engaged in another insidious form of abuse – stealing their parents' feelings.

Ever able to find obscure and Dickensian terms to describe human misconduct, the law describes it as 'fraudulent calumny'. Not many people have heard of this strange legal concept and yet, I suspect, it goes on very frequently in Australian society.

What is this abhorrent conduct? Put simply, it is where one person makes deliberate misrepresentations or tells lies about someone to another person with the intention of causing that other person to change their Will. The classic example is where the conduct is designed to, and does, cause a parent to cut a child out of their Will and to instead favour the child who has been the source of the misinformation.

A court has described it as where A poisons a person's mind against B, who would otherwise be a natural beneficiary of the person's Will by casting dishonest aspersions on B's character. Where someone has conducted themselves this way, the law can find that, as a result, the person's Will is invalid.

In a recent Court case, two sisters spent 8 days in court battling over the significant estate of their late mother. One of the sisters, Andre, alleged that her sister, Niki, had told lies about her to their elderly mother over the course of several months resulting in the mother making a Will in which she left her entire estate to Niki and nothing to Andre. Andre's case was that Niki had convinced their mother that Andre had been stealing large sums of money from her and that Niki had known that this was untrue.

At the crux of the case was the Court's finding that the mother's affections for Andre had been 'poisoned' by the falsehoods told about her and that Niki's lies had induced the mother to make a Will entirely in Niki's favour.

The Court described Niki as 'a thoroughly dishonest and manipulative individual to whom integrity and truth are less important than achieving what she wants, even when she knows she is not entitled to it.' The outcome was that the last Will was set aside and, in the absence of any other Will, the estate passed to the two daughters under the intestacy laws.

It is surprising that fraudulent calumny doesn't feature more often in Australian law.

It is an unfortunate reality of our modern society that elderly people often become the prize in a tug-of-war between warring offspring or other family members. In the effort to win over the elderly person's affections, some family members will paint the opposing family members in a very black light. Sometimes the efforts to influence the elderly person are directed at trying to obtain financial gains from them during their lifetime but they go hand-in-hand with inducements to the elderly person around their estate planning as well.

Unfortunately, we see many cases where a particularly ruthless family member will seek to isolate a vulnerable person from broader family purely with the object of brain-washing them against competing beneficiaries. In situations where the elderly person suffers from some form of dementia related paranoia, it can be easy to plant suspicions in their minds regarding the motives and actions of those around them – often times it is those who genuinely have their interest at heart and who are trying to do the right thing by them who become the brunt of the fabrications.

Alternatively, while keeping your feelings to yourself can be a good philosophy in making your Will, beware of the apparently well-intentioned child who gossips or criticizes others, especially other children (and their partners). They may just be trying to steal your parent's feelings.

SUGGESTIONS

There is no doubt that elder abuse is a family affair initially. It invariably occurs within families by some members of the family. Parents can appear to tolerate it, even if they are aware of it, making in effect a cost/benefit decision – the security of having a family member look after their affairs as opposed to the family destruction and personal grief of speaking out.

As such it behoves the innocent children to do something:

1. Seek the facts from the member of the family. If you get rebuffed (or even threatened) hold your ground. That type of reaction is almost a give away or an admission of guilt.
2. Discuss it with the other members of the family and your parent, if possible.

3. Understand that the financial abuse will have long term adverse implications for a parent especially if it involves having to pay for aged care later and it cannot be afforded.
4. Talk to a lawyer who knows what they are talking about as to your options to stop the abuse and/or to recover what has been lost.
5. Blow the whistle by reporting it to an appropriate authority e.g., in Queensland, the Public Guardian, who can then investigate.
6. Accept there will be long term and serious adverse effects on family relationships from which it will never recover.

CHAPTER 11

SEXUAL EXPRESSION

This may seem like an odd, if not unnecessarily intrusive, subject for discussion in the context of you and your parents. Trust me, it's not.

Web entrepreneurs have spawned a kaleidoscope of on-line dating services, mostly targeted to the young and the less young. These sites and apps tend to feed our apparent irrepressible need for romantic relationships and, ultimately, partnering or marriage. But is this only what older people are looking for? Websites are now emerging focused on the more refined or discrete interests of the older person.

HIGH TOUCH/HIGH TECH

'Stitch.com' is one such site with over 50,000 members. Its core audience and participants are the over 50's. It extols its virtues as facilitating 'company' for older people through companionship, community, activities, interest groups, dinners, friendship and last, but not least, intimacy.

It provides a plethora of individual settings including the ability for you to nominate a preference for 'Non-Romantic'. It is an antidote to social isolation. In 'The Longevity Economy' one of its members commented that she values the platonic friendships she has made through the site having realised that it wasn't a relationship she was looking for necessarily, it was a connection with other people.

DESIRE DENIERS

In the many circles of life that ageing represents—one in particular, perhaps, was your parents initiating 'that' conversation with you about the birds and the bees in your early teens. In another example of the reversal of roles, it can gyrate to you initiating 'that' conversation with your parents. Our parents' frailty can drown any thought that they would be interested in anything but their sheer survival – staying vertical with some forward motion each day.

I have been struck by the number of stories I have come across about intimacy in later life and its idiosyncratic, if not subterranean, presence and significance. I recently read a number of quotes from residents in nursing homes although I cannot locate the source. Here are some of them:

> *I always look for a man under the bed at night ... just the thought that there might be makes me feel better.*
>
> *I can remember it and sometimes even think about it but now—I'm managed.*

I have also read stories on what aged care providers do to suppress any such human urges and thoughts, in an attempt to ensure that there are no 'complications' in the care world. Here are some:

> *Seriously, you would think in their twilight years these people would have better things to do than shag, like writing their histories...'*

Unfortunately, we have to treat sex in high care as just another form of assault and we have to report it.

Dreams and desires are the subconscious moving forces of our human existence. Yet, we tend to assume with older people that their dreams, at best, are of the past, not of the present or the future or that their desires left them when they became consumed by the sheer effort of getting up and getting down. Not surprisingly perhaps, in their protective mode, adult children can be the biggest advocates of ageism – the conviction that their parents are 'past it', if not, 'over it'.

An additional element of this ageist tendency in adult children is their very conventional and rigid view of what sexual expression is – it is sex or copulation. Whereas, in older peoples' lives, it can come in many forms and often is a reflection of their physical capacity. It can be cuddling, canoodling, whispering sweet nothings, eye fluttering, fondling, hand holding, hanging out with, massaging or even sex toys.

Being Alone

We are also bombarded of late with the not surprising news that loneliness in older age is very bad for your health and exacerbates our decline. At any age, and no matter what our circumstances, most of us have a longing for belonging. All the evidence suggests that:
- Sexual expression and old age are not mutually exclusive
- Sexual needs do not decline with age
- Sexual intimacy provides many physical and psychosocial benefits
- Sexual expression can be an antidote to loneliness.

Yet, in nursing homes, sexual expression is a foreign phrase that never appears in the resident's care plan. It is a taboo subject because it does not fit in to the clinical lexicon of an older person's 'needs' assessment or, in any event and to put it more subtly – it's a 'yuk' subject. Besides, it's counter-intuitive to the thrust of aged care – to comfort our decline, not to satisfy our desires. Care is all flaccid, it has no fluorescence – a 'don't mention the war' issue.

This psychosis is facilitated by other factors including no staff or even resident or family education on sexual expression and the very 'built environment' of nursing homes doesn't help:
- No 'quiet time' rooms
- No resident lockable rooms
- No 'knock and wait' policies for staff
- Single beds with bed rails
- Multi-bed rooms.

UNINTENDED CONSEQUENCES

One example may demonstrate the sensitivity of this subject. There was a 40-bed nursing home in a regional centre. It contained 38 female residents and 2 male residents, all with their own individual rooms.

As the doors on the rooms on the male residents could not be locked from the inside, the men were being constantly irritated by female residents entering their rooms, day and night seeking some form of blissful encounter. The concern only came to light when one of the male resident's family members complained about how tired their father was when they saw him. The family member wanted the facility to stop it and do something.

The doors could only be locked from the outside, so the solution was to have them lockable also from the inside. It required a special dispensation from the local council to achieve the solution, but it worked. The men could now get a good night's sleep.

CREATIVE CARE

'Creative care' is a phrase I have invented, as far as I know. How can care be creative or inventive? I encourage you to watch an SBS documentary from some years ago entitled, *The Scarlet Road*. It is a poignant story about a severely disabled man who engaged the services of a prostitute to provide for his sexual needs, once a month. It is eye opening and, to use my favourite word, liberating.

Alas, enter stage right, the adult children, also known as the 'moral police'. For an elderly parent, they can have an unhelpful, if not, unholy alliance with nursing homes in this context. It stems from an innate cleavage in aged care – that between privacy and care. Privacy connotes the absence of other people, whereas care requires the presence of other people. While privacy is at best a right, it comes with a tension – the aged care provider's duty of care. When can the provider take time out for caring or does caring require some privacy?

These are not just academic meanderings. Privacy has tended to be a reclusive subject of discussion in ageing and an elusive goal for residents in aged care. It is about to become an even more rare commodity.

The desire for intimacy is trammelled by processes and procedures which can only be implemented by other people. Now it is proposed to have a 24 hour, 7 day a week visual and sound record of all movement in a resident's room in the form of the push for the installation of CCTV's in residents' rooms (and even in the ensuite). Now that's a classic passion killer.

No doubt, as well, as a reflection of their concerns for the welfare of their parent and in response to the slightly hysterical pall that hangs over the quality of care in aged care, adult children may often be the movers and shakers in this regrettable development. Welcome, dear elders to your bubble wrapped and hermetically sealed future. It just goes to show you that aged care is very much a case of private lives being played out in public places.

To their vicarious caring role, adult children will also bring another fear—that of another person coming into the life of their single parent. Aged care can throw residents together, usually innocently at first for companionship and company. Sometimes this can go further. A relationship will develop between residents that falls into the boyfriend/girlfriend (and variations on that) space.

Some children can be aghast at this prospect and will quickly assume the mantle of 'director of desires' for their parent. Where mum or dad appear to be spending too much time with another resident, a quick and decisive set of instructions will be issued to the facility to 'stop them now!'. Sometimes, these directives can even extend to 'keep them apart!'.

DEMENTIA AND DESIRE

Often times, these scenarios will arise in circumstances where the parent suffers from some form of mental incapacity. It is particularly pronounced for those suffering dementia. They can sometimes sexually 'act out' as they say, and have no understanding of, or not be restrained by, the usual parameters of acceptable conduct. They are not sexual predators, just victims of their disease.

While management of this situation is required in a care, or clinical, sense, it is more fraught where relationships arise between residents suffering from incapacity but who are not otherwise acting inappropriately. The question will then arise for a substitute decision e.g., the parent's EPOA (usually one or more adult children) about what, if anything they should, or could, do. There is nothing inherently wrong with a friendship between residents or even having a 'special friend'.

What if that should extend to an intimate relationship? How would you, the adult children respond? It also raises a number of bedevilling issues:
- The law requires consent between adults to engage in any physical relationship. If there is no valid consent by one person then the other person can be charged with assault.
- You need to have the necessary capacity to consent.
    * What if that consent is hampered by some form of mental impairment?
    * Does an EPOA have power to make decisions for a parent in this situation?

While an EPOA can make decisions for someone who has lost capacity, does that power extend to not only their financial and health affairs, but the affairs of their heart? To put it inelegantly – can you have a 'heart' for it where you don't have a 'mind' for it. As a matter of law, I believe not.

However, that appears to fly in the face of the reality of what is actually going on out there. I am reliably informed, and have heard apocryphal stories about, that, flying under the radar, some of our public protectors, such as public trustees are making what they term as 'comfort' decisions for clients who have lost capacity. This includes engaging sexual services for their clients.

Does that offend you? If it does, you may need a reality check yourself. Put yourself in the shoes of your mum or dad. If you could say, what would you say?

ADVANCE SEX DIRECTIVE?

An American legal academic has suggested that, if we can have an Advance Health Directive, why can't we have one that addresses another aspect of our personal lives, if not our health, why couldn't we have an Advance Sex Directive?

ill remember that an Advance Health Directive is a document in which you can give directions or even express wishes about the sort of health care decisions you would want others to make for you when you can't make them yourself. It is giving consent to health care in advance of the need for the health care. In effect, the consent is not contemporaneous with the decision – it comes potentially well before the decision is required, if it ever is. Those decisions would normally be made by your Enduring Power of Attorney based on the directions in your Advance Health Directive.

There has always some significant doubt as to whether consenting to a physical or other type of relationship for someone who has lost capacity to do so, is properly within the bounds of an Enduring Power of Attorney's power. But, if you accept that sexual expression or personal relationships are an integral part of a healthy life, it could very well be argued that you could even put such directions in an Advance Health Directive.

This is not mere academic mind games. The issue was confronted by the Canadian Supreme Court in 2011. A woman and her male partner had engaged in consensual kinky sexual activities for some years. In particular, she had consented to erotic asphyxiation and to sexual penetration while unconscious. After one particular episode of this practice, Canadian prosecutors, despite the woman's consent, prosecuted the man for sexual assault and argued she could not consent to the activities in advance. One court determined that there is no legal principle which provides that a person cannot legally consent to an activity that takes place when they are unconscious. In the appeal from the decision, the Canadian Supreme Court determined that consent for sexual assault requires the victim to provide actual, active consent through every phase of the activity and an unconscious person cannot do so.

It may sound far-fetched as this particular case no doubt is. But what is its potential application in situations where the 'victim' is suffering from incapacity due to Alzheimer's or

? If they can give consent to other health care that would normally require contemporaneous consent (which they can't provide), why can't they similarly do so for sexual expression?

An interesting subject to raise with your parents when you next see them!

BROADER CHALLENGES

These questions don't just arise in nursing homes. They extend to the broader frontier of later life lifestyles, when mum or dad become single again.

The biggest retirement village in the world is 'The Villages' in the state of Florida, USA. Across a broad range of statistics, it has a reputation for the 'mostest' of all retirement villages. One of those, not mentioned in their marketing material, is that it reportedly has the highest rate of sexually transmitted diseases of any community in the state. It consists exclusively of elderly people. Seems that there may be a general misconception that because they are beyond the age of conception, protection is not required.

Retirement villages can represent a hotbed of intrigue. Traditionally, they are populated by 'independent' retirees, some of whom, male and female, are single or widowed. Needless to say, hearts may flutter from time to time. This can cause happiness for them but anxiety, once again, for their children. The spectre is a legal one. Without getting married, finding and having a relationship in a retirement village can ultimately create a de-facto relationship which, for the purposes of the law can create unanticipated legal rights e.g., such as giving either of them a right to challenge each other's Will.

Some retirees, perhaps aware of this looming problem, go to great lengths to secrete their relationship in the village. We call them 'tip toers'. Amongst other things, they will furtively travel between each other's unit in the dead of the night, about 6pm, and then just as unobtrusively return to their own unit at the rising of the sun.

Becoming older is potentially a loss of some of our faculties or at least a decline in them. Loneliness can arise as a result with all the consequences already discussed. Having you or the grandchildren or even the internet around, will never substitute for the benefits of a true and meaningful relationship. It's healthy.

For older children, the stress comes from the desire to be concerned and, at the same time, to let go of those concerns for the sake of parental happiness. Even if one parent has died, to see the survivor embark on another relationship can seem like infidelity. It will require children to suspend their moral judgements on their parents' activities, the very morals their own parents inculcated into them.

So, ask yourself this question – in looking for an aged care facility for your parent, how would you respond to the following advertisement for such a facility:

Why choose us for your aged care?

We respect your right to sexual expression

We uphold your right to personal and sexual choices

We can facilitate make and female comfort companions

Interested?

Contact us on Ph..........

STORIES

Being Caring or Carefree?

Your dad has had to move into residential aged care. A fate you hoped would never befall him.

It has become just too difficult (if not expensive) for him to stay at home with your mother. It is affecting her health and the quality of their lives. As much as the children say they will help, they usually can't, particularly in those long, lonely nights when he is at his worst.

So now your mum is at home by herself. After being rusted on to each other for so long, it is, to say the least, disruptive if not downright distressing. Psychologists are want to call it an 'adjustment disorder'. That anxiety is not alleviated by the many visits to the aged care facility to see him only to be met by a blank stare of indifference or lack of recognition.

What does your mum do with the rest of her life now? Is it:

- To be a diligent and dutiful spouse albeit separated by circumstance and for her to live for him and not for herself? or
- To adjust and find a new meaning in life for those many extended times when she is not with him?

In many ways, this is not a legal conundrum but more, a moral one, with a bit of pragmatism thrown in. How far do those ancient vows go? Does your mum mothball her life or embark upon another journey?

Sex, Aged Care and the Law

I once gave a speech entitled *Sex, Care & the Law—Managing the Ménage à Trois* to an aged care conference on the Gold Coast.

Not possessing that rare combination of talents of a Bettina Arndt and a Florence Nightingale, you may be wondering what I, a lawyer, was doing pontificating on sex and care. It was the culmination of my accumulated legal experience in advising aged care providers on how to deal with the delicate issue of sexual expression in residential aged care. More importantly, for aged care providers, I thought it was time – time for them to come out, vent the subject and confront it, not avoid it.

My speech was propelled by two universal truths:
1. Sexual expression and old age are not mutually exclusive.
2. Sexual expression can be good for our physical and mental well-being.

The message was that, if sex is good for us then, surely, facilitating it for residents (where possible), rather than suppressing it, is a logical and essential element of good care, i.e., good sexual care. It can make us feel better.

Sexual expression, however, particularly for older people in aged care, is a wide and opaque landscape. It is not confined to copulation but can be simple, subtle human touch or gestures – cuddling, canoodling and even whispering sweet nothings. Trouble is, in residential aged care, the way we care and even the law itself are touch suppressants.

In the care context, even discussing resident sexuality can be taboo, a 'don't mention the war' element of care. The need for human touch tends to be subsumed to the exigencies of clinical touch washing, wiping, pulling, pushing, and lifting. Rarely does a resident's sexuality or wishes feature in their care plans or their 'strategies for loneliness'. Some staff can also be judgemental particularly where they are untrained and may let their moral disapproval infect an appropriate response to resident sexual desires or activities. Alternatively, other staff may seek to avoid it and look at their shoes when confronted by a 'compromising' situation.

Added to this are the environmental antidotes to intimacy in how our facilities are designed and constructed – no 'quiet rooms' or lockable rooms, and no 'knock and wait' policy. Single beds or 4-bed rooms are also hardly conducive to sharing the pleasurable presence of another human.

Even the Federal Government, the great funder and regulator of aged care, appears to adopt a paradoxical position on sexual expression. On the one hand, the ubiquitous accreditation standards applied to aged care providers do not require providers to develop policies on resident sexuality. On the other hand, the very same government helped fund the development of what is known as the 'Sexuality Assessment Tool' a document designed to assist aged care facilities in helping to identify and support residents' sexuality.

As for the law, don't start me up! It is a morass. It sends a push/pull message to aged care providers. Applying the law to sexual expression in aged care is a bit like refereeing a kick boxing match between two pugilists:

- In the red corner we have high sounding rights bestowed on residents contained in such places as the Aged Care Act and Principles, the Charter of Rights and Responsibilities and the General Principles applying to substitute decision makers. Taken together, they are a force for resident empowerment and expression.

- In the blue corner we have the, 'now, just wait a minute' laws. The ubiquitous common law duty of care (sometimes called the law of social control), the mandatory reporting regime, the complaints scheme and doubts and uncertainties about assessing a resident's capacity to consent to sexual contact tend to act as a restraint on a provider's propensity to facilitate residents' expression of their rights.

Overlaying this is a general reluctance by providers to have the courage of their convictions in the face of the potential perceived reputational damage of *A Current Affairs* expose or a marauding and moralistic family. Providers can tend to resort to type and err on the side of caution and control – it is better to stop it now than suffer the slings and arrows of any resident sexual freedom.

I suspect some people may react to this article with a certain amount of tired derision, after all, what would I know – I work every day in an ivory tower don't I, not in an aged care facility. But this article is not intended to open the floodgates of hedonism in aged care. Rather, it is to provoke us to confront the importance of the place of sexuality in that constant quality of care discussion that we must continually have.

Fundamentally, as well, in an environment where private lives are played out in relatively public places, the subject of sexual expression exposes an innate cleavage in aged care – is it more comforting the decline of the frail or accommodating the last vestiges of life's receding pleasures?

If I was a resident in an aged care facility, I know which one I would go for.

'Make War not Love'

I know what you're thinking – you've got that wrong Brian! Well, if you are thinking that, you've got it wrong.

Family relationships especially between an elderly parent and their adult children can take on some ironic dynamics as the older parent's life starts to diminish and the children, by desire, necessity, or even self-interest, become more involved in their parent's life.

In the 1960's, especially in the latter part of that colourful decade, and in my late teens, I sympathised with, and dabbled in, the flower power fever. Decked out in the obligatory braids, beard, bare feet, beads, shoulder bag and imbibing on bunkum, I joined in the youthful movement of peaceful revolution encapsulated in the exhortation – *Make Love not War!*

It was a time of a challenge to, if not derision of, the adult world order as we saw it. It was also a call to arms to free us from our stifling sexual mores and to love one another (and often), not kill one another. It was an era of libidinous liberation. Needless to say, our parents could not understand and were aghast at our aspiration and assertion of sexual freedom. Life can come a full circle, however, when it comes to ageing and morality.

I was recently consulted by two clients (sisters) who were from my generation and may very well have been 'flower power girls' of the 60's. They recounted their upbringing in a conventional family where their father applied strict moral creeds and eschewed any form of so-called liberation for his children. They rebelled to some extent and described themselves as teenage renegades who often defied him and scoffed at his medieval morals.

But they had not come to see me to help them write their family's story. Their concerns were more pressing and, in their eyes, required immediate legal attention.

Their father, aged 84 and widowed some 12 months earlier from his wife of 60 years, had, as they put it, 'fallen into the arms of a 45-year-old gold digger'. They were about to go on a 4 week holiday together and, despite their father's feeble protestations that they were just friends, the daughters could not help but perceive a more insidious agenda especially as he had now decked himself out in a whole new wardrobe that included jeans, albeit with an elasticised waistband.

They expressed their perception of the situation in terms of fear—she was using him to get to his money, next thing they will be moving in together, she just wants him as a bank to pay her debts, she will turn him against us, Mum would turn in her grave etc etc. On the surface, there was an apparent moral irony. Life was indeed coming a full circle. Here were the previously liberated children of the 1960's concerned about their father's apparent latter-day liberation including, they suspected, a libidinous one.

We often confront these family tensions in older people's lives especially where the older person has lost their spouse and looks to create another life for themselves that does not involve just wallowing in a slow slide to single senility. There is no doubt that there are some people out there who dig for gold in the mine of an older person's life and the law can sometimes help redress this especially where issues of undue influence or incapacity are in play.

However, if an older person has all their faculties, the best antidote to loneliness and isolation in later years can be the search for, and discovery of, a loving relationship. It can even add years to your life. We call the conundrum a case of the love or the loot. To the father, it may simply be love but, to the adult children, it can be just a patently transparent thirst for ill-gotten gains.

A subterranean feature of some children's' concerns can be, understandably, that their well laid inheritance plans and expectations may come unstuck or, at best, more complex. It is hard to convince many children in this situation that the law is quite clear. If you have the capacity to make your own decisions at any time in your life, even to the point of your last breath, you are entitled to do so even if the rest of your family, and even the world, think you're sad and silly and 'should act your age'.

The daughters have determined it is a case of usury and undue influence. They will probably do all that they can to prevent their father falling further into the clutches of this Jezebel. This may mean that their old mantra of *Make Love not War* will become *Make War not Love.*

As for me, if I am ever in the situation of that father, I hope my children will allow me to be a hippy just one more time.

Testing Time for Relationships in Later Life

The US Department of Health and Human Services recently imposed a fine of US$83,800 on the owners of an aged care facility because, in the Department's view, the facility had 'inadequately addressed sexual interactions between three cognitively impaired residents'. The Department concluded that the facility's failure to act had put the residents in 'immediate jeopardy', meaning the facility's actions or inactions '...caused. or is likely to cause, serious injury, harm, impairment or death of a resident'.

The relevant facts were:
- There were three residents involved, two men and one woman.
- Each had fairly advanced dementia and suffered from 'behavioural disturbances' or 'inappropriate

behaviour' also known as 'acting out'.
- One of the men performed various sexual acts on the other man and also on the women.
- There was no evidence that there was any objection from the other man or the woman.
- Several staff witnessed the events but did not seek to intervene except to record it in their notes.
- The facility's policy was to allow residents to have sexual interactions and not to intervene or report it unless 'a participant showed outward signs of non-consent'.

The facility appealed against the finding of 'immediate jeopardy' and the penalty. The appeal court dismissed the appeal and, in doing so, appeared to decide that:
- Their policy of only intervening if there were outward signs of non-consent was insufficient to determine consent particularly where there was cognitive impairment.
- The facility had taken inadequate measures to determine if the acts were consensual.

- The non-intervention policy was 'misguided' and left the residents at risk.

Curiously, there was no discussion about whether the conduct caused, or was likely to cause, harm, impairment or death to the participants as required by the definition of 'immediate jeopardy'.

In any event, it has some salutary lessons and insights for us:
- In Australia, the first law of capacity is that a person is presumed capable of consenting to anything unless there is evidence to the contrary. It is not clear in the court case above whether this is the law of America too.
- The case did not decide that persons with a diagnosis of dementia are not capable of consenting to sexual relations.
- What the case seemed to focus on was the failure to follow an appropriate process to determine if the participants were capable of consenting.

It also gives rise to more conundrums which stretch beyond the law and into the morality space:
- What if the facility had undertaken a proper process to assess the residents' capacity to consent to sexual relations and the upshot of that was that they were capable?
- What if the opinion was they were not capable?

These quasi legal/moral/care issues are complex, and we often give little credence to the difficulties aged care providers and their staff have to face in addressing this sensitive issue. The task of trying to balance the right of the resident to decide what to do themselves and the provider's duty of care i.e., to protect the resident is often unimaginably difficult and for which there if often not obvious right or wrong. And, as if it couldn't get any harder, we should not forget the other moral policeman—the resident's family.

There is no doubt that human touch is an essential element of happiness for our human condition particularly to ward off that later day malaise, loneliness and depression. Most touch in aged care is clinical, it is often not affectionate. Indeed, affection in aged care, particularly for staff comes with a fear. It can not only be misinterpreted, it can be dangerous because, for some aged care outside scrutineers who are, perhaps not in touch, it is no less than an assault.

It is a sad day when aged care becomes an affection free zone. If I am ever a resident of an aged care facility, I would definitely want the maximum touch possible (and legal).

CHAPTER 12

THE END

These salient factors may cause you to take a more active interest in the demise of your parents:
- Most people who die each day are 'old'.
- Most of them will have gone through a dying process.
- During that time, they may have lost their capacity to make decisions.

Death is not the starting point but an end point in facilitating your parents to do the right thing, as a last thing. It may appear maudlin but dying is a window of opportunity and, a reason to raise important issues with your parents. Be warned, many parents will not be interested in confronting this even at the start of the dying process. Their failure to do so will frustrate you and your entire family. It could also be a trigger for another family implosion point.

The law has identified crucial dying issues and provided equipment to address them and to avoid the trench warfare that can erupt as a result of do-nothing parents.

THE ESSENTIALS

Here's a legal menu for your, and your parents' table:

Care

While I have addressed aged care in some detail already, if both of your parents, or the surviving one, are still living at home, now is the time to adhere to 'Be Prepared'.

Poor health squarely raises the potentially pressing issue of how to deal with living arrangements as a result of their inevitable declining health and increasing dependency. What are they going to do, where will they go, and how much will it cost – all the familiar exhortations.

For fear of repeating myself, I can say no more.

Advance Health Directive

The coming together of longevity and its illegitimate child, loss of capacity, means that, at some stage in an older person's life, they may not be able to make their own health care decisions.

This can create another implosion point for a family – what would Mum or Dad want in this situation? Of course, the most significant 'situation' would be where a family is asked whether their parent's life switch is left on or turned off. It is hard to imagine a more life-altering decision that someone can be called upon to decide, namely, whether someone else, their mum or dad, should live or die.

Even worse is the prospect that none of the family can agree what mum or dad would want. Picture the scene – the family are circling the wagon of mum or dad's hospital bed and have just been told the 'situation' has arrived and it's time for them to make that decision. Disagreement ensues and disaster follows shortly after. To live or die amidst recriminations and acrimony would not be one of your parent's desired legacies.

In response, the law has interceded to create a tool for family detente. In Queensland, at least, it is known as the Advance Health Directive. It is a legal document containing legally binding directions for the health care you would, or would not want, if ever health care decisions need to be made and you are not able to make them yourself. It speaks for you if ever you cannot speak for yourself. It informs your family and, most importantly, tells your Enduring Power of Attorney what decisions you want them to make. I have often seen families go off to court about a disagreement about what their mum or dad's wishes might be because they have never made an Advance Health Directive. Seems like a good idea and an implosion busting document.

In other states and territories, they are known by various phrases including an Advance Care Directive or just Health Directive. Some large hospitals have even devised their own forms which are given to a patient on admission.

Except currently for Victoria and the ACT, no other Australian state or territory has a right to die law. More than likely, they will have eventually. The right to die of course is not the same as withdrawing or withholding life sustaining measures. For those purposes, the Advance Health Directive serves its purpose.

Will

This section is included for emphasis rather than a presumptive discussion given my previous treatment of the subject, but it is an essential element of the dying discursive. Dying creates a focal point and, apart from dying deniers or reincarnation revivalists, would appear to be a moving force to get this one attended to. A 'der' point.

The Statutory Will

But there's more. You may know that the law prescribes that if you did not have the necessary capacity to make or change your will then, if you try to, it will be invalid. Fortunately, some years ago, in most Australian states and territories, the law introduced the concept of a statutory Will.

Put simply, it allows anyone to apply to a court to have the court make or change another person's Will where that person may have lost the capacity to do so.

When could this possibly be justified? There was a famous case some years ago in Victoria involving a Gloria Kropp. Her husband was having an affair with another woman. Because of the problem she represented to their relationship, the husband and the girlfriend hatched a plot to kill Gloria. At this point, Gloria had done the usual Will giving everything to her husband and then to their two children.

One night, the girlfriend secreted herself in the garage at the Kropp home and when Gloria arrived home, she was mercilessly beaten by the girlfriend with a baseball bat. Believing she was dead, the girlfriend placed Gloria in the boot of the car intending to dispose of her later. Some days later Gloria was found, still barely alive. She was rushed to hospital in a vegetative state.

When suspicion fell on their father, the two daughters, knowing the terms of their mother's Will, applied immediately to the court for it to change her Will before she died. The court duly did and made a new Will for Gloria giving everything to the two daughters. Gloria died shortly after the court order and her husband was charged with murder although he later committed suicide before he was tried.

While this is a dramatic example, there are other poignant reasons to apply to change or make a person's Will. One, in particular, is where a young person has a serious road accident and becomes severely disabled. Being a young person, almost inevitably they would not have made a Will before the accident. It they receive a large compensation payment as is often the case, the question arises as to what happens to that money in the event of the death of the young person. It will call out for someone to make a statutory will application.

Second marriages in later life also may give rise to similar considerations. It is not unknown for a parent to marry in later life and then change their Will to give everything to the new spouse much to the chagrin of the parent's children. If there was any doubt about the capacity of the parent to change the Will, there may be a basis for the children to apply to a court to change his or her Will.

On even a basic level, if your parent has never done a Will and loses their capacity to do so, there may be a cause to consider applying to the court for a statutory Will.

Bear in mind, however, the urgency of such an application because a court cannot make or change someone's Will if they have died. It can even be too late if the person should die in the midst of an application having been made but not yet determined by the court.

Other Things

Many of our parents have created and stored their wealth through more than just the acquisition of personal assets. Some have squirreled them away in such vehicles as family trusts and self-managed superannuation funds. There are special rules that apply to the passing on of the assets of these entities and a failure to understand this can have calamitous consequences for families after a parent's passing.

One of the great myths in this regard is that you can pass the assets of these entities to the chosen ones through your Will. That is generally wrong, and you need to ensure your parents are aware of this before their ignorance leads to major issues for you as the surviving children.

CREATIVE DEATH AND DYING

Our last days on earth are becoming the focus for imaginings and creativity. A form of celebration or, at least, embarking on some reflective musings and pleasures, if possible.

'Death Cafes'

I read a report recently in the Otago Daily Times published in Dunedin, New Zealand, of people gathering at a 'Death

Cafe' to meet and, over green tea, lattes, and gluten free carrot cake, they discuss death. This is apparently one of many such cafes throughout the world founded in 2011 by Shirley Welsh who described them as a '...space for an open, respectful, confidential, facilitated conversation, where people can express their views safely.'

Dying should bring with it a certain insight and honesty with ourselves and others and such a social outlet may well have a useful contribution to make to the transition we all need to make to the ultimate conclusion of our lives.

Can you imagine visiting your mum or dad one day and suggesting an excursion with the words, 'How about we have tea at the Death Café today?'.

Music Thanatologist

Music can also form an integral part of the dying process. It gives pleasure, relives old memories, can bring peace and tranquillity and distract us from the generally morbid atmosphere.

We may be familiar with music therapists. They are often found in hospitals providing familiar tunes and songs to enliven the atmosphere amongst the sick but not necessarily the terminally ill. So it is, we now have the music thanatologist. Thanatology is the scientific study of death.

Music thanatologists specialise in providing music to the terminally ill and those who face imminent death. Their favourite instrument is the harp for its lilting and dulcet tones if not its conjuring of angels and cherubs. But the music is also mixed with song and silence and is designed to imbue a mood of comfort and reflection.

Death Doula

Your parents and their parents may remember Birth Doulas. Now we have Doulas at the other end of life – Death Doulas.

It captures our understandable desire to be at home when we die. These Doulas provide all sorts of special services and have been described as a type of event manager to ease the process and the task of dying.

Their services encompass planning sustainable and environmentally appropriate funerals, being a companion, helping with any aged care processes, decluttering and being an ear and helper in breaking down the fear and uncertainty involved in the dying process. It also extends to assistance in the grieving process for families both before, and after the death.

They may not be for everyone but at least they are helping us identify a common avoided discussion in families about death and dying.

Voluntary Assisted Dying (VAD)

More commonly known as euthanasia or voluntary suicide, as I write, VAD is now legal in Victoria and will be in Western Australia in 2021. All other states are flirting with introducing it as well. While they did previously introduce VAD laws, the respective Territories, the ACT and the Northern Territory, promptly had those laws overturned by the Commonwealth Government and are currently prevented from attempting to reintroduce them.

As the only law currently applying in Australia, the Victorian law provides in summary as follows:

- A person who wants to use the VAD law must be capable of understanding what VAD means for them and must maintain that understanding throughout the process.
- Another person, such as an Enduring Power of Attorney or Guardian cannot make the decision on behalf of the person.
- The person must be suffering from an incurable disease or one that causes intolerable and unrelieved suffering.
- They must not be expected to live for between six to twelve months depending on the nature of the illness.

The prescribed process is a long and contorted one. To date, some 130 Victorians have applied and 52 have used the law to end their lives.

However, if you think you can pop down to Victoria to take advantage of the law, think again. It requires that you have lived in Victoria for at least one year before you can seek to apply the law.

The Way to Go

Objectively speaking, the funeral service and how your parents go to heaven seems, on the surface at least, to be an innocuous issue and not that significant, given their condition at the relevant time.

Again however, while I may still be naive at my advanced age, from my experience it is remarkable how these issues have a tendency to extract the last once of family dysfunction at the very last moment, if not, shortly after that.

The who, where and what of the funeral and the way we go to heaven can cause such acrimony and disputation within families. How unedifying for a family to be involved in litigation while their mum or dad (and some believe, their soul) lies a bit longer in the waiting room on earth. Here resides another point of implosion at a point when your parents can't say who they liked or disliked and how they want to go.

And that's the problem. If only the parents had said something! It's all very well to put some helpful instructions in your Will but, by the time somebody has managed to lay their hands on your Will, you may be up for second drinks in the waiting room.

It sounds uncontroversial but believe me, for many families it is not. Time for parents to be asked, or even better, to tell without being asked.

STORIES

What Happens to a Personal Guarantee on death?

A personal guarantee is a promise to pay someone a debt that is owed to them by somebody else it. Usually a personal guarantee is only called upon if the person who owes the money doesn't pay it when they are required to.

It is remarkable how many parents give personal guarantees for their children's or even their grandchildren's debts. Many of us seem to believe that we never stop being a parent or a grandparent. Personal guarantees, however, can be a serious and risky commitment especially in later life. The worst case we have seen was a personal guarantee given to a financier by a 76-year-old father for his 47-year-old son's $820,000 debt associated with a hydroponic herb farm that went bad.

Of course, if parents have multiple children and provide financial benefit to some and not others when they are alive, the tension that creates in the family is obvious.

Quite apart from the prudence of giving a guarantee, however, there is another tricky issue that can arise, namely – what happens to the personal guarantee a parent has given when they die?

The Effect of Death

A personal guarantee will usually last as long as the associated debt is outstanding. If a person dies while their personal guarantee is still alive, what does that mean for their estate?

In a nutshell, usually, and subject to the terms of the document, the guarantee does not die. Instead, the estate continues to be liable under the deceased's personal guarantee. Can you imagine the consequences of that!

Here are just a few:
- The estate cannot be finalised until the personal guarantee ends i.e. when the related debt is paid or the guarantee released.
- If the debtor defaults in paying the debt, the estate will be called upon under the guarantee to meet the debt.
- If the guarantee was given for the benefit of one of the children, the other children who are beneficiaries of the estate will not be pleased, to say the least, particularly if the guarantee is called upon and as a consequence, they lose some, or all of their entitlements.

The Perils of Passwords for the Disabled and Deceased

Every day our benevolent banks and felicitous financiers exhort us to 'Be Cyber Safe – Never give your password to anyone!'

It is usually very prudent advice when you are alive and able to make your own decisions – but how useful is it if you have died or lost your ability to make your own decisions?

Passwords don't pass with your passing – they stay alive. If you have kept them in a secret place or, even more securely, in that impregnable cyber space called your head, it could create a problem for others if you lose your life or your mind. This is particularly so for those who come after you and have to manage your earthly affairs – such as the Executor of your estate or your Enduring Power of Attorney.

Here's an example of the issue that we had to address recently:

- Some years ago, when she was one of those savvy septuagenarians,

Molly had set up her bank accounts and other investments online via internet banking. She used her computer and her passwords to access and operate her accounts, pay bills and transfer money. In fact, one of her accounts could not be operated at all except online. The trusty companion, the bank passbook was now passé.
- She was 'cyber safe' and kept her passwords to herself despite the salivating urgings of her children to tell them.
- Some 18 years later, as the result of a severe stroke, she lost the capacity to make her own decisions including, of course, her ability to operate her online accounts.
- Some years earlier fortunately, she had the foresight to appoint one of her children, Ezra, to be her Enduring Power of Attorney. At the same time and to be seen to be even handed, she made two of her other children, Erin and Eric the Executors of her Will when she died.

- In light of her situation, as Molly's EPOA, Ezra was now entitled and needed to stand in her shoes and operate her finances.
- Molly's largest investment was held in an account that could only be operated online.
- Ezra was now confronted with a number of challenges and this is just a sample of the imbroglios:

    * Molly had not told anyone what her passwords were or where she had stored them and now she couldn't.

    * Ezra had to somehow prove 'online' that he was the EPOA and entitled to operate the accounts and do this without her password.

    * Not only that, earlier this year before the introduction of the new laws on Unclaimed Money, (which entitles the government to take any money from a person's bank account which has not been accessed for three years (previously seven years), a helpful letter arrived for Molly from one of her banks advising her to do something urgently unless she wanted the

government to get its hands on the money in her bank account that had lain dormant for a long time.

* Ezra responded quickly but without a password to the account he could not access it to make a withdrawal or even to make a cursory deposit.

* Without regaling you with all the other hoops and hurdles placed in Ezra's path by the finance institution, suffice to say that, two months after Ezra's fruitless attempts to access Molly's money, Molly died.

* Her death raised even more complications as suddenly, Ezra's role disappeared and in came the Executors under Molly's Will, Erin and Eric to take control of her affairs.

* Needless to say, they have faced the same mountains and valleys that Ezra had to confront as they also had no access to her account without the ubiquitous password.

When we pack up our life and relocate to heaven or somewhere more remote on earth beforehand, for those of us who have heeded our friendly lawyer's advice, we will no doubt leave our affairs in a neat, tidy and ordered way. More than likely, we would have kept good records about our finances and done a good Will to make things a little easier for that long suffering after life bureaucrat, the Executor.

Really?!

Some of us might proudly assert the famous Bjelke-Peterson catchcry, 'Don't you worry about that!', because we have embraced the electronic age and carefully retained our records on our computer, even scanned bills and other hard copy documents onto it and banked online. But, do we ever think how useless those achievements might be if other people need to (not want to) access the information and can't? We have even seen an example where an Executor didn't even have the password to turn on a deceased's computer let alone access what was on it.

While it may be all resolvable eventually, it takes time and requires your family to expend a significant amount of energy, time and frustration to get on top of your affairs. In some cases, it can even result in the breakdown of relationships between members of the family. Unless you take the laissez faire attitude to life – 'it's their problem', you may not want to leave this morass to your family. If so, think about these things to alleviate the issues for your family:

- Should you tell anyone your passwords particularly the person you have bestowed with the power to make decisions for you if you can't make your own – your Enduring Attorney or for later purposes, your Executor?
- Should you give someone an authority to operate your bank accounts along with you?
- Should you appoint someone as your Centrelink 'payment' or 'correspondence' nominee?
- Should you authorise someone else now to operate your Facebook page, twitter account etc?
- Should you give a copy of your Enduring Power of Attorney

document to your bank/and/or financial institutions?

We don't suggest the answer to all these questions is yes (except the last one). You need to judge what is appropriate and makes you comfortable in your own family circumstances.

I have always liked that age-old mantra, 'Trust me, I'm a lawyer!' You need to decide whether you accept your family's familiar mantra, 'Trust us, we're family!'

You Can Rule from Heaven (or elsewhere)!

While you walk on this temporal earth, you make your Will and it goes to sleep. When you die, it awakes – it comes alive. Others are then often left to ponder the unanswerable question – what were you thinking?!

There is a lot of law about the making of a Will but not much about the thinking that goes into it. When making it, you are usually subconsciously contemplating what you would like to happen when you do peer down from above (or up from below).

It requires a mix of imagination, a dollop of motivation all seasoned to taste with a touch of manipulation.

It is this latter psychological element of influencing others from afar that is the oft neglected aspect of Will-making. Most lawyers are trained, religiously, to advise our clients that you should not try to control your family's fate from heaven in your Will – *Just let go,* they say. But for some of us, while reincarnation remains elusive, celestial control is the next best thing.

Trouble is the courts have long taken a conflicting view on what is described as our 'testamentary freedom'. Yes, you can say what you like in your Will – we live in a free country but, when you die, that freedom dies with you. Thus, the law allows people to challenge your Will at a most inauspicious time for you – you're not here to put your side of the story. In an increasing number of cases as well, the Courts are changing Wills and laying waste to our best laid plans.

While there are a number of grounds upon which you can challenge a Will, there is one particular rule of law that

prescribes that a Will should not be contrary to good public policy i.e., what is good for the community generally. As a consequence, the Courts have struck down provisions in Wills which are seen as discriminatory such as:
- My daughter will only receive her share if she divorces her husband.
- My daughter will forfeit her interest in my estate if she marries a Jewish man.
- My bequest to my sons is conditional on their wives converting to Protestantism.

However, all is not lost. Believe it or not, Courts have also managed to find the following provisions of a Will to be valid:
- A bequest to a son subject to him marrying a Jewish girl.
- A gift to grandchildren provided they were Roman Catholics and not married to Protestants.
- A daughter was not to receive her share of her mother's estate until such time as the daughter divorced her current husband or her current husband died.

It is hard to reconcile the two opposing sets of decisions when, on the face of it, the clauses look remarkably similar, yet they lead to entirely different results. If we can extrapolate a distinction, it may be this – if a condition in a Will requires someone to do something, before they get their share, it may well be invalid. But if the entitlement is simply subject to an event occurring, over which the beneficiary has some control, then it may be valid. The first is best described as a prescription to a beneficiary and the second, a discretion in the hands of a beneficiary.

Needless to say, we would not recommend that you now leap at the opportunity to orchestrate your children's lives from afar. While it is possible, it must be carefully crafted and will almost inevitably be subject to the scrutiny of a Court.

Alternatively, you could just let go and get on with enjoying yourself in heaven (or elsewhere).

CHAPTER 13

THE LAST WORD

I once had a client who was an 'Emeritus Professor', meaning a retired academic. It's a reward for a life-long contribution to a field of academic endeavour and a title bestowed upon the distinguished – an honorific.

EMERITUS PARENTS

I sometimes ponder whether ageing parents think of themselves as 'Emeritus Parents'. Having retired long ago from being a hands-on parent, they are now entitled to the appropriate respect and due deference that comes with that esteemed status.

However, that redoubtable life experience can be accompanied by a certain disdain or dismissal of others making suggestions or trying to help. Hell, why do they need help, they know it all and have done it all, haven't they? Of course, they are still to experience the downsides of ageing and, in that sense, they are still wet behind the ears, undergraduates.

In the famous words of the former US Secretary of State Donald Rumsfeld, there are known knowns, known unknowns and unknown unknowns. While he was describing the state of military intelligence, he could just have easily been referring to ageing.

YOU AS LOSS LEADERS

As much as I would encourage us all to take a positive and proactive approach to ageing, it inevitably comes with loss. Loss of mobility, loss of mental acuteness, loss of the familiar, loss of friends and, ultimately, loss of life.

Loss leading is a common phrase used in the commercial world. Milk is a loss leader for large retail stores (and a loss for dairy farmers). I like to see myself not only as an elder lawyer but also a loss leader in my work with families.

However, top of the tree of loss leaders are you, the adult children. You are the ones on the ground and in your parents' lives who will not only have to confront their future but also be involved intimately when the future arrives. Your parents' losses used to be restricted to just their mortal departure, through the prism of death. Now a more complicated loss can befall them beforehand – the loss of their mental capacity. Death is an event, but incapacity is a stage full of events and infinitely more complicated and demanding.

As adult children, your parents' (and parents-in-laws') circumstances and how to deal with them will not only impact on you personally, but also on your marriage, your relationships, your friends, your work, your siblings, your children, your plans, your retirement, your yoga and pilates, your time (including play time), your own role as a grandparent, your sanity and your bank account.

WHAT'S THE POINT?

The point of this dissertation is to equip you for the future or, indeed, the present. It is not, or will not just be, about you and your children. There is a holy, or unholy, trinity looming in your life and on this earth – the third arm of which, is your parent. It can be a time of regret, of *'wouldas, couldas and shouldas'*. A time exposing in a painful light your lack of preparation and planning. A place where you and I will be one day.

Your family could easily slide into power coalitions, competing alliances and 'goodies and baddies' where all sides share the mantra of 'make war not love' and where battles are won and wars are lost.

I have witnessed many times the failed or fetid family that has descended to the depths of disunity, disruption and destruction because of a failure to confront and collaborate. Even worse is the failure to challenge your parents to become partners in this almost mandatory need to anticipate events, educate ourselves, converse, communicate and action, or implement, a strategic plan.

You may wear the mantle of the one 'that Mum liked best', and while that badge can grate with you and the others, you are, ironically, the best person to activate the task. You will have some credibility, particularly in your parents' eyes, if you have the fortitude to open up the discussion. If not, the legacy of lassitude, lethargy and indeed loss, will haunt you and your siblings long after your parents' passing. It may not be apocalypse now, but it will be shortly.

The message, then, is all about consensus building and acknowledging that conflict emanates from layers of sub text as in any 'normal' family, the unresolved feelings, anger, sleights and distrust. It then requires a certain maturity to grasp the need to cooperate and collaborate and to confront, not in a conflicted sense, but in understanding the dynamics of your parents' needs and your siblings shared concerns.

It's no time to marinate in mediocrity – It's lights, camera, action! (and it really is the end).

Do something!

ABOUT THE AUTHOR

Brian Herd is an experienced and passionate lawyer, working in the frontier of elder law, or law relating to older people and their families involving the new dynamic emerging in families – disputes and dysfunction brought on by ageing parents. He is recognised as one of the leading experts in Australia on elder law, aged care, retirement, estate planning and a regular author, broadcaster and popular presenter on many elder law subjects and issues.

He was exposed to the simmering issues some 20 years ago in his first visit to a nursing home. Confronted by an imploding family of five daughters, a hapless mother and some of the language of aged care – the 'bowel book' and the 'stool tool', he discovered a new calling – change management for families and their ageing parents.

Since then as a lawyer, he has been involved in countless family experiences, some which are truly eye opening.

He has many stories to share. Along with his four siblings, he also has a mother and father aged in their 90's.

Find out more:

CRH Law – website: www.crhlaw.com.au

Email address: bherd@crhlaw.com.au

Facebook: www.facebook.com/brian.herd.35

Linkedin: au.linkedin.com/in/brian-herd-2062aa27

Twitter: brianherd1

For more great titles visit
www.bigskypublishing.com.au

www.ingramcontent.com/pod-product-compliance
Lightning Source LLC
Chambersburg PA
CBHW010555020526
44111CB00054BA/2932